ROYAL HISTORICAL SOCIETY

STUDIES IN HISTORY

New Series

T0355750

WOMEN AND RELIGION
IN LATE MEDIEVAL NORWICH

Studies in History New Series

Editorial Board 2017

Professor Vanessa Harding (*Convenor*)
Dr D'Maris Coffman
Professor Peter Coss (*Past and Present Society*)
Professor Emma Griffin (*Literary Director*)
Dr Rachel Hammersley
Professor M. Hughes (*Honorary Treasurer*)
Professor Daniel Power
Professor Guy Rowlands
Professor Alec Ryrie

This series is supported by annual subventions from the
Economic History Society and from the Past and Present Society

WOMEN AND RELIGION IN LATE MEDIEVAL NORWICH

Carole Hill

THE ROYAL HISTORICAL SOCIETY
THE BOYDELL PRESS

© Carole Hill 2010

All Rights Reserved. Except as permitted under current legislation
no part of this work may be photocopied, stored in a retrieval system,
published, performed in public, adapted, broadcast,
transmitted, recorded or reproduced in any form or by any means,
without the prior permission of the copyright owner

The right of Carole Hill to be identified as
the author of this work has been asserted in accordance with
sections 77 and 78 of the Copyright, Designs and Patents Act 1988

First published 2010
Paperback edition 2017

A Royal Historical Society publication
Published by The Boydell Press
an imprint of Boydell & Brewer Ltd
PO Box 9, Woodbridge, Suffolk IP12 3DF, UK
and of Boydell & Brewer Inc.
668 Mt Hope Avenue, Rochester, NY 14620-2731, USA
website: www.boydellandbrewer.com

ISBN 978-0-86193-304-4 hardback
ISBN 978-0-86193-346-4 paperback

ISSN 0269-2244

A CIP catalogue record for this book is available
from the British Library

The publisher has no responsibility for the continued existence or accuracy of
URLs for external or third-party internet websites referred to in this book,
and does not guarantee that any content on such websites is,
or will remain, accurate or appropriate

TO AUBREY

'But yet lykth hym better that we take full holsomly hys blessyd/ blode to wassch vs of sinne; for ther is no lycour that is made lykyth hym so wele to yeue vs. For it is most precious, and that by the vertu of the blessyd godhead. And it is our owne kynde, and blessydfully ovyr flowth vs by vertu of his precious loue': Julian of Norwich, *Showings*, pt ii, ch. xii, lines 13–19.

Contents

List of Illustrations

Acknowledgements

My thanks are due to many people who have supported, encouraged and informed me during the production of this volume, only some of whom can be mentioned here. First, Professor Carole Rawcliffe, whose infectious enthusiasm for her subject was an early inspiration, and from whose critical scholarship I continue to benefit. I am particularly indebted to Christine Linehan, executive editor for the series, for her guidance and patience in leading me through the territory which must be traversed in order to produce a book ready for the press. I am immensely thankful to The Royal Historical Society for accepting my text, the illustrations for which could not have been published without generous financial support from the Scouloudi Foundation.

I must also express my great appreciation of generous funding from the Centre of East Anglian Studies at the University of East Anglia, which enabled this book's completion and my thanks to Professor John Charmley for facilitating this.

Without the unfailing affirmation of my family and friends the whole project of even becoming an undergraduate at the age of fifty would have been an impracticable fantasy. To subsequently complete a PhD, and then this book, without their continuing encouragement and even more, the staunch support of my husband, Aubrey, would likewise have been impossible. To him this book is dedicated.

Carole Hill,
Norwich
August 2010

The publication of this book has been assisted by a grant from
The Scouloudi Foundation in association with the
Institute of Historical Research

Abbreviations

ANC   Archdeacon of Norwich's court
BL   British Library
Bodl. Lib. Bodleian Library, Oxford
CPR   Calendar of patent rolls (TNA)
EETS   Early English Text Society
NCC   Norwich consistory court
NRO   Norfolk Record Office
NRS   Norfolk Record Society
PCC   Prerogative court of Canterbury
TNA   The National Archives
UEA   University of East Anglia

BAACT   *British Archaeological Association Conference Transactions*
EAA   *East Anglian Archaeology*
JEH   *Journal of Ecclesiastical History*
NA   *Norfolk Archaeology*
RCN   *Records of the city of Norwich*, ii, ed. W. Hudson and J. C. Tingey, Norwich 1906

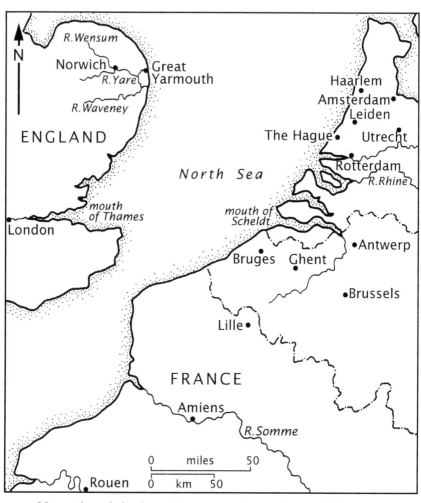

Norwich and the Low Countries: the proximity of Norwich
to cloth-producing towns

Introduction

Incarnational piety and the women of Norwich

'In this god brought oure ladye to myne vunderstandynge. I sawe hir gastlye in bodilye lyekenes, a sympille maydene and a meeke, yonge of age, in the stature scho was when scho conceyvede ... For abovene hir ys nothynge that is made botte the blessyde manhede of Criste.'[1]

This brief quotation from the *Showings* of the anchoress Julian of Norwich (c.1342–?1416) encapsulates a complexity of ideas and concepts that was current in the late Middle Ages and which is now associated with incarnational piety, a form of religious devotion focused on 'the blessyde manhede of Criste'. That is, God becoming flesh, born of a young girl, living on earth as a man among men in the person of Jesus of Nazareth, and dying the death of a convicted felon as described in the synoptic Gospels of the New Testament. In western Christendom, by the late medieval period, such devotion had evolved to include other popular and associated cults. These included devotion to the five wounds of Christ, and the salvific power of Jesus' holy name.[2] Each cult was commemorated by innovative masses and liturgies, incorporated widespread attachment to and veneration of Christ's fleshliness and was inclusive of his extended earthly family, the holy kin.[3] First in the hierarchy of the earthly family was his mother, the Blessed Virgin Mary, whose cult had gathered momentum since the twelfth century until she had become acknowledged as queen of heaven and empress of hell, and, as a

---

[1] *Julian of Norwich: A book of showings*, ed. E. Colledge and J. Walsh, Toronto 1978, pt I, ch. iv, p. 213, lines 24–35.
[2] In the centre aisle of St Andrew's church, Norwich, lies a large marble slab with indents (brasses removed) depicting a kneeling figure before a large cross, with a heart at its centre, and with free-floating dismembered hands in the quarters above, and feet in the quarters below. The slab has been reused and inscribed at a later date than its original manufacture.
[3] Gifts emblazoned with emblems of the holy name and the passion which were to be used or worn during mass are catalogued in W. H. St J. Hope, 'Inventories of the parish church of St Peter Mancroft, Norwich', NA xiv (1900), 153–240 at pp. 197, 201, 203, 206, 209, 211, 212, 216, 222. The silver gilt chalices of Robert and Christian Holdy, for example, were specifically listed as 'longyng to Ihc mase' ('belonging to the Jesus mass') (p. 206). The inventory gives invaluable insights into the cult of St Anne, Christ's legendary grandmother, as well as to the Virgin (pp. 218, 220, 221).

bridge between both, venerated as an intercessor without equal throughout Christendom.[4]

The Annunciation to the Virgin was a major religious feast.[5] The quintessential moment of Mary's conception of Jesus – the incarnation – is captured and repeatedly depicted in the carved stone, painted glass and wooden panels that survive in the late medieval parish churches of East Anglia, and of course beyond, as well as in illuminated manuscripts associated with religious observance. The angelic messenger, Gabriel, is shown as announcing to a very young, possibly prepubescent girl (therefore a virgin) that she is to bear the son of God.[6] This event, and its layered interpretations, became a major international cult, celebrated and enshrined in its highest English form at the Augustinian priory church of Our Lady of Walsingham in North Norfolk, a major site of pilgrimage which came to outrank in popularity and wealth that of Thomas Becket (d.1170) at Canterbury. Christ's incarnation, as the quotation demonstrates with great clarity, was specifically enabled by his young mother's unpolluted flesh; unlike her precursor, Eve, she demonstrated faithful obedience in response to this revelation and was celebrated as the gateway to salvation. Mary was therefore venerated as redemption's precursor and progenitrix.

The climax of a medieval pilgrimage to the Walsingham shrine was the displaying of a crystal phial containing a relic of the breast milk of the Virgin. The spiritual parallel made between Christ's spilled blood and Mary's milk is a recurring theme in late medieval iconography.[7] There was an understanding of the co-action of mother and son in the redemption of the world which is implicit in painting and more explicit in contemporary verse. The Virgin's free submission, physically and spiritually, to the will of God, led ultimately to that of her son. The offices used by the nuns of the Brigettine monastery at Sion reflect this: 'And therefore I may well say that my mother & I haue saued man, as yt had be with one hart I sufferynge in harte & body, & she in sorowe of harte and in loue.'[8]

---

[4] 'Dame du ciel, regente terrienne / Emperiere des infernaux palus': François-Villon (d.1463), quoted in M. Warner, *Alone of all her sex: the myth and the cult of the Virgin Mary*, New York 1976, 299–314.

[5] It was introduced by Pope Sergius I (687–710): ibid. 350.

[6] Such a Mary is shown in the *Bedford hours*, in an illumination showing the St Anne trinity, with a suppliant duchess kneeling at Anne's feet, as the diminutive Virgin and infant Christ stand on the side of her chair, all three raising their hands in blessing: BL, MS Add. 18850, fo. 257; *The Bedford hours*, ed. J. Backhouse, London 1990.

[7] An example is the triptych of Goswyn van der Weyden, commissioned by the Cistercians, and currently housed in the Museum of Ancient Art, Brussels. See C. Hill, 'Incarnational piety: women and religion in late medieval Norwich and its hinterlands', unpubl. PhD diss. UEA 2004, plate 12 at p. 96. See also S. Beckwith, *Christ's body: identity, culture and society in late medieval writings*, London–New York 1993, 58.

[8] *The myroure of Oure Ladye: containing a devotional treatise on divine service, with a translation of the offices used by the sisters of the Brigittine monastery of Sion, at Isleworth, during*

At another level the Annunciation also signified the indwelling of the Holy Spirit in Mary and its availability to all who would receive the gift, a prerequisite of salvation. Julian of Norwich even goes on in her text directly to connect the creation and Christ's passion with this conceptual moment, each one destined to lead to the other. Icons of the Annunciation and the crucifixion were universal. In every parish church of the time could be seen, between nave and chancel, the holy rood, a large-scale representation of the crucifixion showing Christ in his passion displaying his wounds. On either side of the cross his mother and the beloved Apostle John witnessed the end of his mission as a man on earth and the beginning of his eternal work of redemption. Simultaneously, the image of the mother witnessing her son's death made clear Mary's enormous investment in the accomplishment of this destiny. She it was who had, in the theological hermeneutic of the day, reinforced by contemporary understanding of Aristotelian and Galenic medicine, bestowed upon him his body – flesh, blood and bones – which, now crucified, was to be the means of salvation for all humankind.[9] Any mass, celebrating the power of Christ's wounds and passion to save mankind, implicitly venerated the woman who had provided that body. Central to this concept was the 'spending' of Christ's blood, which, as Julian wrote, was 'our owne kynde'.[10] The mass was the religious and cultural heart of the culture that this book examines, celebrating an incarnate God who spends himself physically for his creation: Christ as *caritas*. Christ as love, as self-giving, was a concept with which many women could readily engage and sought to express in their own daily lives.

Medieval thought, heavily dependent on Aristotelian theory, attributed to women the fleshly, damp and mutable aspects of reproduction and to the male the superior heat and energising life principle that engendered spirit.[11] This construct was reinforced by traditional patriarchal theology which regarded women as lesser and more imperfect beings, primarily designed for the physical and the domestic spheres: birth, nursing, feeding, child-rearing and attendance on the sick, dying and dead. Women were also thought to be, by their innate nature, like their fallen grandmother, Eve, more suscep-tible to moral corruption and sexual voraciousness.[12] Such thinking was compounded by the legal system: a woman had no status or identity outside

---

the fifteenth and sixteenth centuries, ed. J. H. Blunt (EETS e.s. xix, 1873), 25. These offices were used by the sisters of the Bridgettine monastery of Syon, in Isleworth, Middlesex.

9 R. Swanson, 'Passion and practice: the social and ecclesiastical implications of passion devotion in the late Middle Ages', in A. A. McDonald, H. N. B. Ridderbos and R. M. Schlusemann (eds), *The broken body: passion iconography in late medieval culture*, Gron-ingen 1998, 1–30 at p. 8 n. 18.

10 Julian of Norwich, *Showings*, pt ii, chapter xii, p. 343, lines 15–19.

11 P. Brown, *The body and society: men, women and sexual renunciation in early Christianity*, New York–Chichester 1988, 9–10.

12 Ibid. 108–9, 111–12.

that subsumed in her husband or father, and could never attain parity in any official or judicial sense, even if wealthy. The prevalent devotion to the tortured body of the mortally wounded Christ, which extended to his mainly female relatives, has been described as indicative of a 'feminisation of religion', with which, because of their allotted role, many women identified. Something of that thinking, or more precisely their response to that thinking, promoted much practical charitable activity among women in late medieval Norwich. It also enhanced to a substantial degree their attachment to and veneration of certain female saints, biblical, legendary and contemporary.

Charity was practised within the Christian context of the seven corporal works of mercy, which, on pain of damnation if in default, heavily emphasised the spiritual value accorded to the practical service and support owed to the marginalised by those able to pay for or execute it.[13] While the Church taught that all surplus wealth should be given to the sick and indigent, this spiritual ideal was clearly not always realised.[14] As preached the Dominican friar, John Bromyard, 'Where are the evil lovers of the world who a little while ago were with us? ... who ruled their subjects harshly and cruelly to obtain the aforesaid luxuries, and fleeced them? ... the false merchants who knew how to deceive a man to his face ... the cruel executors who increased the sorrow of widows?'[15] And if the onus placed upon the mercantile elite to succour the poor was great, the demands made upon their wives were greater still. Women's domain, as officially endorsed by the Church and understood by custom, was service to the body. And women in Norwich, especially those rich in resources and time, were, it seems, able and willing to engage in such personal service; indeed, they may have valued the mobility and autonomy such philanthropy required in a period when a respectable woman's place was at home attending to her household.[16] On a more quotidian level, the rolling up of sleeves and practice of the comfortable works by somewhat lower-status women also provided an opportunity for them to earn extra income.[17]

---

[13] Matthew xxv.34–46. The comfortable works were to give food to the hungry, drink to the thirsty, clothes to the naked, to visit the sick, aid the prisoner, shelter the homeless and bury the dead.

[14] This is endorsed in the will of Richard Caister, the venerated vicar of St Stephen's, Norwich: 'Item, ex pro bono Eccleis secundum canones sunt bona pauperum, omnia cetera bona mea pro maiori partie lego pauperibus sic quod paupers parrochie mee preferantur': NRO, reg./4, bk 8, fo. 135 (Castre), 1420.

[15] G. R. Owst, *Literature and pulpit in medieval England: a neglected chapter in the history of English letters and of the English people*, 2nd edn, Oxford 1966, 293.

[16] See, for example, the will of Margery Dogett: NRO, ANC, reg. Cook, fos 46–7 (Dogett), 1515.

[17] Many will remember women in the 1950s who were still identified in their locality as available for a small fee to attend a lying-in or a laying-out.

A range of lay female activities was associated with incarnational piety. These were multi-faceted, focusing upon the eucharist, but also embraced acts of spiritual and corporal mercy. They included the commissioning of saints' *Lives*, the donation of stained glass, the gift of a cherished rosary to a saint's image to promote intercession, the dispensing of bread to paupers, the tending of the sick poor and the washing of the dead. A survey of these undoubtedly gives a disproportionate view, skewed as the evidence must be towards those women with both time and money at their disposal and whose engagement or intention was recorded or left some tangible mark.[18] Those women who left no mark, and their activities, remain invisible. The practice of the seven corporal works of mercy was not, however, confined to the elite as recorded in public or corporate benefaction. These tasks were practised as a matter of course in many small ways by any woman who tended an old or ailing neighbour, or helped out at the lying-in or laying-out of a friend.[19] Such had always been the case, but, arguably, late medieval attitudes to the wounded body of Christ placed these activities in a heightened framework of redemption based on charitable reciprocity, which was reinforced by the richness of visible iconography and vernacular preaching.[20]

Context

Norwich merchants had long-standing international trading networks. As a consequence many became immensely rich, largely, and initially, through trade connected with textiles and their production, but also by diversifying their business interests. Inevitably much of their prosperity was accrued at the expense of the lesser, poorer artisans involved in some level of cloth production, whether broadcloth, worsted or humbler cloths, but still, through poverty, unable to rise to the status of full citizenship, or even, on occasion, to maintain their urban customer base. It has been estimated that by 1525 the wealthiest citizens of Norwich, who owned moveable goods to the value

[18] An example is Katherine Brasyer (d.1457) of St Stephen's parish, Norwich, whose lengthy will provided gifts across a wide social and economic divide, but all with a similar focus: NRO, NCC, reg, Brosyard, fos 58–9 (Brasyer), 1457.

[19] Margery Kempe describes how, after a journey, she was taken home, washed, dressed in fresh clothes, and looked after by another woman: *The booke of Margery Kempe*, ed. S. B. Meech and H. E. Allen (EETS o.s. ccxii, 1940, repr. 1997), i, ch. viii, p. 241, lines 28–30. Unless otherwise stated all references to the *Book of Margery Kempe* will be to the Meech and Allen edition.

[20] J. A. F. Thomson notes that it is spurious to separate 'pious' benefaction from 'charitable' gift or deed, as no such disjunction existed in the mind of the donor: 'Piety and charity in late medieval London', *JEH* xvi (1965), 178–95 at p. 180. For the influence of iconography see E. Duffy, *The stripping of the altars: traditional religion in England, c. 1400–1580*, New Haven–London 1992, 186–7, and 'De festo Sancti Nicholai', in *Mirk's festial: a collection of homilies of Johannes Mirkus (John Mirk)*, i, ed. T. Erbe (EETS e.s. xcvi, 1905), 12–13.

of between £100 and £1,000, comprised only 2 per cent of the population but owned between them 40 per cent of the taxable wealth. A further 4 per cent were assessed on sums of between £40 and £90.[21] These groups had for long constituted the leading men of the city, the mercantile elite being coterminous with the city's ruling body, thereby reinforcing the power of oligarchy and the *status quo*. Charitable bequests by the wealthy, initiating or augmenting provision for the poor, reflected this hard reality and, perhaps, the guilt induced by a nagging awareness of the great socio-economic divide. There is no disputing the fact that the entrepreneurial nature of successful Norwich men of business was enriching the *milieu* in which their womenfolk were finding opportunity to nurture and practice charitable work, even while their husbands were amassing the wealth that, arguably, may have made such charity necessary.

From Norwich's early days as an Anglo-Scandinavian settlement its links with the continent were always important and should not be underestimated in assessing the city's religious culture in the later medieval period.[22] For years a city second or third only to London in size and prosperity, Norwich was geographically well-placed for both domestic and international commerce, its situation on the banks of the Wensum giving ready access to the port of Yarmouth and its many trade routes, while also maintaining Norwich's own links with the Low Countries and Germany. In many senses Antwerp and Bruges were quicker and easier of access to the Norwich merchant than Exeter or York, making it a vibrant *entrepôt* for continental goods. Such links also became the conduit for ideas and innovations that, by the early fifteenth century, made Norwich a vector of what might be termed cutting-edge piety, especially among women.

By water, Norwich could also provision and trade with London speedily and safely. The commercial development and wealth of the city, as a regional centre of religious and secular government, rested firmly on its busy staithes, sought-after licensed property, those downstream of Bishop's Bridge being its most important.[23] Like the religious houses, many mercantile properties in the city, especially those with useful proximity to the river, boasted spacious stone or brick-built undercrofts the better to receive and store imported goods as well as prepare commodities for export and to enable the trader to engage in expeditious front-line trading: sixty of these, dating from the early fifteenth century, have been documented within the walls of Norwich,

---

[21] J. Pound, *Tudor and Stuart Norwich*, Chichester 1988, appendix 2, pp. 179–82.

[22] B. Ayers, *Norwich, a fine city*, Stroud 2003, 27–9. Ayers points to place-name evidence, and also to the pre-Conquest churches in Norwich dedicated to St Vaast of Maastricht and St Amand, as well as the surviving St Clement Fyebridge, all sited near the river.

[23] S. Kelly, 'The economic topography and structure of Norwich *c.* 1300', in U. Priestley (ed.), *Men of property: an analysis of the Norwich enrolled deeds, 1285–1311*, Norwich 1983, 13–39. See also P. Dunn, 'Trade', and R. Frost, 'The urban elite', in C. Rawcliffe and R. Wilson (eds), *Medieval Norwich*, London 2004, 213–34, 235–53.

mostly on the southern bank of the Wensum in the four most prestigious parishes of the city.[24]

Clearly the successful merchant families of Norwich, with an ambitious foot in both town and country properties, many of them spending considerable time trading abroad, either as factors or masters, were far from parochial or provincial in their experience or aspiration.[25] This is also true of the journeymen, craftsmen and craftswomen who had to travel in order to earn a living. There was much international influence and activity among locally-employed glaziers (including a female one) and painters.[26] Likewise the transmission has been identified of the favoured styles of art of the Low Counties through painters fulfilling commissions for rood-screen panels, especially in areas around Norwich known for their expertise in cloth production, such as Aylsham, Cawston, Ranworth and Worstead.[27] Such was the background which cultivated a demand for, and enabled the commissioning of, many of Norwich's surviving medieval religious structures and artefacts. Arguably, too, this *milieu* nurtured and influenced a lively and interactive piety pursued and expressed in different ways by its citizens, male and female. It is, however, the women of Norwich and its environs who are the subject of this work, the 'silent' half of this entrepreneurial and in many ways exceptional population. Was there a distinctive local 'female piety'? What, if any, were its distinguishing qualities? How far did the often inherently misogynistic theology of the period become integral to popular observance?

Sources

Inevitably, where a woman's identity is ultimately subsumed in that of her husband or father, her public life or private thoughts can never be fully recovered; documentary evidence for women is sparse, and it is therefore necessary to look elsewhere for sources of evidence for their activity. And indeed the rising merchant classes and their craftsmen-employees in and around the city, both men and women, did leave evidence of a different sort to that normally used by historians, thus bridging the gap in the written evidence: their commissions, charitable, commemorative or literary, as well as architectural, are examples. Norwich still retains well over half of the

---

[24] Ayers, *Norwich*, 121–5. There is a map of the sites of the undercrofts at p. 124.

[25] R. Frost, 'The aldermen of Norwich, 1461–1509: the study of a civic elite', unpubl. PhD diss. Cambridge 1996, passim.

[26] D. King, *The medieval stained glass of St Peter Mancroft, Norwich*, Oxford 2006, p. lxxiii n. 106, and passim.

[27] J. Mitchell, 'Painting in East Anglia around 1500: the continental connection', in J. Mitchell (ed.), *England and the continent in the Middle Ages: studies in memory of Andrew Martindale: proceedings of the 1996 Harlaxton Symposium*, Stamford 2000, 365–80.

forty-six parish churches that stood within its walls in the 1520s.[28] Many possess brass memorials, some their medieval glass and wall-paintings, or vestiges of chapels. Medieval churches in the weaving hinterlands of Norwich also retain stunning examples of past investment, including rood-screens and glass.[29] Thus the focus of female devotion, as demonstrated in works of mercy and acts of charity to the body, is still clearly visible in glass, wood and stone.[30] Archaeological research carried out in Norwich over the last three decades has also been invaluable in 'pinning' accumulated knowledge to precise locations, for example the excavations within the north-east bailey of the castle and, later, the Magdalene Street sites, as well as more recent work on the sites of the Franciscan and Carmelite friaries.[31] Palaeontological analysis has further supplied information about lifespan, physical activity and trauma, as well as evidence of neo-natal mortality of mother and infant.[32]

Norfolk and Suffolk also produced poets, dramatists and authors within and without the cloister whose works provide glimpses into women's lives at many levels of society, insights into their attachments and priorities. Such are Osbern Bokenham and his contemporary, John Lydgate, both professed religious, and the unknown authors of the *N-town* and the *Digby plays*.[33] The texts written most famously by Norfolk women, Julian of Norwich's *Book of showings* and the autobiographical *Book of Margery Kempe*, have come, understandably, to dominate and colour many studies of religion in the period without necessarily placing them in their urban context among

[28] N. P. Tanner, *The Church in late medieval Norwich, 1370–1532*, Toronto 1984, 2. This book was based on Tanner's 1973 Oxford DPhil. diss. 'Popular religion in Norwich with special reference to the evidence of wills, 1370–1532'.

[29] P. Cattermole and S. Cotton, 'Medieval parish church building in Norfolk, *NA* xxxviii (1983), 235–79; S. Cotton, 'Medieval roodscreens in Norfolk: their construction and painting dates', *NA* xl (1989), 44–54; W. W. Williamson, 'Saints on Norfolk rood-screens and pulpits', *NA* xxxi (1957), 299–346; E. Duffy, 'The parish, piety and patronage in late medieval East Anglia: the evidence of rood screens', in K. French, G. Gibbs and B. Kumin (eds), *The parish in English life, 1400–1600*, Manchester 1997, 133–62.

[30] An example is the window panel showing the life of St Elizabeth of Hungary in St Peter Mancroft parish church, Norwich, and the wall-paintings at Potter Heigham church. For examination of performance of the comfortable works see chapter 5 below.

[31] B. Ayers and others (eds), *Excavations within the north-east bailey of Norwich castle, 1979*, Norwich 1985; M. Atkin, A. Carter and D. H. Evans (eds), *Excavations in Norwich, 1971–8*, pt II, Norwich 1985; P. Emery and E. Rutledge (eds), *Norwich Greyfriars: excavations at the former Mann Egerton site, Prince of Wales Road, Norwich, 1990–5*, Norwich 2007.

[32] J. Bown and A. Stirland, 'Criminals and paupers: excavations at the site of the church and graveyard of St Margaret in Combusto', unpubl. report, Norfolk Archaeology Unit 1987.

[33] *Legendys of hooly wummen by Osbern Bokenham*, ed. M. S. Serjeantson (EETS o.s. ccvi, 1938, repr. 1971); *Lydgate's minor poems*, ed. O. Glauning (EETS e.s. lxxx, 1900); *The N-town play: Cotton MS Vespasian D.8*, ed. S. Spector (EETS s.s. xi, xii, 1991); *The Digby plays*, ed. F. J. Furnivall (EETS e.s. lxx, 1896, repr. 1967).

their 'even chrsitians'.[34] But while the works of these very different and exceptional authors share many similar preoccupations, where stand the rest? Mary Erler's recent research on Margaret Purdans (d.1483), a pious and book-owning widow of Norwich, has uncovered important and interesting connections in her circle which may go some way towards answering that question.[35] Her remarkable network might yet be extended, or be shown to be replicated in the lives of other women of the city, and may thus throw light on the acitivities of the less exceptional.

An attempt has been made in this book to balance the physical and literary evidence with the valuable testamentary and other documentary evidence left by Norwich women. While an extensive examination of the archive of the Norfolk Record Office cannot be claimed, a selection of testamentary material from registers held there, and proved in the Norwich consistory court and in the archdeacon of Norwich's court, has been used. The wills of some women in particular are cited because they yield signs of personal piety or inclination to specific charitable benefaction. From many, little if any such information can be gleaned. This is a local and regional study; although some women living in Norwich in the late Middle Ages left wills that were subsequently proved in the prerogative court of Canterbury, these were generally the exception.[36]

Norman Tanner's survey of 1,515 late medieval wills of the laity from between 1370 and 1532 estimated an approximate ratio of 3:1 male to female (379) testators. He selected 615 of these (of which the male to female ratio is unstated) and added the 289 surviving wills of the secular clergy.[37] His sample of female wills was, therefore, inevitably very under-representative of female testators in Norwich generally. For this book the wills of fifty-two Norwich women living or with interests in the city, and further wills of women from neighbouring districts, have been used, while the records of the city of Norwich have supplemented the accumulating sightings of Norwich's working female population.[38]

However, the use of wills alone as a source for such research is hedged about with limitations, not least because of the widowed status of most female testators,[39] who were thus essentially more independent, and hence

---

[34] For further discussion of Julian and her contemporaries see C. Hill, 'Julian and her sisters: female piety in late medieval Norwich', in L. Clark (ed.), *The fifteenth century*, vi, Woodbridge 2006, 165–87.

[35] M. C. Erler, *Women, reading, and piety in late medieval Norwich*, Cambridge 2002, 68–84.

[36] The will of the widow, Agnes Thorpe (d. 1503), was one of these: TNA, PCC, reg. Moone, fo. 19 (Thorpe), 1500–1.

[37] Tanner, *Church in Norwich*, 113–14.

[38] These are held at the Norfolk Record Office: *RCN*. For examples see pp. 360–1, 365, 384.

[39] C. Peters, *Patterns of piety: women, gender and religion in late medieval and Reformation England*, Cambridge 2003, 44.

more visible,[40] than their married sisters, who had no legal power to administer property without the consent of their husbands. On this basis, and from the evidence of their testaments, there might indeed be an argument for a discrete, or at least a more identifiable, 'widows' piety'. Norwich women who were widowed, and who chose to remain so, were perhaps able to pursue and develop a life akin to the *devotio moderna*, a life balanced between contemplative prayer and piety and active charitable deeds. In this context the fourteenth-century *Book of vices and virtues*, known by the fifteenth century in many vernacular redactions throughout Europe, including England and the Low Countries, is of relevance. It speaks of widowhood as the fourth state of chastity:

> Thre thinges longen to the estate of widowhode. The first is to hide hire and be prieliche (private) dwellyng in hire place and nouzt for to folewe suspecious felawschep ... wherfore seynt Poule vndertaketh thes yonge wommen widowes that weren idel & besy to go alday hider and thider and iangelode & speke to moche, but thei schulde schut hem with-ynnehouses and entende and be besy to do goode dedes, as Seynt Poule techeth. [these young widowed women that were idle and busy to go all day hither and thither to gossip and talk too much, should rather stay indoors and give heed to be occupied to do good deeds as St Paul teaches].[41]

That said, and illustrative though wills are of some female concerns and attitudes, whether these women were married or not, they alone will never conclusively reveal the stuff of daily precept and practice that preoccupied women during their busy, and sometimes short, lives. While the social, political and economic *milieu* of late medieval Norwich supplies the topographical context of women's work and worship, in particular how their activities were funded,[42] other means have to be found, assessed and contextualised in order to estimate whether or not women had spiritual priorities or expressions of devotion that differed from those of their menfolk.

Historiography

A project such as this would not have been possible without the comprehensive study of the Church in late medieval Norwich undertaken in the 1970s and 1980s by Norman Tanner. To his assessment of the surviving wills of the period every medieval historian of the city repeatedly returns.

---

[40] C. M. Barron and A. F. Sutton (eds), *Medieval London widows, 1300–1500*, London 1994, p. xiii. See also K. Lacy, 'Margaret Croke (d.1491)', ibid. pp. 143–64.
[41] *The book of vices and virtues*, ed. W. N. Francis (EETS o.s. ccxvii, 1942, repr. 1968), 250–1.
[42] Rawcliffe and Wilson, *Medieval Norwich*. This contains essays by thirteen scholars. See also Hill, 'Incarnational piety'.

In the area of commercial enterprise Ruth Frost's dissertation on Norwich's aldermen-merchants has proved an invaluable resource,[43] while the publication in 1992 of Eamon Duffy's *Stripping of the altars* presented all students and scholars not only with a mind-altering experience, but also with a lively synthesis of disciplines.[44] His study offered a fine example of what might be possible in the task of attempting (to use an apt metaphor) to put flesh on old bones, whether or not one agrees with his revisionist conclusions. Such productive interdisciplinarity was taken further by Carole Rawcliffe in her study of the Great Hospital in Norwich, which drew together so many aspects of the dynamic of Norwich life and experience, and revealed a hitherto unrecognised seam of female investment and activity.[45] Duffy's work on East Anglian churches and their benefactors has been reinforced and complemented by the more recent study of lay piety and commemoration in Suffolk undertaken by Judith Middleton-Stewart. [46] With what appears to be a cast of thousands, this book unfolds a medieval pageant of wool-enriched inhabitants who rebuilt their magnificent parish churches, and embellished both the buildings and their liturgical worship with their wealth.

No proper student of Norwich and Norfolk's religious history can afford to ignore Francis Blomefield (1705–52), the great eighteenth-century recorder of Norfolk's ecclesiastical treasures.[47] While neither his accuracy nor that of his co-editor, Charles Parkin, can be uncritically relied upon, the vast canon of Blomefield and his associate eighteenth- and nineteenth-century antiquarians has to be consulted, especially as much that they saw and recorded has not survived.

Finally, Mary Grace's edition of the records of the prestigious gild of St George in Norwich supplies insights into the social and political culture of the city, including the cult of St Margaret of Antioch, especially when examined in conjunction with the contemporary legendary literature featuring the saint.[48] It is in the interstices between the documentary, the legendary and the political that challenging and perhaps unexpected glimpses into the life of the city can be achieved.

---

[43] Frost, 'The aldermen of Norwich'.
[44] Duffy, *Stripping of the altars*.
[45] C. Rawcliffe, *Medicine for the soul: the life, death and resurrection of an English medieval hospital: St Giles, Norwich, c. 1249–1550*, Stroud 1999.
[46] J. Middleton-Stewart, *Inner purity and outward splendour: death and remembrance in the deanery of Dunwich, Suffolk, 1370–1547*, Woodbridge 2001.
[47] F. Blomefield, *An essay towards a topographical history of the county of Norfolk*, 2nd edn, London 1805–10.
[48] *Records of the gild of St George in Norwich, 1389–1547: a transcript with an introduction*, ed. M. Grace (NRS ix, 1937).

Norwich women: devotional patrons and exemplars

This, then, is the context in which the study of Mary moves on to an exploration of the cult of her legendary mother. Norwich's prosperous mercantile community, like its trading partners in the Low Countries and Germany, exhibited a strong devotion to St Anne that placed her at the pinnacle of the heavenly hierarchy of intercessors, next to her miraculously-born ever-virgin daughter. Differences can be perceived between male and female concepts of the *cultus*. St Anne was invoked by women with acute concerns about conception in particular, but also about childbirth generally, as was St Margaret of Antioch, though for a multiplicity of different reasons. The fifteenth-century *Legendys of hooly wummen* by Osbern Bokenham, Austin canon of Clare, in Suffolk, who incidentally had wide-ranging connections with female patrons, contains a life of St Anne that gave hope to the infertile, particularly the rich desperate for an heir.[49] It gives further insight into a devotion that was enormously popular locally, but which, sadly, has left little material trace in Norwich, probably because of the scorn felt by reformers towards Anne's non-biblical identity.

The Virgin and her mother were, however, not the only female saints venerated by the populace of Norwich. The ancient cult of St Margaret of Antioch has, fortunately, left significant surviving material evidence throughout Norfolk, even if few signs now remain in the city. As the patron of safe childbirth she was ubiquitous. In an age when the neo-natal death of mother and/or child was a common occurrence that crossed all socio-economic boundaries, the saint's legend and familiar iconography offered hope to the fearful in life and assurance in death. A quite different aspect of the cult is connected to that of St Jerome, which might suggest a focus especially attractive to the pious widow or vowess. Episodic outbreaks of plague in Norwich were concurrent with an increasing elaboration of civic ritual, incorporating gild processions and masses. Such is the context for St Margaret's role in the legend of the highly popular St George, patron of the city's elite gild.[50]

The local cult of St Margaret was complemented by that of a biblical saint, Mary Magdalen, and of the very recent and influential married saint and author, Bridget of Sweden (d.1373), whose book of revelations was in wide circulation in East Anglia by the mid-fifteenth century. Aside from the individual interest of these cults as promoters of various kinds of devotion and behaviour, it seems that together the three saints provided an interesting nexus around which women could operate on a distinctive and independent level. Although not every woman in Norwich was intent upon seeking higher spiritual development, this was a culture that enabled and supported

---

49 *Hooly wummen*, 38–58.
50 *Gild of St George*, 16–18.

women in their daily lives and allowed pragmatic engagement at times of crisis: in their various ways these three saints provided the substructure for this.

The unique iconography inspired by the cult of Mary Magdalen once visible in the city churches is there no longer, but it is still possible to glimpse her image in the cathedral, in a fourteenth-century painted panel in the Norman chapel of St Andrew in the north transept. It is her association with the body and blood of the crucified Christ that traditionally imbued her image with sacramental significance. Two small defaced donor figures, a man and a woman, are tucked in at the foot of the cross, the veiled woman wedged in by Christ's feet and turned towards the Magdalen. Further, the saint's legendary association with leprosy and her patronage of a *leprosarium*, which offered material support for the diseased in Norwich, formed part of the framework of spiritual redemption and the *devotio moderna* with which she was so closely identified. The appeal of her cult to women, especially to those attempting to combine an active and contemplative piety in their mode of living, is validated by Bokenham's verse *Life*, his longest,[51] while the *N-town play* and the *Digby plays*, all of East Anglian provenance, in which the Magdalen significantly features, offer valuable insights into contemporary perception.[52]

Here too the voices of Julian of Norwich and Margery Kempe cannot be ignored. Significantly, each puts the Magdalen at the top of her list of saints to be regarded as successful and inspiring exemplars for other sinful 'even christians' in search of salvation.[53] Margery's personal role model, St Bridget of Sweden, recorded in her own visionary writings that Christ had revealed to her

That there were thre that plesdi hym byfor all other, 'Mi modir … John Baptist, and the Magdalane'… wen the Magdalane was conuertid, than saide the fendes, 'How sall we do? We haue lost a fat pray. Scho wheshes hir so white with terres that we dar not luke on hyr. Sho couers hir so with gude werkes, and sho is so warme and feruent in suruys of Gode, that we dar noyt com ner to hir'.[54]

---

[51] *Hooly wummen*, 136–72.
[52] T. Coletti, *Mary Magdalene and the drama of saints: theater, gender and religion in late medieval England*, Philadelphia 2004, 22–49.
[53] Julian of Norwich, *Showings*, pt II, ch. xxxviii, p. 446, line 15; *Book of Margery Kempe*, i, ch. xxi, p. 49, lines 23–6. In the 'final page' of her book, in a section called 'Prayers of the creature' (ii. 253, lines 9–22), Margery names four saints beginning with the Magdalen, three of whom are noted for their sexual sins, and asks for the mercy shown to them. She proclaims herself 'qwyk & gredy to hy contemplacyon in God', a very physical expression of religious hunger.
[54] *The liber celestis of St Bridget of Sweden: the Middle English version in British Library, MS Claudius Bi, together with a life of the saint from the same manuscript*, ed. R. Ellis (EETS o.s. ccxci, 1987), iv, ch. cix, p. 347, lines 27–8; 348, lines 2–6.

It was a model that Margery was to adopt, very literally, as her own, repelling as many neighbours and fellow-travellers as fiends. The influence on Margery and other mothers of the writings of St Bridget seems to have been quite specific, if, in fifteenth-century reality, terrifying in its enormity. Bridget placed the weight of responsibility for the spiritual salvation of all children firmly in the lap of their mothers. This was their ultimate and ineluctable role, one which caused the saint years of *angst*, mirrored in Dame Margery's uncompromising relationship with her adult son.[55]

The threat of sudden, unshriven death, which was never far distant in the late Middle Ages (and its accompanying 'fendes' looking for 'fat pray'), spurred many people to plan strategies to promote prayers of intercession, if possible combined with charitable works. In such a context, women's lack of autonomy, even in their personal movement, may have been a catalyst in their growing involvement in, and attachment to, charitable activity. Certainly it was so with the restless Margery Kempe and, though not necessarily typical in expression or degree, there is little reason to think that her aspirations were much at variance with those of many of her contemporaries. Since her detractors have often argued a contrary view, this study may go some way towards redressing the balance in favour of the 'undocumented' women of Norwich.

How exceptional was Norwich in its manifest piety? Arguments have been made in favour of a substantial claim to unequalled spiritual standing in late medieval western Christendom, citing, for example, not only Julian's text and her sphere of influence, but also Norwich's other anchorites, some female, and its hermits, as well as the possible existence of several beguinages.[56] The enigmatic groups of lay holy women living a life of apostolic poverty under self-imposed rules, rather than under the authority of the established (male) ecclesiastical hierarchy, which, unique to Norwich, survived for over seventy years, are also cited. The beguines on the continent were, by the fifteenth century, long formalised and enclosed in orthodox religious orders, often Cistercian, but there remained a legacy of innovative religious thought and writing which seemed to find uniquely fertile ground in late medieval Norwich.[57] It may be that Julian of Norwich represented its greatest flowering. Certainly her writings, like her visionary experiences, all bear the same characteristics as those of her earlier continental sisters: ecstatic, one-to-one communion with God, visions and preoccupation with the life, and particularly the redemptive wounds and death, of Christ. Unlike most of the beguine and other female continental mystics, though, Julian was nurtured as a recluse in the context of her highly industrial location, at St Julian's cell, near the busy quays of King Street, Conesford. Her influ-

---

[55] *Book of Margery Kempe*, ii, ch.ii.

[56] N. P. Tanner, 'Religious practice', in Rawcliffe and Tanner, *Medieval Norwich*, 137–55.

[57] D. Devlin, 'Feminine lay piety in the high Middle Ages: the beguines', in J. Nichols and L. T. Shanks (eds), *Medieval religious women*, I: *Distant echoes*, Kalamazoo 1984, 190.

ence is undoubted: as Norman Tanner has noted, after two brief mentions of anchorites in the leet rolls of Norwich, in 1287/8 and 1312/13, no further examples are documented in the city until Julian at the end of the fourteenth century. Thereafter there appears to be a burgeoning of around ten anchorites and anchoresses who were concurrent in Norwich.[58]

This apparent steady increase in numbers cannot be categorically identified as a 'movement' perhaps triggered by Julian's vocation, but the possibility cannot be dismissed. Nor can possible spiritual links with the shadowy 'beguinages'.[59] These groups of lay women, like their solitary sisters and brothers, must have placed special value on a direct unmediated relationship with God. That they attracted bequests, as did Julian and her reclusive contemporaries and successors, there is no doubt.[60] Alderman John Gilbert, for example, in making his bequest, tacitly requested the prayers of nuns and the anchoress of Carrow and 'hir maydens', as well as those of the 'sisters of St Laurence'. Indeed, one in five of the city's parishioners left bequests to the city's solitaries, a much greater incidence than in other urban centres, including London.[61] Clearly, the presence and intercession of a variety of people following exceptional religious vocations were greatly valued in Norwich.

There is also evidence of the lively and extensive regeneration of Norwich's many parish churches, while the prevalence of book ownership may also function as an indicator of spiritual awareness and aspiration.[62] Many more books may have been in circulation than surviving wills seem to indicate. There was also a steady increase in the number of graduates among the secular clergy of Norwich (twelve out of 158 between 1370 and 1449, rising to twenty-five out of sixty between 1500 and 1532),[63] which, along with the presence of four friaries, may have been a factor in promoting better access to books and the teaching of their contents to the population, particularly women. Margery Kempe herself exemplifies the possibility of such relationships through her literary dealings with various 'reading priests', which included the transmission of knowledge of the continental female mystics.[64] The wills of some women in Norwich record the exchange and circulation of books, and it may be that many undocumented women were part of such

[58] Tanner, Church in Norwich, 58. Tanner's argument for increased numbers is based on the paucity of surviving will evidence prior to 1370, and the incomplete leet rolls of Norwich, which name offending anchorites only, of which there are just two. This does not necessarily mean that there were no others: Hill, 'Julian and her sisters', 170–1.
[59] For specific testamentary references see Tanner, Church in Norwich, 64–5.
[60] References to bequests to anchorites are given ibid. appendix 7, pp. 198–203.
[61] Ibid. 150–5.
[62] Erler, Women, reading, 68–9.
[63] Tanner, Church in Norwich, 28–32.
[64] Book of Margery Kempe, i, ch. xvii, p. 39, lines 23–5; ch. lx, p. 147, line 2; ch. lxii, p. 154, lines 10–14.

networks.[65] In contrast, there is no evidence of such practices among the godly women of late medieval Bristol, for example, apart from bequests to churches of a few service books.[66] This is one of several differences that are surprising in a mercantile community which, like Norwich, was engaged in international commerce at the water's edge.

In Norwich the expression of pious devotion by both sexes was marked by a 'feminisation of religion'. It was characterised by the veneration of the wounded physical body of Christ and the emphasis on the matrilineal line of his earthly family. Women in the city found practical expression for their piety in charitable works that were perceived as an extension of his redemptive passion, and conformed to his injunction in the Gospel of St Matthew. Women who paid considerable sums in advance to become resident nursing sisters in Norwich hospitals exemplify this pragmatic piety.[67] Perhaps the question to be asked should not be whether Norwich was Europe's most religious city, but rather whether its women were the fulcrum of a highly innovative lay piety as well as personal participants in an evolving and vibrant religion.

[65] For example Margaret Purdans, NCC, reg. Caston, fos 163–5 (1483).
[66] S. J. Adams, 'Religion, society and godly women: the nature of female piety in a late medieval urban community', unpubl. PhD thesis, Bristol 2001, 64.
[67] Rawcliffe, *Medicine for the soul*, 173.

1

St Anne

Almost all traces of the once ubiquitous cult of St Anne are now gone from Norfolk churches. Her image would once have been venerated with lights in churches throughout the county.[1] But all that now survives of her is the odd small panel of medieval painted glass, a few pieces of sculptured stone and only three or possibly four rood-screen panels.[2] The detailed sixteenth-century inventories of the parish church of St Peter Mancroft stimulate speculation as to what may for other city churches have been forever lost.[3] The glass panel there of St Anne teaching the Virgin to read, a fragmentary piece of this scene at Mulbarton, the Flemish glass roundel at Ketteringham and the German glass panel at Hingham;[4] Blomefield's report of the saint with her daughter and the twelve Apostles in an east window in the chapel of St Anne at Fersfield, where he was priest: all hint at lost treasures.[5] Any comprehensive assessment of Anne's popularity is thus greatly compromised. Norwich, it seems, was thoroughly purged of any sign of her after the Reformation. Her apocryphal identity and association with the cult of the Virgin would have made her an early casualty of the reformed Church, which was quintessentially a religion of the word, no longer characterised by image or painting. The dangers of arguing from negative evidence are manifold, but the disappearance of St Anne's image in Norfolk, and particularly Norwich, speaks volumes in view of what is known of earlier devotion to her there and elsewhere.

The role of St Anne in the religious observance, personal and commercial life of Norwich, and in artistic and spiritual commemoration, is complex and inter-related. As the legendary mother of the Blessed Virgin Mary and her

---

[1]   Duffy, *Stripping of the altars*, 182 n. 73.
[2]   W. Martin, 'Some fragments of sculptured stone found in a barn at East Barsham', *NA* xi (1892), 257–8; Williamson, 'Saints on Norfolk rood-screens', 299–346. The painted panels are at Elsing, Harpley, Houghton St Giles and probably Horsham St Faith. For the glass see A. E. Nichols, *The early art of Norfolk: a subject list of extant and lost art including items relevant to early drama*, Kalamazoo 2002, 49–50.
[3]   Hope, 'Inventories', 153–240. The inventories were made in the very early sixteenth century. Inventories also survive for the churches of St Andrew and St Mary Coslany, though recorded much later, and under very different circumstances, in 1548–52: J. L'Estrange, 'The church goods of St Andrew and St Mary Coslany, in the city of Norwich, Temp. Edward vi', *NA* vii (1872), 45–78.
[4]   For Mulbarton see Nichols, *The early art of Norfolk*, 49–50. On the glass at Hingham and Ketteringham I am grateful for personal communication with David King.
[5]   Blomefield, *History of Norfolk*, i. 105.

two sisters, Mary Cleophas and Mary Salome, grandmother of Christ and, as it was understood, six of his male Apostles, she was often portrayed as a prosperous thrice-married merchant's wife, the matriarch of a powerful, indeed world-changing male dynasty.[6] Her life story therefore had many resonances for the ambitious mercantile families of the city. Much more important, her first-born Mary being the vessel of the saviour of the world, placed Anne firmly in the role of the progenitrix of the incarnate God, and therefore instrumental in the redemption of mankind, in a real sense mediating it. And this she achieved without the need of the dynamic of virginity, which alone earned for women spiritual parity with men.[7] She offered a powerful interpretation of female spiritual potential.

The veneration of St Anne was established in East Anglia earlier than elsewhere in England. Her feast had been flourishing in Bury St Edmunds since 1309, though it remained unconfirmed by papal edict until 1378. In 1382 Urban VI, as a compliment to Anne of Bohemia, new queen of Richard II, ordered the observance of the feast throughout the English Church.[8] This can only have given renewed impetus to an already well-established devotion and celebration of St Anne's special place in the affections of her devotees. Locally, such a boost must have been apparent when Anne, with Richard, visited Norwich in 1381, and she bestowed her patronage (including a new ceiling lavishly decorated with her heraldic eagle) on St Giles's hospital, her name-saint being its co-dedicatee.[9]

More widely, participation in trade, particularly with the Low Countries and Germany, assured much cultural and social exchange and had considerable significance in areas of personal choice, such as devotion to particular saints. St Anne was venerated universally in the Low Countries and Germany as the woman at the pinnacle of a spiritual dynasty vibrant with incarnational and redemptive power.[10] Numerous surviving fourteenth- and fifteenth-century free-standing images of her and magnificent gilded altarpieces in which she is the focal point, as well as paintings commissioned from the foremost artists of the time, vividly demonstrate her position and authority as precursor of Christ. Fine examples still abound, particularly in

[6] Mary Cleophas, married to Alpheus, was the mother of James, Joseph, Simon and Jude; Mary Salome, married to Zebedee, was the mother of James the Great and John the Evangelist. During the Middle Ages these 'subsidiary' Marys came to be identified with women of that name mentioned in the Gospels.
[7] C. W. Bynum, *Holy feast and holy fast: the religious significance of food to medieval women*, Berkeley 1987, 261–2.
[8] *The Middle English stanzaic versions of the Life of St Anne*, ed. R. E. Parker (EETS o.s. clxxiv, 1928, repr. 1971), introduction at p. x.
[9] Rawcliffe, *Medicine for the soul*, 118.
[10] T. H. Lloyd, *England and the German Hanse, 1157–1611: a study of their trade and commercial diplomacy*, Cambridge 1991, 164.

Belgium and Germany.[11] Clearly, such striking images influenced visiting Norfolk merchants as well as local craftsmen who travelled abroad and the 'alien journeymen' commissioned to work in Norfolk churches.

In the fifteenth century the city possessed at least three gilds dedicated to St Anne and a minimum of nine chapels under her patronage.[12] The evidence of wills shows a particularity of attachment to the saint's patronage and protection,[13] and at the affluent end of parish life devotion is demonstrated in the surviving inventory of St Peter Mancroft, in which artefacts and images associated with their St Anne gild and chapel were listed as being carefully stored and in use during the fifteenth century.[14] In the wider county, a further twenty-seven gilds and chapels can be identified, but this list is unlikely to be comprehensive.

The incarnation and the matrilineal line

The frequent and familiar depiction in glass, brass and painting of St Anne teaching the Virgin to read characterises her place in incarnational devotion. She is to be found engaged in this task on the screen at Harpley St Laurence, uniquely in Norfolk, together with her husband, a youthful Joachim (*see* plate 1); at Elsing St Mary (beautifully drawn but almost gone); and at Houghton St Giles. Each of these churches is close to the shrine of Our Lady of Walsingham, and thus would have been a possible stopping place for rest and intercession for the pilgrim either *en route* to the shrine or returning home, full of positive images.

Hence the depiction of the Virgin with a book in almost every late medieval north European Annunciation. The Annunciation is the moment of conception, of incarnation, the path to which has plainly been prepared by Anne. The archangel Gabriel is the messenger, conveyor of inward knowledge. Many stained-glass Annunciations – for example the window at Bale church – depict the Holy Spirit as a dove, entering the Virgin's eye-line, signifying conception through sight. At another level of understanding, this was perceived as the reception of the indwelling spirit of God through interior or spiritual insight; the feast of the Annunciation marked the universality

---

[11] For example, the triptych of the confraternity of St Anne in Louven, *c.* 1509 (inv. 2784); St Anne with the Virgin and Child and St Joachim, by Joos van der Beke, *c.* 1540 (inv. 565), both currently in the Royal Museum of Ancient Art, Brussels: T. Muller, *Sculpture in the Netherlands, Germany, France, Spain, 1400–1500*, trans. E. Scott and W. R. Scott, Harmondsworth 1966, plates at pp. 105, 114, 189.

[12] References for the evidence of the cult of St Anne throughout the county are listed in appendix 1 below.

[13] The wills of Annor and John Gilbert (1466), for example, which are discussed at pp. 44–5 below.

[14] Blomefield, *History of Norfolk*, iv, passim; Hope, 'Inventories', 159, 161, 170, 172.

of this gift for all.[15] This echoes the belief that simply seeing the sacring at the mass was a means of obtaining redemptive grace.[16] The window at Bale All Saints is composed of at least five, possibly six, Annunciations, all of Norwich School glass (*see* plate 2). In the fifteenth century every window in the church probably displayed such a scene, thereby enhancing the experience of the female pilgrim, and, no doubt, that of all pious visitors, irrespective of gender.[17]

In the 'Anna and Joachim' play from the *N-town play* Anne's announcement and definition of her name to her husband brings to attention the wider significance of her spiritual role and its implications for the play's medieval audience. That the cycle is of East Anglian provenance also speaks to the extent of St Anne's cult locally. The role assigned to St Anne in the play, and in the legends and English stanzaic poems of the fifteenth century more generally, is revealed from the outset as divinely inspired, miraculous and with specific intention: to be no less than the conduit of God's grace to the world. Imperfect humankind, perpetually doomed to sin by the action of Eve, and its subsequent estrangement from God, required grace to achieve redemption and salvation: 'My name is Anne, that is to sey, "grace"', says St Anne, 'We wete not how *gracyous* God wyl to us be.'[18]

The *N-town play* consists of forty-two mini-plays written down by various scribes over a period of years from 1468, each play enacting a part of the history of the world from the creation of heaven and earth through to judgement day.[19] Based mainly on biblical stories and characters embellished by legend and tradition, and, as the stage directions make plain, intended for performance, it combined teaching of the faith with entertainment. The tale of Joachim and Anna is the eighth play and links the Old Testament, connecting the authority of preordained and prophetic genealogy ('Jesse Root', play seven) through Anne to the fulfilment of the Gospel in the subsequent plays. Anne signifies and embodies 'the grace of God'. What, in the late medieval Christian context, was meant by 'grace', the concept which lay at the heart of Anne's appeal in Norwich, as reflected in her iconography and that of her first-born daughter?

As defined by Thomas Aquinas (c. 1225–74), God's grace was a necessary aid to the attainment of eternal life: man alone had no power over what happened after death and could not 'by his natural powers produce meri-

---

[15] *Golden legend*, i, 'The advent of Our Lord', 5. Voragine writes of the incarnation of Christ, quoting Psalm xiii.4: 'Enlighten my eyes'. Later (p. 6), he says that 'even after we are set free from prison, we still have to have our eyes opened to the light, so that we may see where we ought to go'.
[16] *Mirk's festial*, 41, 169–70, lines 30–9.
[17] My thanks to David King for this information. His uncle, G. King, the Norwich glazier, dismantled this glass for the duration of the Second World War.
[18] *N-town play*, i. 73, play 8, lines 67–8 (my italics).
[19] Ibid. i, pp. xxxviii gives a date of 1468 through to the early sixteenth century, but linguistic evidence hints at earlier roots (p. xl).

torious works commensurate with eternal life'.[20] Aquinas argued that 'the humanity of Christ does not cause grace by its own power, but by the power of the divinity conjoined with it, through which the *actions of the humanity of Christ are redemptive* … Grace is caused instrumentally by the sacraments themselves, yet principally by the power of the holy spirit operating in the sacraments'.[21] In effect, then, 'grace' is coterminous with the active third person or principle of the Trinity, the *pneuma,* or Holy Spirit, which can only be manifest on earth through the physical body, be it of Man or Church or, more particularly in this case, Woman. The legend of St Anne thus provided a model whereby women, even if married, could achieve spiritual status, even sanctity.

Such a positive theological interpretation of female spiritual potential did not go unchallenged. The Holy Spirit, while also central to Pauline theology, was, in his thinking, in conflict with the domination of the flesh that is common to all humanity, but especially associated with women: 'Are ye nott ware that ye are the temple of god, and how that the sprete of god dwelleth in yow? Yf any man defyle the temple of god, him shall god destroye';[22] 'So then they that are geven to the flesshe, cannot please god.'[23] It therefore allowed no salvation except by total dependence on the merits of the passion of Christ, whose activity was, for Paul, as with Aquinas, closely bound up with that of the Holy Spirit. Women must have found little to comfort them in Paul.

St Anne's own life story is apocryphal, the Virgin's mother (and father) being noticeable by their absence from any of the four Gospels. The Greek *Proto-evangelium of St James* (c. 150), where she makes her first appearance, was of Syrian or Egyptian origin; later writings were based on the Latin redaction, the *Pseudo-Matthew*.[24] The parallel concerns of salvation on one hand, and a pragmatic approach to matters dynastic and familial on the other, run throughout the legend. Anne and Joachim, married many years, remained infertile, resulting in public shame and humiliation for Joachim, a priest, at the Temple and grief for Anne. 'The fawte is in me', she says, emphasising the necessity of the female fleshly part in the incarnation of God.[25] The still current physiological theories of Aristotle about gender married

[20] *Nature and grace: selections from the Summa theologica of Thomas Aquinas*, ed. and trans. A. M. Fairweather, London 1954, 12ae, q.109, art.5: whether a man can merit eternal life without grace (pp. 145–6).
[21] Ibid. 12ae, q.112, art. 1, p. 175 (my italics).
[22] 1 Cor. iii. 16. The William Tyndale version of the New Testament (*The New Testament 1526, translated by William Tyndale*, ed. W. R. Cooper, London 2000), had been used throughout for the authentic and most contemporaneous 'voice'.
[23] Romans viii. 8.
[24] Jan Gijsel dates the reworking of the early manuscripts to between 550 and 700: *Die unmittelbare textüberlieferung des sogenannte Pseudo-Matthaüs*, Brussels 1981, xliii.12, no. 96.
[25] *N-town play*, i. 73, play 8, line 67.

well with the theological association of the female with bodily matter and the male with soul and spirit: man as the activating and heat-energising principle in conception, associated with the production of *pneuma*, or soul; woman supplying the crucible of flesh through her own cool liquidity.[26]. Even Galen's view of human reproduction, which required sperm from both parents for conception, ultimately did nothing to undermine the theology of parthenogenesis, since the male role in conception was dominant. As Christ was believed to have been engendered by the activating principle of God, his human flesh and physicality were seen as exclusively provided by his mother, Mary. His link with female flesh and the dependence of his incarnation upon it is thus clear. As Aquinas, following Aristotle, defined it, Mary 'effected the matter to be apt for conception'.[27]

Driven by the pragmatic necessity of the virgin birth of Christ as a prereq-uisite for the creation of a spotless redeemer without the stain of original sin, the Virgin herself, created from the flesh of her mother, was quasi-miracu-lously conceived.[28] Her parents prefigure her own experience. Like her they were vouchsafed a prophetic angelic visitation and a mysterious conception, in their case as the result of a chaste embrace at the Golden Gate of Jerusa-lem.[29] In a sense they thus personified the golden threshold to the *sanctum sanctorum*: St Anne was to become the gateway through which a powerful holy kindred, as well as the redeemer of the world, was ultimately to emerge and change the spiritual and physical destiny of humanity.

---

[26] N. G. Siraisi, *Medieval and early renaissance medicine: an introduction to knowledge and practice*, Chicago 1990, 109–13; J. Cadden, *Meanings of sex difference in the Middle Ages: medicine, science, and culture*, Cambridge 1993, 24, 115, 172–3.

[27] *Summa theologica of Thomas Aquinas*, part II/1, ed. Fathers of the Dominican Province, London 1915, q. 81, art. 5, p. 413.

[28] Celebration of this originated in the Eastern Church around the fourth century, although Byzantine iconography did not highlight aspects of her extended family or of the holy kin as later in western Christendom, and by the eighth was being celebrated in Constantinople. It first appeared in England around 1030, and was re-established and promoted by a Frenchman, Anselm of Bury St Edmunds (d.1148), initially simply as a celebration of the Virgin's conception. The formulation of a doctrine of virgin birth, by Eadmer of Canterbury (c.1060–1128), caused great academic controversy with vehe-ment opposition from such as Bernard of Clairvaux (1090–1153) and Thomas Aquinas. Aquinas, in his commentary on Galatians, attacked both the *trinubium* (Anne's three marriages) and the Immaculate Conception, expounding an alternative concept of Mary's sanctification which took place when her spotless soul joined her body in Anne's womb, freeing her flesh from the consequences of the Fall and restoring it to that pre-lapsarian state of grace. The doctrine attracted devoted clerical advocates, while the pious laity clearly had preferences and attachments that fostered Anne's high place in the heavenly hierarchy. See K. Ashley and P. Sheingorn (eds), *Interpreting cultural symbols: St Anne in late medieval society*, Athens, GA 1990, 9, 16; M. Clayton, 'Aelfric and the nativity of the Blessed Virgin Mary', *Anglia* civ (1986), 286–315.

[29] *N-town play*, i. 74–81, play 8, 'Joachim and Anna'; *Hooly wummen*, 45–55; *Life of St Anne*, 2, 100, 110.

Thus Anne represented two parallel concerns: on the one hand the centrality of redemption and the possibility of eternal life which continued to require the intercessory prayers of succeeding generations, especially of heirs and kindred; on the other, more quotidian issues arising from childlessness and its significance, whether in royal house or journeyman's workshop, which, at a time when fecundity remained the marker by which a wife was judged a success or a failure, blighted the lives of many women in the Middle Ages.

Marriage, childbirth and the family

A powerful element in the great popularity of the cult of St Anne, particularly among women at an everyday, practical level, surely rests on the status accorded by her legend to marriage, even multiple marriage, fertility, pregnancy and childbirth (both miraculous, as in the case of her first-born, and natural, with her subsequent two daughters) within an extended and productive matrilineal group of great influence. This elevation of serial marriage in the face of elements of biblical disapproval regarding women's remarriage at all would have been very significant in urban communities ravaged by epidemic disease and frequent premature death.[30] In Norwich, third, fourth and even fifth marriages were not unusual among the mercantile elite, fostering complicated family networks of sibling and in-law relationships that continued to bind.[31]

Such issues found expression, for example, in the painted glass in St Peter Mancroft parish church, where the St Anne chapel featured a series of Norwich School glass panels showing the holy kindred, as well as St Anne teaching the Virgin to read.[32] A Visitation panel continues the theme of the ancestry and the kinship of Christ through the matrilineal line, the Virgin being greeted by a very pregnant St Elizabeth wearing a finely drawn and expanding laced maternity gown. A similar gown is also shown in a contemporary Visitation window at East Harling church.[33] The story of the Visitation describes an exclusively female experience: the embryonic Christ causing the quickening in Elizabeth's womb of the foetal John the Baptist. As Luke records, Elizabeth was filled with the 'holy goost', on hearing the

---

[30] For example, 1 Cor. vii.25–40, esp. verses 39–40.

[31] For example, Agnes Thorpe, Norwich widow (see pp. 55–6 below), who was Robert Thorpe's third wife; he was her second husband: PCC, reg. Blamyr, fo. 26 (Agnes Thorpe), 1501/3. Elizabeth Drake, kinswoman of Margaret Paston, was married five times, each marriage improving her social and material status: NCC, reg. Spyltymber, fos 66–70 (1507/10). Several aldermen matched this pattern.

[32] King, St Peter Mancroft, p. ccxxi.

[33] G. M. Gibson, The theater of devotion: East Anglian drama and society in the late Middle Ages, Chicago–London 1989, 102, fig. 4.12.

word of Mary's salutation, and describes with delight how 'the babe lepte in my belly for ioye (joy)'.[34]

Devotion to the saint is also a reflection of the anxiety experienced at every level of Norwich society by women of childbearing years who had not yet produced a healthy son. Such a woman was trapped in the dilemma of needing one heir at least, and knowing that her value as a wife and daughter depended on her fertility. In the 1440s, for example, Katherine Denston of Long Melford, in Suffolk, commissioned Bokenham to write the *Life* of St Anne.[35] She already had a daughter, Anne, named, Bokenham tells us, in honour of the saint. The *Life*, written in the vernacular, begins 'If *grace* my penne vochesaf to illumyne', asking for the saint's 'specyal grace ... To oure bothe confort & solace',[36] and ends with a prayer to St Anne, which makes plain the motive for Katherine's commission: 'if it plese the *grace* of God above, thorgh thi merytes (to grant her) a sone of her body'.[37] Powerful though St Anne's immediate patronage was perceived to be, this is a reminder that her ultimate destiny had been to prepare the way for a spotless male heir. Katherine Denston hoped to share some part of the saint's potency in this regard, so that through the spiritual merits of St Anne, Katherine herself would conceive a son and heir. Doubtless her daughter had been named with an eye on the saint's dynastic potential. This example gives a moving insight into the equation of a married woman's status with her ability to bear healthy sons. Something of this tension is heard in the text of the *N-town play*, when an anguished St Anne cries: 'A, mercy, Lord! Mercy, mercy, mercy! We are synfolest it shewyth that ye send us all this sorwe (sorrow). Why do ye thus to myn husbond, Lord? Why? Why? Why? For my barynes? (Ye) may amend this thiself, and thu lyst (desire), tomorwe.'[38]

Although St Anne's legend tells of her three daughters and their three fathers, it is in the birth of her seven grandsons that her power and standing reaches its apotheosis. Thus, in the culture of the fifteenth century, Katherine Denston's inability to provide her husband with even one son marked her as a less-than-blessed wife. One daughter did not constitute a family in such perilous times, and dynastic ambition, be it for reasons of state or the continuation of a family's name or specialist trade or business, primarily required sons. Whether she went on pilgrimage to this end is unknown, but many did, men and women alike.[39] Katherine was in an unenviable position, and despite her efforts to honour two powerful saintly intercessors through

---

[34] Luke i. 41.
[35] Katherine was the sister of John Clopton who left a bequest to 'Saynt Anne's aulter' at Long Melford church. The family chapel at his house 'Lutons' was also dedicated to St Anne, indicating a serious family attachment to the saint as sponsor and intercessor: Gibson, *Theater of devotion*, 82 nn. 59–60.
[36] *Hooly wummen*, 40, lines 1468, 1475.
[37] Ibid. 57–8.
[38] *N-town play*, i. 77, play 8, lines 165–71.
[39] C. Rawcliffe, *Medicine and society in later medieval England*, Stroud 1995, 178–9.

her literary commissions, remained so. In this context too, women embarked on pilgrimage to Our Lady of Walsingham, in order to ask for the intercession of the Virgin, as well as that of her mother and St Margaret.[40] The pregnant Margaret of Anjou, wife of Henry VI, came to Norfolk on such a quest in 1453, in urgent need of a male heir. She marked her pilgrimage to Walsingham by the gift of a magnificent pearl, ruby and sapphire-encrusted jewel depicting an angel with a cameo head, perhaps in honour of the Annunciation, and costing a staggering £29, equal to the annual income of a substantial landowner.[41] The queen was safely delivered of a son the following autumn.

Having successfully conceived, in the late Middle Ages, as throughout time, every pregnant woman would anxiously await the physical sensation of the first fluttering of life, the only reassurance that the foetus was alive and thriving. Hence the importance, both physical and spiritual, of the Visitation as a special and life-affirming event, given ecclesiastical endorsement by the feast of the Visitation, kept on 2 July, which was promoted by the Franciscan order and officially recognised in 1263.[42] The office most widely accepted was that of the Benedictine Cardinal Adam Easton, himself from Norwich.[43]

The burden of anxiety attending any woman in an age when pregnancy and parturition were life-threatening continued.[44] Indeed, without the protection of the Church, even her soul was at risk. If the foetus died and she experienced a stillbirth rather than an intact abortion, the probability was septicaemia and death.[45] An incomplete abortion carried similar risks of infection and fever, or haemorrhage; maternal death after an incomplete

---

[40] For the reference to the presence of St Margaret next to the Virgin on the altar at the shrine, 'alle these gold', see C. L. S. Linnell, 'The commonplace book of Robert Reynes of Acle', NA xxxii (1961), 126.

[41] A. R. Myers, 'The jewels of Queen Margaret of Anjou', Bulletin of John Rylands Library xlii (1959–60), 115. It is fascinating to speculate on Margaret's possible meeting at Walsingham with the prolific Cecily Neville, duchess of York, and wife of Richard, subsequent contender for the throne of Henry VI. Cecily was then pregnant with her last-born son, later Richard III, who was to be accused of killing Margaret's son, Edward, at the battle of Tewkesbury. Richard subsequently married Edward's widow, Anne Neville.

[42] Prescribed first by Urban VI and later by Boniface IX (1389), the feast was not formally established until after the Council of Basle, in 1441, by Pius V: Oxford dictionary of the Christian Church, ed. F. L. Cross, 2nd rev. edn, Oxford 1983, 1446. See also R. W. Pfaff, New liturgical feasts in later medieval England, Oxford 1970, who claims it (pp. 40–61) as a rare 'top down' innovation, to invoke the Virgin's aid in ending the schism.

[43] He wrote it for Pope Boniface, who restored Easton's dignities after his imprisonment and torture by Urban: Pfaff, New liturgical feasts, 44.

[44] Medieval English prose for women: selections from the Katherine group and Ancrene Wisse, ed. B. Millet and J. Wogan-Browne, Oxford 1992, 31–2.

[45] A leechbook, or a collection of medical remedies of the fifteenth-century, ed. W. R. Dawson, London 1934. See 'ffor swelt of womb, pound rue wt wyne eyther with ale and drynke it oft' (812 at p. 252); a remedy for leucorrhea 'for to dry the supfluytees of the moder, Seth calamynt in water and therewith washhe hym (her) byneyth forth' (592 at p. 188).

abortion could, theoretically, make the mother spiritually unclean.[46] In such a situation St Anne was a stiffener of the upper lip, a soul-companion who offered hope to the hopeless in matters of conception, while St Margaret of Antioch promised protection and intercession through the birth process itself.

From the point of view of women generally, July was a month full of feasts with which they could identify and wherein they might find support. After the Visitation, on 20 July came the feast of St Margaret of Antioch, virgin patroness of women in childbirth, closely followed on 26 July by that of St Anne, and between the two St Mary Magdalen on 22 July.[47]

In this context the wooden screen panels behind the Lady altar of Ranworth St Helen (*see* plate 3)[48] may well have constituted a special focus for pregnant women and nursing mothers when they were painted in the 1470s and 1480s. Here Anne's three daughters and their little sons are to be found in their most sensitive and touching surviving East Anglian representation.[49] The small sons of Mary Cleophas are still just visible playing with their toys around her feet, while in the last panel on the right sits St Margaret of Antioch. Triumphant over her vanquished dragon, the young Margaret in this context has been appropriated to the holy kin.[50] Her presence unites this essentially female-led family group and confirms that such a complex icon must have had a special appeal to women of childbearing age, whatever dynastic interpretations male parishioners may have placed on it. Anne herself is absent from this family group, probably because there was a separate image of her in the church, which was an object of particular veneration during the fifteenth century.[51] (She is still, however, to be found, a young first-time mother flushed with achievement in successful childbed in a beautifully preserved illumination in the fifteenth-century Ranworth antiphoner [*see* plate 4].) Women would almost certainly come to the Lady altar after childbirth for purification and thanksgiving, and to offer a candle in imitation of Candlemas and the Virgin's own Presentation at the Temple.

---

[46] *John Mirk's instructions for parish priests*, ed. G. Kristensson, Lund 1974, 180, lines 98–106.

[47] Although he does not mention any of these female festivals, Ronald Hutton describes the ritual year as it was celebrated in late medieval towns in *The rise and fall of merry England: the ritual year, 1400–1700*, Oxford 1994, 1–48.

[48] John Mitchell has identified the artists who painted the Ranworth screen panels as belonging to a workshop active in the 1470s and 1480s; they were also associated with painted panels at Filby All Saints, near Yarmouth, Southwold St Edmund, North Elmham St Mary, Thornham All Saints, Old Hunstanton St Mary and Norwich St James: Mitchell, 'Painting in East Anglia', 369.

[49] Ibid. 371.

[50] Ibid. 182–3.

[51] Duffy, *Stripping of the altars*, 182, n. 73.

Anne and her books

Although almost all traces of Anne's cult are gone from the city churches, a glimpse of her status among city parishioners and their financial invest-ment in devotion to her may still be gained, for the paucity of surviving material culture and artefacts is in some measure compensated by the wealth of contemporary East Anglian texts honouring her, whether for personal, contemplative use, for instruction or for public performance.[52] By examining these a clearer picture of her suppliants emerges and augments that hinted at by traces of painted panels, windows and altar and chapel dedications.

By the end of the thirteenth century until well into the sixteenth, vernacular poems of celebration and supplication to Christ's grandmother were being composed in England, mostly of unknown authorship.[53] The best-known to which an author can be ascribed are those by John Audlay (writing in the 1420s), the Benedictine poet-monk John Lydgate (c. 1370–c. 1450) and Osbern Bokenham. Bokenham's *Legendys of hooly wummen*, and the hugely influential thirteenth-century *Golden legend* (*Legenda aurea*) of Jacobus de Voragine (d. 1298), a comprehensive collection of saints' *Lives* and expositions of the church feasts, arguably provided the substance of most lay people's knowledge of Anne even among those who were unlettered, as well as being integral to their entertainment in mystery plays, *tableaux vivants* and processions mounted by gilds.[54] The *Golden legend* circulated and was read in various forms: the nuns at Bruisyard, Suffolk, in the diocese of Norwich, for example, possessed a copy in English.[55] It was also widely used for the instruction of the laity and as the basis for sermonising, as for example in the successful promotion and reception in Norwich of the cult of St Elizabeth of Hungary, in particular on the practice of charitable works of mercy as an imperative for personal salvation.[56] This was endorsed by the financial deployment ascribed to Anne and Joachim in the *Golden legend*, and cited in Robert Reynes's stanzaic *Life*, whereby they reserved a third of their income for such works: 'And they (Anne and Joachim) haddyn werdely ryches ful gret plente / But that ryches they partyd on three maner wyse / On parte they youyn to god. With hert good and fre /To the meyntonawnse of holy chyrche and godds seruyse.' The second part of their fortune went on alms to the poor: 'Fulfyllyng the vii dedys that ben of mercy / But many fol on days wyl not do thes (but many folk these days will not do this)/ That

---

[52] This is discussed in Gibson, *Theater of devotion*, 83–4.

[53] *Life of St Anne*, p. xi.

[54] *Hooly wummen*, 38–58; *Jacobus de Voragine: the golden legend: readings on the saints*, ed. W. G. Ryan, Princeton 1993, i. 149–58.

[55] R. Gilchrist and M. Oliva, *Religious women in medieval East Anglia: history and archae-ology, c. 1100–1500*, Norwich 1993, 54.

[56] Elizabeth's *vita* was commissioned by Elizabeth de Vere, countess of Oxford: *Hooly wummen*, p. xxi.

han welth and weelfare ful plentewously.' The third part only was for Anne and Joachim for 'her (their) owyn fode' and for their servants: 'And thus schuld every man that hath mekyl (much) goode / Be the wyl of god dapart his good in three.'[57]

The *Golden legend* was also very influential in presenting Christ as a product of the matrilineal rather than the patriarchal line of the Gospels. The Gospels of Matthew and Luke are the only sources for the myths surrounding Christ's birth and carefully list the forefathers of Joseph to emphasise that he was a scion of the house of David. The only account given of Mary is that she was espoused to Joseph. Luke's Gospel precedes the account of Jesus' birth with that of the miraculous birth of his cousin and herald, John the Baptist. The story of John's conception and nativity is again told very much from the viewpoint of the father, the sceptical Zacharius, who comes from one of the twenty-four divisions of the priesthood.[58] His wife, Elizabeth, claims her descent from the priestly stock of Aaron, so their childless state and subsequent shame at what was perceived to be the judgement of God on them provided an exact model for the circumstances of Anne and Joachim in the *N-town play* and in the *Golden legend*.[59]

Anne and the mass

Without St Anne there is no Virgin, no Annunciation, no passion, no mass and no redemption. Given St Anne's role in incarnational piety, and the importance of the matrilineal line in the descent of Christ, it comes as no surprise to find her continually associated with the ritual and celebration of the mass, an association which can be traced in Norwich in particular through the textiles, altar frontals and vestments worn by the celebrant. Thus, the inventories of St Peter Mancroft provide details of the embroidered designs featuring the saint on textiles that were commissioned for the church, including but not exclusively for the chapel of the gild of St Anne, a rich investment in silks and damasks.

There were five main altars to be dressed in St Peter Mancroft. The inventories describe the frontal for Our Lady's altar as being embroidered with the images of St Anne and the Virgin, while the Trinity altar frontal was decorated with depictions of the coronation of the Virgin above and of St

---

[57] *The commonplace book of Robert Reynes of Acle*, ed. L. Cameron, New York– London 1980, 201–2 (my italics). Reynes was a prosperous churchwarden, tradesman and family man with a devotion to St Anne. His source is unknown but there are close similarities to another manuscript version of the poem, MS Harley 4012: G. M. Gibson, 'St Anne and the religion of childbed: some East Anglian texts and talismans', in Ashley and Sheingorn, *Interpreting cultural symbols*, 108 n. 14.

[58] 'The Gospel according to St Luke', ed. W. Baird, in C. M. Laymon (ed.), *The interpreter's one volume commentary on the Bible*, Nashville 1992, 672.

[59] Luke i.1–25; *N-town play*, i. 71–81; *Golden legend*, 149–58.

Anne below; sponsorship and endorsement came no higher. Of the church's nine recorded banners, one was dedicated to St Anne. It had 'litell gold in it frengid wt threde wight rede & grene'.[60] Among the many copes owned by the church, to be worn as the over-garment by the priest during mass, St Anne featured on at least two. These could and did carry the donors' initials and their chosen saints and symbols, all visible to the assembled congregation. An inventory describes one cope as being 'of whight damaske wt M & A of golde croned (crowned) wt orpheras brodered of postelles & virgynes (with orphreys embroidered with apostles and virgins) and in the cape sent Anne. Of the gifte of (deleted)'.[61] The other cope is similarly recorded except that one description of an orphrey has been struck out, again probably by a reformer who wished to eliminate the now heretical observances associated with this kind of imagery. It was appreciated, too, that recording the donor's name made a bede-roll of the inventory, such a list thereby itself becoming a doctrinally suspect document after the Reformation. The inventory also lists 'a single vestment of wight damaske wt orpheras rede damaske wt a ymage of sent Anne upon the bake / belonging to sent Anne is gilde'. How much more powerful must have been the call to remember names embroidered on copes and vestments alongside images of a venerated saint, especially when they were displayed in proximity to the host, the redemptive body itself? [62]

It was believed that the cope worn by a celebrant might well absorb the incarnational power inherent in the mass because its wearer had handled Christ's sacrificial body and blood at the time of its transubstantiation. However this was understood, 'the sacring' was universally acknowledged as a numinous moment imbued with mystery. Such vestments were sometimes used in other parts of Europe to treat the sick and to aid women in childbirth:[63] the belief that Mary deferred the pains of parturition until she experienced the passion of her son may be bound up in this utilisation of copes as a type of spiritual theriac. They were, after all, worn specifically to honour the repeated celebration of the passion. The popular image of the Virgin giving her protection to suppliants by enfolding them in her cope-like cloak may well have propagated these ideas.[64] Such imagery also helped to reinforce the idea central to incarnational piety that as she 'clothed' Christ in her flesh, Mary was also mother of all in the enfolding protection that she offered. It reminds that the Virgin's role was that of nurse to Christ the

60 Hope, 'Inventories', 221.
61 Ibid. 196–7.
62 This thinking is apparent in many gifts used near the high altar, such as the Reedes' and the Westgates' altar cloths at St Gregory's and the donation of communion vessels inscribed with the donors' names, for example the 'pair challis gilte pondez of the gifte of Robert Holdy and Christiane his wiffe whos names be written in the fote': ibid. 206.
63 C. von Burg, 'Le Témoignage des sources: 1530 Baar', in C. Dupeux, P. Jezler and J. Wirth (eds), Iconoclasme: vie et mort de l'image medievale, Berne 2001, 130.
64 Such an image survives from the early sixteenth century on the altarpiece of the Blessed Virgin Mary at the Heiligen-Geist Hospital, Lübeck.

Physician, and that spiritual health was inextricably enmeshed with physical well-being.[65]

None of the luxurious textiles of St Peter Mancroft survive, but comparative contemporary material is available elsewhere. A set of English embroidered silk panels, or orphreys, dated to 1415–30 and thus nearly contemporary with the altar frontals at St Peter's is extant, now attached to the front and back of an Italian dalmatic believed to have belonged to the Cistercian house at Whalley, in Lancashire.[66] This vibrant and extremely intimate series conveys a very clear idea of the genre. What is so vividly depicted here, apart from affirmation of marriage, family and domesticity, is St Anne's role as the primary mediator of God made flesh, each fine and elaborately-stitched orphrey showing an event in the life of the saint and her family. The depiction of the marriage of Anne and Joachim endorses the elevated view of marriage as a state in which sanctity and grace may be attained within the marital household, and the family as the context within which grace is received and nurtured under the mother's hand. The continuance of this context into the afterlife is significantly demonstrated in the will of Joan Chamberlayn of York (1502):

> Also I wit my weddynge ring of golde, a gyrdill the tushoye theroff of gold of Vynes harnest with sylver and gylt, and a payr of corall baydes gaudiett wt sylver, unto ye blessid ymage of Saynt Anne wt in the said monystorie of our Lady: and I wyll that the rynge the day of my bureall, be put on hir fynger, the gurdyll abowt hir, and the baydes in hir hand.[67]

The symbols of Joan's marriage (ring), childbearing (girdle) and intercession (beads) are thus given an eternal dimension. To the professed and others viewing this image in the monastery, St Anne was Joan Chamberlayn. In arranging for the image of the saint to be a theatrical representation of herself Joan was clearly claiming Anne as model and patron. Similarly, for the community at Whalley that owned this vestment, the appeal of the orphreys resides in the assumption that the professed would pray for the salvation of the world, as if for the souls of their own spiritual children. In the late thirteenth century, the beguine mystic, Mechtild of Magdeburg (1210–80) wrote:

> I must give them my heart's blood to drink. If I pray for them because of their great need and see the bitter fate they must suffer for every sin, then I suffer as a mother. Yet it pleases me that for real sin they should suffer pain

---

[65] For example, Piero della Francesca's 'Madonna della misericordia' (c. 1445–8). See *Henry of Lancaster: Le Livre de seyntz medicines*, ed. E. J. Arnould, Oxford 1940, 233.

[66] Burrell Collection, Glasgow, cat. 29/2.

[67] *Testamenta eboracensia, or, wills registered at York: illustrative of the history, manners, language, statistics, &c. of the province of York, from the year MCCC downwards*, ed. J. Raine (Surtees Society liii, 1868), 200–2. This will is cited in Peters, *Patterns of piety*, 50.

to honour God. If this child is to recover its mother must be faithful and compassionate.[68]

Other orphreys in this set depict the chaste embrace of St Anne and Joachim at the Golden Gate, signifying the Immaculate Conception of the Virgin and paralleling the Annunciation.[69] The Nativity of Mary is shown, as was traditionally the case, with a formidable-looking midwife in attendance on St Anne, much in the manner that Margery Kempe imagined herself in her visualisations (see plate 5). The series is characterised by homely, colourful presentations, typical of which is the holy family together, with the toddler Mary with a wooden 'stroller' being taught to walk in the ways of God. The Presentation at the Temple of the three-year-old Mary by a solitary St Anne is the final orphrey (the N-town play includes a scene where the parents jointly present Mary, in fulfilment of their vow to dedicate her to God's service[70]). The depiction of this scene on the Whalley dalmatic, however, clearly hints at Anne's Old Testament precursor, Hannah, mother of the prophet and priest Samuel, thereby emphasising the fulfilment of Anne's preordained and prophetic destiny as the progenitrix of a holy priesthood rather than a subordinate figure at the Temple behind her husband:[71] 'Thys gloryous Anne, happy, full of grace, / Ys caryed up most worshipfully / To the hyest of seynts in that place / With the seruyce of aungelles truly / Unto the euerlastyng company / Of patriarks and prophets old, / She ys comyn with ioes (joys) manyfold.'[72]

In the context of the mass, when these orphreys would be visible on the celebrant's moving body (most notably at the sacring and the moment of elevation), it is significant that the matrilineal line is so powerfully emphasised as the predestined channel through which salvation is mediated. St Bridget's understanding of St Anne's message to her rendered this awe-inspiring theological concept in reassuringly human terms: a mother's greatest responsibility was to bring up her baptised children in the worship of God, without which there could be no salvation.

This was a teaching reinforced by the mendicants' promotion of devotional images to be used in the home, particularly with the young (male) in mind, the image being regarded as a much more efficient tool than the word or text at this early stage. Thus, in his Rule for governing the family, the fifteenth-century Florentine Dominican Giovanni Dominici (d.1419) commended the use of images of the young Jesus and other young saints, 'in

---

[68] Mechtild of Magdaburg, Flowing light of the godhead, 5, ch.viii, 136, quoted in C. W. Bynum, Jesus as mother: studies in the spirituality of the high Middle Ages, Berkeley 1982, 236.
[69] Golden legend, ii, 152.
[70] N-town play, i. 81, play 9.
[71] 1 Samuel i.20–4.
[72] Life of St Anne, 93, lines 113–19.

which your child may recognise himself'.[73] The Ranworth and Houghton screens should at one level be understood with this in mind. Norwich, before the Reformation, would have possessed many such educational images.

An altar frontal from the Carmelite Marienburg convent at Boppard on the Rhine – the sort of textile that members of Norwich congregations would frequently have seen on business trips to the Low Countries – further demonstrates the pivotal role of St Anne and conveys a sense of the iconography of the lost artefacts of Norwich.[74] (Though it has to be said that even the wealthy parishioners of St Peter Mancroft are unlikely to have commissioned anything quite so grand.) Anne takes the central place on this frontal, as the matriarch with a diminutive crowned Virgin on her left hand, bearing up the infant Christ in the crook of her right arm, high above his mother's head. St Anne is flanked on her left by St Dorothy (a patron to the poor) leading a child with a flower basket, and St Barbara, protector against sudden death, holding her book and tower. On the right stands St Katherine with her wheel, sword and a trampled king, and St Agnes with her lamb. All are depicted in vibrant coloured silks against a black ground sprinkled with flowers, this tapestry being embroidered, not woven. The inclusion of Barbara and Katherine, both also associated with the mass, emphasises St Anne's status as precursor of the incarnate redeemer.[75] Christ here is presented to the viewer by his grandmother, rather than his mother.[76]

The significance of the grandmother's role is continued in the iconography of the screen panels at Houghton St Giles, with the appearance of Esmeria, legendary mother (or sometimes sister)[77] of Anne and another significant female precursor of Christ. Esmeria occupies a panel with her daughter Anne next to St Elizabeth, mother to St John the Baptist (see plate 6). For both Anne and Elizabeth, tears of contrition and compassion prefigure the waters of baptism and redemption.[78] Of deeper spiritual significance is the clear confirmation that the indwelling spirit of God, the incarnation in Everyman and Everywoman betokened by the embrace at the Golden Gate, the Annunciation to Mary and the quickening of Elizabeth's child at the Visitation, is achievable through the feminine and fleshly, through humility and receptivity, not through the more traditional and overtly assertive masculine attributes. Redemption by and through the flesh is linked with

---

[73] J. Tripps, 'Les Images et la devotion privee', in Dupeux, Jezler and Wurth, Iconoclasme, 38–45.

[74] Burrell Collection, cat. 46/16.

[75] St Barbara was also venerated as a protector from sudden, that is unshriven, death. A chapel dedicated to her, co-founded by the Brouns and the Gilberts, was in the Guildhall, Norwich, for the use of the prisoners incarcerated there.

[76] For similar iconography but with a royal lay provenance see the Franco-Flemish tapestry, Burrell Collection, cat. 46/14. Illustrations of both may be found in Hill, 'Incarnational piety', 208.

[77] Sister, according to the Golden Legend.

[78] N-town play, i. 79, play 8, lines 213–16; i. 132, play 13, lines 51–8.

aspects of incarnational devotion that were also at the heart of the veneration of the Magdalen. This concept surely illuminates the burgeoning of
female mysticism both in England in the fourteenth and fifteenth centuries
and, even more, in the Low Countries and Germany during the thirteenth
and fourteenth.[79]

Anne and the family: mothers and salvation

In the early 1400s, when Margery Kempe of Bishop's Lynn was contem-
plating the birth and upbringing of the Virgin as part of her extended meditation on the holy kin, she was also simultaneously attempting to put her
own marriage on a celibate footing, in imitation of her saintly exemplars,
Anne and Bridget. In pursuit of a special and singular relationship with
Christ, Margery visualised her own motherly care of the Virgin for the first
twelve years of her life, imagining herself providing good food and clean
linen for Mary and thereby becoming St Anne in all but name. Whereas St
Bridget of Sweden envisaged the Virgin acting as her midwife in her difficult
last confinement and birth of her daughter, Marte, Margery was, in her own
meditation, the midwife to St Anne at the birth of the Virgin.[80] No doubt
she felt that her meditation on the next twelve years of Mary's life was a
natural extension of this self-proclaimed 'special relationship'. Subsequently,
Margery pre-empts even the archangel Gabriel by herself announcing to
Mary that she is to be the mother of God, thereby taking upon herself not
only St Anne's role in educating the Virgin, but that of God's mouthpiece.[81]
In effect she was exploring the models of St Anne 'teaching the Virgin to
read', that is to receive God, and St Bridget's injunctions on the mother's role
in her children's salvation, which reinforced St Anne, the primary exemplar.

In marked contrast to the more maternal St Bridget, Margery never
mentions her own fourteen children in her book, with the exception of
her ailing adult son. It may be that none of the others survived infancy.[82]
Whether or not this was so, in lacking compassion she could have been
judged to have missed the point of her spiritual exercise. An unnatural lack of
maternal affection could be one interpretation of her refusal to visit her sick
son before he had confessed and been absolved. Another could be that she
was following to the letter Bridget's teaching on a mother's supreme responsibility for the salvation of her child's soul. Yet Margery also saw herself as
something greater than the conduit of grace to her children. Margery's goal
was nothing less than to be handmaid to Christ in the salvation of the world:
on being urged 'And therfor, dowtyr, aske what thow wylt, & I xal grawnt

---

[79] Bynum, *Jesus as mother*, ch. v.
[80] *Book of Margery Kempe*, i, ch. vi, p. 18; *Liber celestis*, p. 1, lines 25–30.
[81] *Book of Margery Kempe*, i, ch. vi, p. 22.
[82] Personal communication with Robert Swanson.

the thyn askyng', Margery replied to Christ, 'Lord, I aske mercy & preseuyng fro euyr-lestyng dampnacyon for me & for all the world.'[83]

It is most likely that she saw her maternal duty to her son in the eternal perspective; she was much more concerned with his spiritual health than his earthly comfort, and had, at an earlier time, prayed for his punishment if he fell from grace (and thus disobeyed her injunctions). This is an apparent dichotomy, but only to modern eyes. Margery would not have seen her son's physical well-being as in any way separate from the spiritual, rather the reverse. As St Bridget's revelations instructed her, 'parfitt cheritie is, whan non thinge is so swete to man as God. This beginnys in this present liff, and is endid in heuen'.[84] Perhaps such an obligation to intercede for the world was felt by many married women who pursued a life of charity and prayer, not unlike their professed sisters, and was not, therefore, merely a unique manifestation of Margery's spiritual pride, even though she did place herself at the head of the queue.

St Bridget records that she had a vision of St Anne while she was in Rome obtaining 'relikes of hir', an experience depicted on a panel of the St Anne altarpiece at Frankfurt-am-Main.[85] The saint informed her that 'I ame Anne, ladi of all weddid folke that were byfor the lawe', and went on to teach Bridget to pray to God: 'for the praiers of Anne, haue merci of all thame that are in wedeloke or thinkes to be weddid, *that thai mai bringe furth froite to the wirshipe of Gode*'.[86] This was the crux of St Anne's importance to most women and was expressed in her iconography. The emphasis on the mother's responsibility before God for her children's spiritual health and status is inescapable, however the individual woman accomplished it. The far from saintly but devout Margaret Paston (1422–84) displayed her own awareness of this duty in the last lines of one of her many letters, when she bestowed a mother's traditional blessing: 'God have you in hys kepyng and make yow a good man, and gyf yow grace to do *as well as I wold ye shuld do*.'[87]

While the pious focus on the fleshly incarnation and body of Christ, as transmitted through St Anne and her daughter, was not completely exclusive to women, those males who espoused a similar devotion, such as Richard Rolle, hermit of Hampole (1300–49), St John of Bridlington (d.1379) and Richard Methley of Mount Grace (b.1451), each shared specific spiritual qualities with the feminine ecstatics and visionaries who by far outnumbered

---

83 *Book of Margery Kempe*, i, ch. vii, p. 20.
84 *Liber celestis*, iii, ch. xxix, p. 240, lines 26–7.
85 K. Ashley and P. Sheingorn, 'Locating St Anne in gender and cultural studies', in their *Interpreting cultural symbols*, 18. Both Chartres and Aachen laid claim to owning her head.
86 *Liber celestis*, i, ch. cii, p. 467, lines 25–8 (my italics).
87 *Paston letters and papers of the fifteenth century*, ed. N. Davis, Oxford 1971– , i at pp. 27, 244, 443 (my italics); a recurring theme. See also J. T. Rosenthal, *Telling tales: sources and narration in late medieval England*, University Park 2003, 95–147.

them, and with whom they were familiar.[88] Rolle's writings, for example, show his own obsessive preoccupation with, and response to, the wounded body of Christ; and he marked his new life in religion by wearing his sister's adapted clothes. St John of Bridlington, like Margery Kempe, Elizabeth of Schonau , Marie d'Oignies, Angela de Foligno and the blessed Dorothea of Montau, had the gift of tears, an acknowledged sign of redemptive grace.[89] What remains to be asked, however, is whether such a theology was understood and accepted by all women, or whether it was a preoccupation of the few relatively affluent women with enough time and money to invest in it. It may well be that more practical women, identifying with Martha of Bethany, and taking a less sophisticated view of St Anne and her part in the mediation of redemption, were the rule rather than the exception.[90] The mindset of the twenty-first-century historian, with its tendency to compartmentalise the pragmatic and the spiritual, must be set aside in order to avoid an anachronistic conclusion. Medieval pragmatism was extremely inclusive.

A few women who sought to observe a contemplative life mixed with charitable activity – the *devotio moderna* – while remaining 'in the world' as matriarchs are known to us because of their elite status and patronage of various kinds, whether of religious foundations or through book-ownership.[91] Those of the merchant class and below, being generally far less well documented, are much harder to identify, but may be glimpsed occasionally in the wills of others. Margaret Purdans, for example, widow of a Norwich alderman, was a beneficiary of the wills of both Richard Fernys, a Norwich hermit, and of John Baret, an extremely wealthy and intensely pious merchant of Bury St Edmunds. As well as making bequests to three fellow male hermits and an anchoress, Fernys also remembered other, more obscure women in his will. They may well have belonged to the same 'inner circle of piety' as Dame Margaret, Fernys and his eremitic peers: Alice Kyngessey; Katherine Kerre (formerly Moryell); her sister, Cristiane Veyl; Sister Agnes Shotesham of St Paul's hospital and Basilie of St Gregory's parish. Whatever their immediate circumstances, these women mainly belonged, like Margaret Purdans, to a fairly tight-knit group of identifiable city merchants and leading tradespeople. Margaret, in her turn, left a revealing collection of books to her son,

[88] J. Hughes, *Pastors and visionaries: religion and secular life in late medieval Yorkshire*, Woodbridge 1988, 298–346.

[89] *English writings of Richard Rolle, hermit of Hampole*, ed. H. E. Allen, Oxford 1931, repr. Gloucester 1988, 34–5; *The book of Margery Kempe*, ed. B. Windeatt, Harmondsworth 1985, introduction, and notes to ch. lii at p. 320.

[90] Luke x. 38–42.

[91] Cecily, duchess of York, is a prime example: C. A. J. Armstrong, 'The piety of Cicely, duchess of York: a study in late medieval culture', in his *England, France and Burgundy in the fifteenth century*, London 1983, 145. Rowena Archer takes a different view in 'Piety in question: noblewomen and religion in the late Middle Ages', in D. Wood, *Women and religion in medieval England*, Oxford 2003, 118–40.

various religious and friends.[92] Significantly, she owned a vernacular version of St Bridget's *Liber celestis*, a work with which Margery Kempe was herself familiar.[93]

Alderman John Gilbert and his wife, Annor, who both died in 1466 but were survived by at least six sons, as well as three daughters, one named for her mother and St Anne, provide another example of the appeal of the saint. Anne and her prodigious family were likely to have been an attractive role model to this prosperous and prolific mercantile dynasty. Annor was specific, despite her illness, about the fate of her rosaries, aware of their spiritual power as tools for prayer, in addition to their aesthetic appeal, material worth and sentimental value. Family continuity in the broadest sense is apparent in her every word. To her daughter Alice she bequeathed 'a paire of bedes of corall with a coste (cross) of perles' and to Annor Gilbert she left a 'paire of bedes of silver which *hir godmoder has giv'*. To daughter Cateryn was given custody of the 'bedys of corall *which were my moderes'*. Annor also bequeathed a coral rosary 'of thryse ffifty', three times the standard length, to Annore Ssalyate [*sic*], perhaps her goddaughter, and almost certainly a relation of Master John Selatt [*sic*], archdeacon of Norwich and master of St Giles's hospital, who was one of John Gilbert's executors.[94] Such a splendid collection of 'bedes' marked Annor Gilbert as one who demonstrably belonged to 'the purple of commerce'. Simpler bone or wooden beads were probably more usual among the less well-off.[95] She was aware, too, that tools for intercession that marked family continuity also had a special place in the accomplishment of her daughters' salvation. On a more mundane level, Annor left her 'scarlett kirtell', a high-quality woollen dress for daily wear, to the wife of Thomas Cambridge, a relative of the aforementioned John Cambridge, demonstrating the tight-knit interaction of this affinity.

Jewellery indeed, usually with sacred connotations, featured significantly in many bequests. It was often bequeathed to decorate images or shrines, and also with a view to being loaned out and used as an amulet for protection, for example, during childbirth. Girdles bequeathed to, and worn by, the images of saints were often hired out for a fee, or loaned freely for this purpose.[96] Elizabeth Paston, later Poynings, then Browne, in her will written in 1487,

---

[92] NCC, reg. Caston, fos 163–5 (Purdans), 1481/3.
[93] *Book of Margery Kempe*, i, chs xx, xxxix; ii, ch. vii.
[94] NCC, reg. Jekkys, fo. 49 (Annor Gilbert). A standard rosary has five sets of ten Ave beads, each set being divided from the next by a Pater Noster bead. Hence the longer the rosary, the longer the time to complete saying it. The extra length of beads would also look very elegant hanging from a decorated girdle. John Selot (d. 1479), one-time chancellor of Bishop Lyhart, later master of St Giles's hospital, began the repair of Bishop's Bridge in 1472, as Gilbert's executor: Rawcliffe, *Medicine for the soul*, 36.
[95] A. Winston-Allen, *Stories of the rose: the making of the rosary in the Middle Ages*, University Park 1997, 11–122.
[96] C. Rawcliffe, 'Women, childbirth and religion in later medieval England', in Wood, *Women and religion*, 91–117 at p. 107.

bequeathed to her daughter, Mary, along with other lavish jewels and silver, 'an Agnus with a baleys (ball or globe), iij saphires, iij perlys, with an ymage of Saint Antony apon it', together with a 'tablet with the Salutacion of Our lady and the iij Kingis of Collayn'.[97] The *Agnus Dei*, or Lamb of God, was a symbol of the sacrificial Christ, the bearer of the sins of humanity who offered redemption through his blood and Passion, and closely associated with the spiritual protection desired during childbirth.[98] This tablet bearing images of the Annunciation and the Epiphany is thus an icon of incarnational piety honouring God made man and the universal offering of his saving gift, symbolised by the 'Kingis of Collayn'.[99] Both of Elizabeth Browne's jewels would have been perceived as very powerful amulets as well as beautiful icons for personal prayer and meditation. Elizabeth, significantly, left them to her daughter, rather than her sons and their wives, and in her will arranged that, in the event of Mary's death, they should go to Margaret Hasslake, 'my kynnyswoman', and only when she died to Isabell Poynings, her daughter-in-law. Elizabeth Browne regarded these jewels as personal to her, belonging to the sphere of female devotion and activity, not simply as valuable items of adornment and family prestige. It would have been unusual if they were not seen as objects of power, or at least 'comforters', during childbirth or other times of perceived physical and spiritual danger.

Carpenters and coronets

St Anne was, among her other attributes, the patron saint of woodworkers, perhaps because she was mother-in-law to one carpenter and grandmother to another. The implications of the wood and tree metaphor resonate at many levels. The most obvious relates to the Old Testament tree of life,[100] the tree of Jesse as family tree, and its iconographic successor, the tree of Calvary with its redemptive associations. Anne here embodies the root or progenitor of an omnipotent redeemer whose ability to save branched out through his extended blood-kin among the Apostles. And this tree of life was characterised by the transmission of an incarnational dynamic through

---

[97]   *Paston letters*, i, no. 123, 211; PCC, reg. Miles, fo. 12 (Browne) 1487.

[98]   The Agnus was also a rebus of Elizabeth's mother's name, Agnes, though beaten and incarcerated as Elizabeth was in her young adulthood she may not have sustained feelings of maternal affection. The Agnus Dei was also a popular subject depicted on paxes: N. F. Layard, 'Notes on some English paxes', *Archaeological Journal* lx (1904), 120–30. It was also central to the engraved design of the fifteenth-century Middleham jewel, confirming its talismanic potential. There, is, however, no evidence to confirm the jewel's original ownership.

[99]   For a woman's bequest to the prioress of Carrow of a cloth painted with images of the three kings see the will of Elizabeth Yaxley (d. 1533), NCC, reg. Platfoote, fos 104–6.

[100]   Genesis iii. 22.

its matrilineal branches:[101] 'Blyssed Anne, whyche in operacion / Of oure redempcion ys gone out / Lyke as the rote hath dominacion / Of the tre and the braunches rounde about / Ys comen out that most blyssyd virgyne / Seynt mary, thys derk world to enlumyne.'[102] As Mirk's homily for the feast of St Anne noted, 'Of a good tre comythe good frute', a succinct appraisal of her role as a conduit of grace.[103] The tree as a symbol of genealogy is very signifi-cant in St Anne's iconography, as is apparent from medieval illuminations as well as verse. The *Hours of Catherine of Cleves* (Utrecht, *c.* 1440) has a page devoted to this explicit image of the saint surrounded by a tree of Jesse with many branches on which are displayed her patriarchal ancestors, of whom she is shown as the culmination.[104] The use of books of hours for personal prayer and the reading of the daily offices by the wealthy, and therefore probably literate, should not be understood in terms of the text alone, but also of the illumination as a primary aid to meditation and contemplation.[105] The power of the image was an accepted commonplace, as the ubiquity and impact of the *pietà* shows: Mary bearing her crucified son, 'thys derk world to enlumyne'.[106]

Pamela Sheingorn argues that such matrilineal images, such as female-emphatic family trees, were defined by, as well as defining, shifts in what constituted 'the family' in the fifteenth and sixteenth centuries.[107] This was a period when many people were married three or four times, either because of death in childbirth or death caused by infectious disease or violence. A matrilineal focus may be read as a rebuttal of institutional patriarchy, but it may equally be read as a rejection of dynastic rivalry: 'She (Anne) … In whom the herytage most surely doth stand / Of oure fadyr Iacob, lowsyng the bond / By hyr most ennoblyd magnificence / Puttyng awey clene all vyolence.'[108]

Yorkist and Lancastrian feuding in fifteenth-century England, and civil violence in the Low Countries, demonstrated that political and dynastic rivalry was frequently complicated by degrees of kinship between major players on opposing sides. Individuals theoretically offering protection or allegiance within the networks of kinship were often in reality the enemy. And, at a regional level, the county of Norfolk and the city of Norwich had

---

[101] Isaiah xi.1–10.
[102] *Life of St Anne*, 94, lines 155–61.
[103] *Mirk's festial*, 216, line 2.
[104] There is just such an illumination in *The hours of Catherine of Cleves*, ed. J. Plummer, London 1966. The original is in the Pierpoint Morgan Library, New York.
[105] S. Penketh, 'Women and books of hours', in J. H. M. Taylor and L. Smith (eds), *Women and the book: assessing the visual evidence*, London–Toronto 1997, 266–80, esp. p. 272, fig. 99 a, b.
[106] *Book of Margery Kempe*, i, ch. lx, p. 148.
[107] P. Sheingorn, 'Appropriating the holy kinship', in Ashley and Sheingorn, *Interpreting cultural symbols*, 169–98.
[108] *Life of Saint Anne*, 96–7.

witnessed short but intense outbreaks of disorder during this period.[109] St Anne, perhaps fortuitously in such a ruthlessly competitive context, was also patron of the 'good death'.[110]

The extent of investment in, and the popularity of, the cult of St Anne in and around Norwich in the fifteenth century cannot be assessed as a discrete development removed from this wider context. It has also to be seen in the broader context of Yorkist and Lancastrian feuding in a competitive and adversarial society. In a time of much 'cross-fertilisation' between the Lancastrian and Yorkist parties in the manipulation of what became spiritual propaganda, it is illuminating to see Osbern Bokenham, a Yorkist, being commissioned to write vernacular saints' *Lives* by Elizabeth de Vere and Katherine Denston, both with strong Lancastrian connections.[111] Bokenham may indeed have helped to reinforce the Yorkist claim to the throne by using his life of St Anne to validate the matrilineal function in the transmission of legitimate, even transcendent right, and thus lend support to the title of Richard, duke of York. The claim of his son, ultimately Edward IV, like his own, depended on two points of succession through the female line.[112] On the other hand Bokenham also expends much ink on Joachim's ancestors and the angelic annunciation to him as father.[113] Moreover, the Lancastrian claim to the throne of France was through a woman. Whatever the allegiance, the cult of St Anne could be deployed and 'spun' by the sparring political factions. The saint's veneration by the Yorkist elite, in any case, assumed a powerful political dimension.

The promotion of this cult ostensibly connected Edward IV with his predecessor Richard II, whose queen, Anne of Bohemia, had been honoured in 1382 by official sanction of the feast of St Anne throughout the English Church. The conscious 'attachment' by Edward to Richard was intended, in a sense, to emphasise the illegitimacy of the intervening Lancastrian occupants of the throne and draw a veil over Edward's own usurpations of Henry VI in 1461 and 1471. A Yorkist chronicler and propagandist describes an incident in Daventry parish church on Palm Sunday 1471, where Edward was hearing mass: an enclosed tabernacle had suddenly opened to reveal an image of St Anne, and afterwards just as suddenly closed again. This was

---

[109] Tanner, *Church in Norwich*, 141–58; P. Maddern, *Violence and social order: East Anglia, 1422–1442*, Oxford 1992, 175–205. See also P. Dunn, 'Discord and dislocation: relations between Norwich and the crown, 1400–1450', unpublished MA diss. UEA 1999, passim.

[110] Ashley and Sheingorn, 'Locating St Anne', 50.

[111] S. Delany, *Impolitic bodies: poetry, saints, and society in fifteenth-century England*, New York–Oxford 1998, 147–8.

[112] These two women, through whom the direct line was transmitted, were Philippa, granddaughter of Edward III, and Anne Mortimer, Edward's paternal grandmother.

[113] Bodleian Library, Oxford, MS Aubrey 31, fo. 31, contains a telling illumination of St Anne and St Joachim (nimbed), with an unusually prominent Joachim nursing the infant Mary, while Anne's attention is totally concentrated on her book: the Word. The text beneath describes her as 'Anna mater magne prolis'.

construed as a mark of the saint's support and blessing.[114] The significance of placing this incident on Palm Sunday, when Christ, lauded by the fickle populace, had made a triumphant entry into Jerusalem, should also be noted.

Names: patronage and protection

The choosing of a Christian name and thereby a spiritual protector and advocate assumed great importance in this period. This is confirmed by surviving books of hours which accord particular prominence to the name-saints of the owners, St Anne among them. 'Then schal zy know that we redyn of v holy woymen that werne cald Anne' preached John Mirk.[115] Christian names also honoured a godparent or other earthly patron, whose temporal duties toward the godchild were expected to mirror those of the heavenly sponsor and constituted a serious life-long relationship.[116] Women's baptismal names reflect the esteem in which these saints were held and the hope that special guardianship would follow such a choice. Annor Gilbert and her daughter Anne exemplify this thinking.

Another Anne, the thrice-married but childless Anne Harling (later Lady Scrope) of East Harling, Norfolk, in her will of 1498, finally opted instead for spiritual children, on whose prayers she could depend.[117] She re-established a college at Rushworth to take thirteen children from the Norwich diocese, a significant five of whom (for the joys of Mary or the five wounds of Christ or both) were to be poor children, clothed, fed and raised by the college and known as 'Dame Annys Childeryn'.[118] The balance of spiritual merit initially acquired by Anne Harling would be supplemented by relays of intercession from generations of young beneficiaries, even more so if her support helped

[114] *Historie of the arrivall of Edward IV in England and the finall recouerye of his kingdomes from Henry VI: three chronicles of the reign of Edward IV*, ed. J. Bruce, Gloucester 1988, 160. See also J. Hughes, *Arthurian myth and alchemy: the kingship of Edward IV*, Stroud 2002, 223 (at p. 227 for an illumination of the birth of the Virgin, with a border decoration containing Edward's arms, the garter and the sun and rose of York).

[115] *Mirk's festial*, 213. Mirk's dates within the fifteenth century are uncertain, but there were more than eighteen editions of the *Festial* between 1485 and 1532: *Mirk's instructions*, 11.

[116] The godmother's gift of a rosary was a tool for (eternal) life.

[117] Anne Harling was a substantial heiress, the last of her family, hence the need for an heir. She owned nineteen manors and five advowsons in Norfolk alone. She requested burial in St Anne's chapel at East Harling church, which was 'joyned to the chauncell of the churche', within the tomb of her first husband, as promised: C. Woodforde, *Norwich school of glass-painting in the fifteenth century*, London 1950, 43. Her will is printed in *Testamenta eboracensia*, 149–54.

[118] H. S. Bennet, 'Notes on the original statutes of the college of St John Evangelist of Rushworth, Co. Norfolk, founded by Edmund Gonville, AD 1342', NA x (1888), 277–382.

to educate any potential priests, for it was from such foundations that promising recruits were harvested.[119]

St Anne and Robert Reynes

The commonplace book of Robert Reynes of Acle, in the Hundred of South Walsham, Norfolk, a 'churchreeve' (churchwarden), born about 1445, throws significant light on devotion to St Anne in the county through the affinity felt by Robert and his wife Emma for the saint. They were married, he writes, two days after her feast, that is on 28 July 1471, a time of great festivity in Acle in the saint's honour. Coming so soon after the restoration of Edward IV, the nuptial celebrations may have been heightened by the prospect of a more settled realm.[120] Reynes's book contains a stanzaic verse *Life* of the saint, probably for recitation at festal meetings of Acle's gild of St Anne, of which Robert and Emma were almost certainly prominent members.[121] Evidence of gild use is apparent from the poem and this was probably its *raison d'être*: 'Now blyssyd be sent anne that brouth forth this berth / And blyssyd be these dowterys and her (their) chylderyn infere (together); / And blyssyd be all tho that make (h)onest mirth / In the worchepe of sent anne in thys tyme of yeere.'[122] And as the poem comes to an end: 'And mary and her moder maynteth this gylde / to the worchep of god and of his plesaunce / and alle that it mayntene it be it man or chylde / god of his hey grace geue hem good chaunce.'[123]

Significantly, Reynes's book also contains a lengthy prose account of the life of St Bridget, another well-known married saint and mother much favoured in East Anglia and beyond, whose book of her *Revelations* was obviously as influential in Acle as it was in Lynn: Margery Kempe, like Robert and Emma Reynes, was devoted to both.[124] Both Anne and Bridget were seen as matriarchs whose primary concern for the spiritual welfare of their respective families was to become an exemplar for every mother. The two saints' spiritual gifts made them a court of first resort in matters dynastic or familial; men and women are 'Cardyd (carried) and holdyn vp both fer and

---

[119] Tanner, *Church in Norwich*, 32–3; Gibson, *Theater of devotion*, 105–6, 96–106; Blomefield, *History of Norfolk*, i. 320–1.

[120] Another wave of the pestilence came that winter and hit hard in Norfolk.

[121] Bodl. Lib., MS 10234 (Tanner 407) at fo. 21. See *Commonplace book of Robert Reynes*, 191–228.

[122] *Life of St Anne*, 112, lines 53–7.

[123] Ibid.126, lines 453–6.

[124] *Book of Margery Kempe*, i, chs vi (St Anne), xx, xxxix (St Bridget). While on pilgrimage in Rome, Margery Kempe even stood as godmother to a child named Bridget, in honour of the saint, she says, having been invited by people who had known Bridget personally. Significantly, Margery also emphasises (i, ch. xxxix, lines 25–9) the high social standing of the family upon whom she conferred this honour.

nere / By hyr suffragys, and that in every thyng' says the poem of St Anne's intercessory powers.[125] With such perceived correspondences between Anne and Bridget, it was inevitable that some confusion should arise among the laity as to their discrete identities. This is apparent in rood-screen depictions, where one is sometimes confused with the other.[126]

Robert and Emma Reynes had five sons whose names he records. He also commemorates his parents, Alice and John, an earlier churchreeve, in his book.[127] Robert's strong sense of family and lineage and possibly the fact that he and Emma had many sons, may explain something of the couple's attachment to St Anne, perhaps reflecting that of the Gilberts of Norwich. Robert was himself one of five brothers but he also had five sisters, a large family for John and Alice Reynes to support, especially if, implausibly, John had started out as a simple carpenter.[128] Plainly, John became a comfortable member of the Acle establishment, and Alice would have occupied an influential position in the community, as wife of a churchwarden and as matriarch of this large and prospering family, almost certainly with servants, journeymen and apprentices to organise, house and feed. John Reynes, together with two other churchreeves, contributed no less than £16 in 1472 (the year following Robert and Emma's marriage) to 'maken the Batylment of the Stepyll', another indication of his standing.[129] Two years later, Robert, with his fellow churchreeves, outdid his father's gift to the steeple project with a combined donation of £23 for a set of red velvet vestments for high mass.[130]

St Anne's patronage of woodworkers may also have prompted the family's attachment, especially if Robert Reynes followed his father's trade. John had obviously seen that Robert received enough education to compile his book and read those books that interested him, including some in basic Latin. Whether he was literate in the medieval sense is, however, open to question. It may be that the Latin he recorded had for him a quasi-magical kinship with the charms against sickness, death in childbirth and danger that he also noted down. The notes concerning land tenure as well as lists of saints' days, sacraments, sins and commandments would be useful *aides memoire* for a busy churchwarden, but the other items reveal more personal preoccupations.[131] Emma Reynes died only eight years after her marriage, possibly in childbed. One of the two sons named John appears to have died in infancy. Robert, unusually, seems to have remained a widower; he certainly records no further marriage.

---

125 *Life of St Anne*, 94, lines 129–30.
126 An example is the rood-screen at Horsham St Faith, where the third and seventh panels are identified as St Anne and St Bridget respectively; I suggest, rather, that the third is Bridget and the seventh, Anne.
127 The sons were two Johns, William, Thomas and Lewis.
128 'Commonplace book of Robert Reynes', 111–27.
129 Ibid. 111.
130 Duffy, 'Parish, piety and patronage', 150–2.
131 'Commonplace book of Robert Reynes', 114, 120.

Acle's gild of St Anne may have been based at the Reynes's parish church of Acle St Edmund.[132] Every year the feast of St Anne was celebrated by the gild with gusto, perhaps with the performance of the play of Anna and Joachim from the *N-town play* or other theatricals, but almost certainly by the recitation of the verse *Life* as recorded in Robert's book. It is known that the gild of St Anne in the city of Lincoln was active in similar productions throughout the fifteenth century.[133]

St Anne: Norwich gilds and chapels

The saint and her cult were established in city churches from early in the fourteenth century. According to Francis Blomefield, a church dedicated to St Anne had been closed by 1370 and combined with St Clements, Conesford.[134] That her cult had appeal to many people at all levels of society through gild performances and the written word is demonstrated by surviving poems, plays and parish devotions. Evidence of testamentary bequests from both men and women reveals a string of Norwich parish churches with a particular attachment to the saint. By various altar dedications, painted glass, image and gild, St Anne encompassed the city like a totem of assurance and stability. St Anne was a popular gild patron and, while chapels and many altars were dedicated to her in Norwich churches, they are particularly notable in well-endowed parish churches associated with rising merchants and artisans, such as St Peter Mancroft, St Stephen, St Andrew and St Michael Coslany.[135]

The gild of St Anne at St Peter Mancroft, of course, was finely furnished, with visual aids in the form of the Norwich School glass.[136] Another gild of this dedication was based at St Martin-in-the-Bailey,[137] an ancient foundation, and a third at St Martin-at-the-Palace-Gates.[138] The church of St John the Baptist with the Holy Sepulchre, Ber Street, had an image of St Anne in a niche or tabernacle in the nave, where it would be visible and accessible,

---

[132] An argument for a different venue has been made by Gail Gibson. She opts for Weybridge Priory, a small house of Augustinian canons in Acle parish: *Theater of devotion*, 83. See also Blomefield, *History of Norfolk*, xi. 93, where this gild seems to be connected with the fact that the priory was in the patronage of the earls of Norfolk.
[133] A. Leach, 'Some English plays and players', in F. J. Furnivall, (ed.), *An English miscellany presented to F. J. Furnivall on the occasion of his seventy-fifth birthday*, Oxford 1901, repr. New York 1969, 233.
[134] Blomefield, *History of Norfolk*, iv. 7.
[135] Ibid. ii. 670.
[136] NCC, reg. Aubry, fo. 32 (Kempe), 1479; reg. Haywarde, fo. 149 (Petifer), 1529.
[137] NCC, reg. Heydon, fo. 24 (Ladde), 1378.
[138] Blomefield, *History of Norfolk*, iv. 121; NCC, reg. Ryxe, fo. 194 (Daywel), 1505/6.

especially to women, who would not be encouraged to linger in the chancel or sanctuary, Anne's usual location.[139]

The foundation of the chapel of St Anne on the north side of St Stephen's parish church began as an act of devotion for which Lettice Pain is remembered. The arms of Robert Brasyer and his family featured in this chapel as well as in the north aisle, as if marking out the territory and almost laying siege to the saint whose protection and patronage they sought.[140]

A chest placed behind the altar of St Anne's chapel in St Andrew's parish church became the site in 1442 of what today might be termed a business starter scheme, when Alderman John Cambridge requested burial next to his wife there. He gave 10s. to be kept in the chest and lent out on security by the churchwardens to the poor of the parish.[141] This became known as Cambridge's Chest, and, in a sense, made St Anne the patron of a modest bank-loan system. That the money was a loan rather than a gift indicates that it was meant to aid those setting up in business, and capable of future repayment. A distinction was being drawn between the allocation of charity to the destitute poor and the struggling but ambitious artisan. Such provision was, none the less, understood as a deed of charity.

St Anne's implicit patronage of this loan scheme reinforces the distinctly commercial aspects of her cult which might appeal to a successful merchant and his wife. (Robert Reynes of Acle was succinctly to note later in his commonplace book that St Anne and her husband Joachim 'weren ryght ryche folke'.[142]) While gaining spiritual merit for their work of charity, the Cambridges had, in choosing St Anne as the patron of their scheme, hitched their wagon to a star. As time passed others added bequests of their own to Cambridge's chest, reinforcing the inextricable linkage between the temporal and spiritual.[143] The church's gild of St Andrew regularly met in the chapel of St Anne to fulfil its spiritual obligations of intercession, and perhaps the members thereby secured priority when it came to obtaining a loan for themselves or their dependants.

John and Annor Gilbert chose to be buried in this chapel, perhaps because of the affinity Annor felt for her name-saint, or her hopes for her protection. Annor's will was drawn up on 5 November 1466, while John's was completed two days later. They had arranged for a priest, wearing a vestment of their gift, to sing masses for their souls for ten years, for which they had left the remarkable sum of 100 marks (£66 13s. 4d.).[144] By comparison, a leading

139 Blomefield, *History of Norfolk*, iv. 141.
140 Ibid. iv. 150.
141 NCC, reg. Doke, fos 192–5 (Cambridge), 1442.
142 Linnell, 'Commonplace book of Robert Reynes', 115; *Life of St Anne*, 110, l.13.
143 PCC, reg. Ketchyn, fo. 18 (Katherine Rogers), 1556. Katherine left £20 to the chest, to be loaned out in sums not exceeding 40s., to the poor parishioners of St Andrew's church. This was nearly a century after the charity was founded.
144 NCC, reg. Jekkys, fo. 47 (John Gilbert), 1466.

mason of the period might earn £7 5s. for 290 days work in an accounting year.[145] John Gilbert was quite specific in requiring a 'tryntyll [trental] ... in the chapell of Seinte Anne in the church of Seint Andrewe ... And a honest priest to syng & pray for me and my wyf and all my good frends soules ... x yers in the chapell of Seynt Anne.'[146] The chapel location is written twice, once at the beginning and again at the end of this directive; the thirty masses were to be celebrated there, and emphatically not elsewhere. John Cambridge and John Gilbert both chose burial next to their wives, who had first elected to be interred in this chapel, presumably after prior discussion. The Cambridges and the Gilberts stood at the apex of the civic governing class, and it is interesting that they chose interment and remembrance in this chapel of St Anne, at St Andrew's church, rather than at the more fashionable, if ostentatious, St Peter Mancroft.

John Gilbert also left £10 to the hospital near the priory precinct, founded by Walter Suffield (1249), who had placed it under the patronage of St Giles. Its co-dedicatees were the Virgin and her mother, St Anne, to whom he had a particular devotion. St Giles, patron of cripples and lepers, was also protector of another vulnerable group: nursing mothers. Although women were forbidden access to all other parts of the hospital and its precincts, they were permitted, from about 1270 onwards, to enter the nave, where later much of the imagery was of female subjects. St Anne is featured on a ceiling boss showing the holy family in Bishop James Goldwell's (d. 1499) chantry chapel in the south transept of the nave.[147] The saint's central position between her daughter and Joseph in this compact composition, makes her the focal point, as she holds out a towel with which she intends to receive the Infant, or from which she has just passed him to his mother. The ambiguity of this incarnational iconography is important and deliberate. St Anne, while the acknowledged precursor of God made flesh, was also by the same token receptive to the Holy Spirit. She was both enabler and receptor. This integrity was her benchmark, as the stonemason who made this boss surely understood. St Margaret and St Katherine were also among the saints carved on the chantry bosses, the inner circle of which features scenes from the life of Christ and his mother, beginning with the Annunciation and ending with the Coronation of the Virgin, situated in a central position.

A finely carved pew-end, depicting St Margaret and her dragon, commissioned by John Hecker (hospital master, 1519–32), which thus post-dates the chantry chapel, placed this helper-saint in close proximity to any pregnant women who might have frequented the nave. In addition to her boss, by the end of the fifteenth century, and probably long before, St Anne's image was kept in the chancel of the hospital church, where an altar and

[145] C. Dyer, *Standards of living in the later Middle Ages: social change in England, c. 1200–1520*, Cambridge 1989, 227.
[146] NCC, reg. Jekkys, fo. 48 (Gilbert), 1466.
[147] For illustrations see Rawcliffe, *Medicine for the soul*, 118.

lights were maintained in her honour.[148] If it was of the same calibre as the rest of the carving in this church, it must have been exceptional. As the musical tradition of the hospital grew more sophisticated, and an additional pair of organs was purchased from the bishop of Norwich's palace at Hoxne, it is no surprise to find this fine acquisition placed next to Anne's image, as it were, under her protection.[149]

The saint's appeal to the merchantile elite of Norwich rested on her family's material and spiritual success, the promotion of matriarchy, marriage and what seemed like an affirmation of wealth if properly deployed. This aspect of the St Anne cult is exemplified in the 'Name of Jesus' window in St Peter Mancroft, begun around 1453, beneath which the elite St Anne gild met.[150] The extensive kindred of St Anne in their sartorial splendour, their success signalled by their evident physical and economic productivity, could readily be interpreted by members of this prosperous congregation as affirming dynastic aspiration, the accumulation of wealth by commercial entrepreneurs, such as Mayor Robert Toppes, its donor, and even political ambition. That this south chancel chapel was the location of an active centre of female piety is also a distinct possibility.[151]

Whatever precious ornaments and vestments honoured the saint also honoured the donor, whether an individual or a gild and its members. The remarkable collection of artefacts gathered by the parishioners of St Peter Mancroft enhanced worship in what had become such a prestigious parish church that, during the fifteenth century, it was a successful rival to the cathedral. So numerous were the treasures given that the inventory suggests a highly competitive community engaged in a spiritual alms race. The accumulated riches of plate and textile, so carefully commissioned, stored and accounted for, were used in multiple masses intended to achieve the salvation of the donors.[152] The paradox posed by such superfluity in the face of a devotion to spiritual poverty, that is Christ embodied in the indigent and sick, can only have driven the desire for yet more intercession and perpetuated further acquisition of commemorative goods.[153]

---

[148] NCC, reg. Brosyard, fo. 288.
[149] NCR, 24A, Great Hospital general accounts, 1510–20, receiver general's accounts for 1511–15, cited in Rawcliffe, *Medicine for the soul*, 125.
[150] Alderman Henry Wilton (d. 1507), who was a councillor for Mancroft ward, requested burial in St Nicholas's chapel at St Peter's, but also left gifts rich with incarnational imagery to Great Plumstead St Mary, primarily 'an image of alabastre of Seynt Anne': NCC, reg. Spyltymber, fos 42–6.
[151] David King's theory is given greater, if non-specific, credence by Mary Erler's work on the affinity of Margaret Purdans (d. 1483): *Women, reading*, 68–84.
[152] An increasing repertoire of liturgies, including new and fashionable settings of the mass, is evident from the goods assigned to them, indicating a high level of lay investment and choice.
[153] The entries on one half page of inventory alone list gifts of engraved silver gilt items, including basins, paxes, a holy water stoop, verger and cruet, given by John and Margaret Cutler, Thomas Alen, John Dereham, Robert Bour and William Ellys, respectively: Hope,

Annor and John Gilbert both left detailed instructions to their executors, probably because they were ailing together. This exemplifies the difficulties of defining who was influencing whom, and how men and women might differ in the nature of their spiritual focus and devotion. John's will provided for a greater number of charitable bequests because he held the purse strings. Nor can their commitment to charitable activity while alive be fully assessed. It is significant that each of them left money to three women sharing a life of poverty and chastity, called in this particular instance 'the sisters of St Laurence'. These unnamed women were then living in this parish in a tenement recently owned by John Asger (d.1436).[154] He (or his son, also John, who also died in 1436) may have been known to the Gilberts in their youth, while his strong continental links and the Gilberts' own commercial connections with the Low Countries may have helped to shape the couple's religious inclinations. Annor was in fact one of two Norwich women, both wives of former mayors, for whom evidence survives, who are known to have made bequests to such 'beguinages', variously designated as 'sisters' or 'poor women' dedicated to chastity or dedicated to God.[155] Of seventeen surviving bequests to such communities, seven were made by clerics: John Riche, rector of St Michael Coslany, John Dyra, rector of St John Maddermarket, and the bishop's registrar, John Excestre, as well as four unbeneficed priests.[156] It is significant that these devout women were aligning themselves with an elite band of clerical testators.

Mancroft ward

It can be fairly assumed that chapels dedicated to St Anne contained her image, probably in statuary form, but sometimes in a wall-painting, on a painted cloth or in a stained glass window. A series of wall-paintings at Potter Heigham St Nicholas, in Norwich's hinterland, was identified in the 1950s as portraying scenes from the life of St Anne.[157] Now fading rapidly,

'Inventories', 213. Christine Peters links this desire for personal commemoration with the more intimate nature of some women's gifts to saints' images: *Patterns of piety*, 50.

[154] Testators leaving gifts to this household are listed in Tanner, *Church in Norwich*, 203 n. 60.

[155] Ibid. 65. The other was Alice Broun (NCC, reg. Cobbalde, fo. 68, 1465) who was also a co-founder of the St Barbara chapel in the Guildhall.

[156] NCC, reg. Hyrnyng, fo. 151 (Riche); reg. Aleyn, fo. 61 (Dyra); reg. Wylbey, fo.107 (Excestre). Rectors of St Michael Coslany may have been on the innovative wing spiritually; Riche's predecessor, Roger Reede, left the first recorded bequest to Julian of Norwich and, in 1498, Thomas Drenthale oversaw an oath-taking at a convocation of aldermen, when one of their number undertook a journey to the Holy Land: *RCN*, ii, no. cclix at p. 156.

[157] E. W. Tristram, *English wall painting of the fourteenth century*, London 1955, appendix F.

this extensive sequence may have incorporated many images and themes, but seems to feature depictions of the seven comfortable works, which were closely identified with expressions of female piety. Much that remains is now unclear or just inaccessible to the eye, although the still-visible and recurring strongly-drawn figure of a woman is clearly the predominant and active element in every scene demonstrating charitable activity.

Blomefield observed that the chapel dedicated to St Anne in the north aisle of the parish church of St Stephen in Norwich once contained an image of her by the altar, reflecting her association with the mass. In 1523 Alice Carr, widow, left her small coral rosary to be placed daily upon this image, to be replaced by Alice's best coral beads on the feast day of the saint (26 July).[158] She also requested that her beads should decorate the images of the Virgin and the virgin martyrs, Margaret and Katherine, on their feast days. It may be assumed that Alice thereby hoped to benefit from a powerful battery of heavenly intercession, while at the same time ensuring that her beads were very close to the celebration of the mass and to the host. It is notable that three of Alice's saintly beneficiaries, Margaret, Anne and the Virgin, had definite associations with protection in childbirth.[159] This very literal act of putting beads into the hands of a saint's image, or draping a statue with the 'tools' of intercessory prayer, demonstrated on one level a need for suffrage and remembrance. On another, an implicit expectation that intercession, or corporate focus on it, might become even more powerful on feast days is apparent from such a very personal, and, at this period, not uncommon female legacy. Alice is only unusual to the extent that she records so specifically where and when her beads are to be used. To the eyes of her fellow parishioners, the coral beads were not only a visible expression of her status and remembrance, but also a powerful reminder to her friends to do as the saint's image appeared to be doing and intercede for her in communion with her saintly patron, an act which earned salvific grace for the intercessors as well as for the departed.

As a result of the plummeting population following successive outbreaks of the plague, the parish church of St Anne, near King Street, Norwich, was united by 1370 with St Clement's, Conesford, commonly called St Clement's at the Well, where a chapel was subsequently dedicated to St Anne.[160] Nearly ninety years later, in 1458, Katherine Marshall gave to this chapel a silver tablet and chain, though whether it was intended to decorate St Anne's image or to lend out, or to be sold to pay for other projects, remains

---

[158] NCC, reg. Grundisburgh, fo. 8 (Carre, d. 1523).

[159] The major feasts of the Virgin Mary were the Purification (2 Feb.), the Annunciation (25 Mar.), the Visitation of Mary to Elizabeth (2 July) and the Assumption (15 Aug.). St Margaret's day was 20 July, and St Katherine's, 25 November. Alice's beads were, therefore, a very visible reminder to all those celebrating the feasts to pray for her throughout the year.

[160] Blomefield, *History of Norfolk*, iv. 78.

unknown.[161] St Anne's chapel, however, patently continued for many years as a strong focus for commemoration and requests for intercession.

In addition to chapels dedicated to the Holy Trinity and the Blessed Virgin (south and north transepts respectively), the parish church of St John Baptist and the Holy Sepulchre in Ber Street, commonly called St John at the Gates, had in the nave, where it was accessible to the women of the congregation, a niche or tabernacle containing an image of St Anne.[162] Here, women could see and touch the image and pray before it, unlike such tabernacles kept in close proximity to the altar, where women were forbidden to venture unless they were of very high status.[163]

Close by another set of city gates the prestigious St Stephen's church, site of the grave and shrine of its former vicar, the saintly Richard Caister, similarly contained a chapel dedicated to St Anne on the north aisle. Margery Kempe gives an account of her first encounter with Caister at this church, late one Thursday morning, which seems at first reading in conflict with his subsequent long-term support for her spiritual aspirations. Margery asked him if he could spare her an hour or two in the afternoon, so she could speak to him of the love of God. He replied: 'Benedicite. What cowd a woman ocupyn an owyr er tweyn owyers in the lofe of owyr Lord? I xal neuyr ete mete tyl I wete what ye kan sey of owyr Lord God the tyme of on owyr.'[164] That this approach was one of humorous irony, meant to tease and encourage confidence, is perhaps confirmed by her subsequent lengthy outpouring to him.

A site close to this chapel was chosen by the Brasyers, Alderman Robert (d. 1435) and Christian his wife, for their chantry and burial. Their family arms were later emblazoned throughout the chapel and in the north aisle by other, later Brasyers, keen to identify with the extended holy kin and the network of spiritual intercession this implied. Francis Blomefield records that the chapel was originally founded as a chantry in 1313 by Lettice Pain (d. 1317) of Norwich, widow of William, together with another chapel in St Peter Mancroft, for which she obtained a licence of mortmain from Edward II.[165] Lettice settled on her chantries and their chaplains a messuage in the parish of St Peter Mancroft, situated in Upper Newport street, and also the rents of what appear to have been commercial properties in Cotelerowe (cutler row), Lower Newport street, Sadlers-rowe, Cordwayner-rowe, the Flesh-market, Sheregate, and in St Gregory's, Pottergate, amounting to a substantial £6 6s. 8d. per annum. The chaplains were to celebrate each

---

[161] Ibid. iv. 79.

[162] Ibid. iv. 141.

[163] See M. Aston, 'Segregation in church', in W. J. Sheils and D. Wood (eds), *Women in the Church* (Studies in Church History xxvii, 1990), 237–94 at pp. 238–9.

[164] *Book of Margery Kempe*, i, ch. xvii, p. 38, lines 25–8.

[165] Blomefield, *History of Norfolk*, iv. 163. For chantries in Norwich, although of a slightly later date, see also Tanner, *Church in Norwich*, 92–4.

morning, one at each chantry, for the souls of Lettice and William, their ancestors, successors and all Christian souls.[166] Lettice appears to have had no surviving children herself, her heir being her great-nephew, Jeffry de Wyleby. It is interesting to note that, when Lettice's own dwelling in Newgate Street, St Stephen's parish, was sold by her executors in 1318, it was bought by Sir Walter and Lady Katherine Norwich, a woman whose accounts show that she daily practised the comfortable works for the poor.

Wymer ward

Across the town in the parish church of St Gregory, in Pottergate, there was a north aisle chapel dedicated to the Virgin and a large south aisle chapel dedicated to St Thomas Becket (d.1170), the altar of which was jointly dedicated to St Anne and St Thomas.[167] Their images were displayed in niches on the wall by the altar, their pairing presenting an initially puzzling iconography to the modern eye. St Thomas is a logical candidate, in view of the dedication of the church to Pope Gregory the Great: Thomas died for the principle of supremacy of Church over State as the ultimate temporal as well as spiritual authority.[168] It might be argued that St Anne, as the earthly precursor of the incarnate and final authority, was here endorsing Thomas rather than the other way around. Clearly, she was a figure of some consequence, being displayed on the south side of the church, traditionally masculine territory, next to a saint who had strong (but not exclusive) appeal to the upper echelons of the male patriarchy. Anne's appeal was plainly not gendered. A chapel dedicated to the Assumption of the Virgin, containing her image and honoured by perpetual lights, was located at the west end of the steeple and opened out into the 'common passage'. The surviving stone vaulting of this chamber indicates something of the level of invest-ment it attracted. The steeple of St Gregory's (which stands on a hill above the Wensum) would provide an apt symbol for the Assumption, a suitable launch-pad of bells and worship carried skywards and a key feature in the decent burial of the dead, the seventh corporal work of mercy.

In the context of the fleshly clothing of Christ by his mother and, ulti-mately, St Anne, this church possessed fine textiles to 'clothe' the dead as they lay before the altar of St Anne and St Thomas Becket. Blomefield

---

[166] The first chaplains were Sir Henry de Thornham and John Brond of Norwich: Blomefield, *History of Norfolk*, iv. 165. Lettice's chantry was still functioning in 1397, as a payment by its chaplain of 1*d.* is noted in *RCN* ii, no. ccccvi, pp. 251–2.

[167] Blomefield, *History of Norfolk*, iv. 273.

[168] In recent years some finely executed wall-paintings have been partially recovered in this chapel, high up overlooking the altar area, and representing the early Fathers of the Church. Becket's intercession, like that of St Anne, was sometimes invoked in childbirth: Rawcliffe, 'Women, childbirth and religion', 94; H. Leyser, *Medieval women: a social history of women in England, 450–1500*, London 1995, 129.

1. Unique screen panels at Harpley St Laurence, Norfolk, *en route* to Walsingham, showing a young Joachim and Anne teaching a prepubescent Mary to read (C. Hill).

2. Annunciation window, detail of a collection of at least five Annunciations at Bale All Saints, north Norfolk, *en route* to Walsingham. Conception could be a fraught issue and here is emphasised what today would be called 'positive imaging' before arriving to petition at Walsingham (D. King).

3. Fifteenth-century screen backing the altar at Ranworth St Helen, Norfolk, showing the three Marys and their seven little sons, accompanied by St Margaret and her dragon. Photography cannot clearly convey the fine drawing of these figures, which is visible where paint has gone (R. Batchelor).

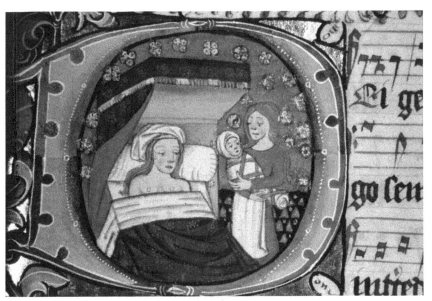

4. St Anne and the birth of Mary from the fifteenth-century antiphoner at Ranworth St Helen, Norfolk, still kept in the church nave. Reproduced by kind permission of the PCC of Ranworth St Helen.

5. St Anne in an English silk orphrey on a dalmatic from Whalley Abbey, Yorkshire, showing the birth of Mary (with midwife), similar and contemporary with those described on vestments in the inventory of St Peter Mancroft church, Norwich (Burrell Collection, Glasgow). Reproduced by kind permission of Culture and Sport Glasgow (Museums), cat.29/2.

6. Lady screen at Houghton St Giles, *en route* to Walsingham, showing all Christ's major female relatives, Gospel-recorded and legendary, with their children, including St Anne and the Virgin (C. Hill).

7. St Margaret panel on the screen at North Walsham St Nicholas, Norfolk, with other female saints. Note the carefully mutilated faces (R. Batchelor).

8. St Margaret with cross staff on the screen at Wiggenhall St Mary the Virgin, Norfolk, with 'Gloucester Old Spot' dragon. Note the screen benefactor's name (C. Hill).

9. Painted panel of St Margaret, now in Norwich Cathedral, formerly at St Michael at Plea, Norwich, showing, unusually, a dragon unlikely to recover (C. Hill).

10. Carved boss of St Margaret on the ceiling of the Bishop Goldwell chantry chapel in St Helen's church at the Great Hospital, Norwich (C. Rawcliffe).

11. Screen panels at Foxley St Thomas, Norfolk, showing SS Jerome and Ambrose, with their suppliants, Anne and John Baymont (C. Hill).

12. Detail of the donor, Anne Baymont, from plate 11.

13. Painted panel in the chapel of St Andrew in Norwich Cathedral, a singular surviving image in Norwich of St Mary Magdalen, with her legendary 'ex-fiancé', John the Evangelist, and two mutilated donor figures, one male, one female (C. Hill).

14. The Magdalen and Lazarus on the screen side by side at Thornham All Saints, north Norfolk, gift of John and Clarice Miller and others (C. Hill).

15. St Mary Magdalen on a fifteenth-century screen at Bramfield St Andrew, Suffolk, forming a central focus of a permanent 'tableau' of the passion (C. Hill).

16. The remains of the medieval cultic cross at Bramfield church, which attracted bequests, as did a similar one at St Giles, Norwich, which does not survive (C. Hill).

17. Margaret Purdans (in vowess's mantle): fifteenth-century funerary brass commemorating alderman Richard Purdans and his widow, Margaret, at St Giles, Norwich. Margaret was a friend and follower of the hermit Richard Fernys, who lived in this churchyard in around 1428/9. Margaret became a vowess after his death, in 1436.

18. St Elizabeth of Hungary, aristocrat and Franciscan tertiary, whose iconography was used to promote the corporal works of mercy, in the Norwich School glass at St Peter Mancroft parish church, Norwich, commissioned in the 1450s (D. King).

19. Sitha, patron of household servants, with her keys and rosary, on the screen at Barton Turf St Michael and All Angels, Norfolk, alongside another 'helper saint', Apollonia, and her extracted tooth (C. Hill).

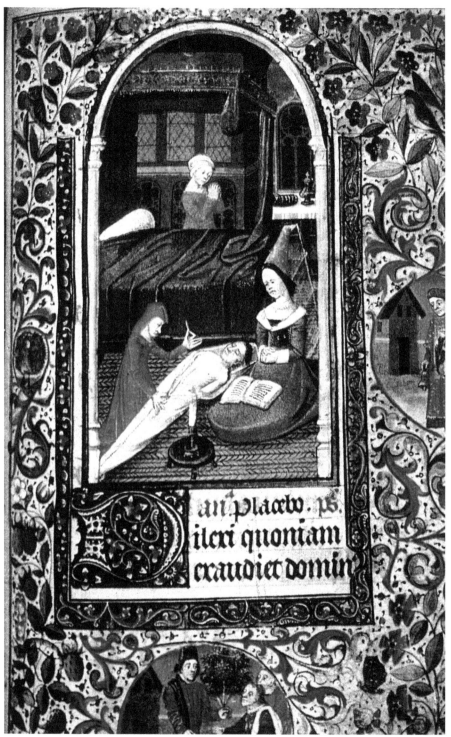

20. Illuminated manuscript, possibly the Master of the Bedford Hours or his circle, Paris, fifteenth century, showing women preparing for a body burial. One stitches him into his shroud while two others pray for his soul.

describes a funeral pall, which is still extant, belonging to St Gregory's, made of black silk and intended for use at funerals and masses of the dead.[169] '[A]dorned with dolphins embowed, embroidered thereon, each having a fish in their mouths half-devoured; there also many angels, each holding a sheet, and those like men, having a demi-man naked, in each sheet, and those like women, having a demi-woman, naked in each sheet ... that by their ministrations, the souls of the righteous are conducted to heaven'.[170] The pall was donated by John Rede, 'Cytesen of Norwich Fysshmonger', in 1517, and originally exhorted 'Pray for the Sowle of Jhon Reede and Agnes his Wyff'.[171] Agnes died in 1522 and in her will asked to be buried next to John (d. 1517) in the churchyard of St Gregory's.[172] John's trade might account for the 'dolphins embowed' on their gift; that dolphins also figured as a symbol with royal connotations may have appealed to the Reedes, or even amused them. It is unlikely that the symbol was a grand gesture of aspiration in view of their desire for churchyard burial, a significant choice that may reflect humility in the face of death, since many of their peers were planning burial in the church, visibly close to their commemorative gifts.

Similar images were used in late medieval illuminated books of hours, the sheet bearing up the souls being resonant of the houseling cloth used during holy communion to prevent crumbs of the host falling to the floor,[173] but also associated with the veil in which the Virgin wrapped her son at birth and, again, during his crucifixion, imbuing it with the saving power of the passion.[174] Thus he was 'clothed' by Mary, signifying her own flesh that had provided Christ's. Symbols of this kind were chosen after some deliberation.

Agnes Reede referred to St Gregory in her will as 'my advoyer'; he was, after all, a canonised pope, a spiritual giant upon whose shoulders many in this congregation may have hoped to climb. The considerable sum of 20s. was Agnes's legacy to the 'reparacion' of this church; it compared favourably with the more modest 6s. 8d. which she left for maintenance of the cathedral

---

[169] This is now in the possession of Norwich castle museum and art gallery.

[170] Blomefield. *History of Norfolk*, iv. 284. The pall is linen and worsted cloth, intended to last. Like others similar to it, it obviously provided the local silk and textile workers with much detailed design and needlework in their relatively well-paid niche market. For an illustration see P. Lasko and N. J. Morgan (eds), *Medieval art in East Anglia, 1300–1520*, Norwich 1973, item 99, pp. 63–4. This pall was once embroidered with the names of the donors, which, Blomefield records, were removed after the early eighteenth century.

[171] NCC, reg. Haywarde, fo. 121 (Reede), 1517.

[172] NCC, reg. Alblaster, fos 132–3 (Agnes Reede), 1522.

[173] See the 'Dormition of the Virgin' from 'The psalter and book of hours of Yolande de Soissons', Amiens (*c.* 1280s), Pierpoint Morgan Library, New York, M.729, fo. 305.

[174] Jan van Eyck, 'The Madonna with Joris van der Paele' (*c.* 1346), Groeningemuseum, Bruges; workshop of Robert Campin, 'Virgin and Child' (*c.* 1435), National Gallery, London; fifteenth-century nativity window, East Harling church; Jan Provoost, crucifixion (*c.*1465–1529), Groeningemuseum, Bruges; Giovanni Bellini, 'Pietà', Gallerie dell'Accademia, Venice.

church. Her will itemises all of what may be termed her 'spiritual' legacies before she proceeds to her family bequests. The former include gifts to the four orders of friars, to lepers, 'ankers', and to 'yche of my godchildren, xijd'. That they were not individually named may indicate that she had many.

Choosing her saintly beneficiaries with care, Agnes Reede specified that six altars or images in St Gregory's church were to be honoured by votive lights: the 'perke lyght' in honour of the passion, and five saints, perhaps for the five wounds. She left the same amount (12d.) for each saint's candle as she did to each of her godchildren and each of the two anchorites who received her charity. One votive light was dedicated to an image of the Virgin in the churchyard, which may well have been a factor determining her choice of this location for burial. Mary, indeed, being regarded as the premier and most powerful saint and intercessor for mercy upon benighted humanity, could be said to have provided the catalytic spark igniting the prayers of all Agnes's other chosen patrons. The other lights were for St Peter (who held the keys to heaven and was a predecessor of St Gregory, her 'advoyer'), St Margaret (after whom her daughter was named) and St Anne, progenitrix of Christ. It seems that Agnes Reede kept a nice balance between the Church's patriarchy and more intimate but potent spiritual patrons who might be deemed sympathetic to female and family concerns, like St Anne. Agnes, like so many of her peers, bequeathed sets of coral and amber rosary beads, both of which she left to her daughter Margaret, her daughter Katherine possibly being already well-provided for.

Another altar cloth, this time of gold brocade, was similarly embroidered: 'Pray for the Sowle of John Westgate Alderman & Mawde hes Wyff.' [175] John Westgate died in 1538, both he and his wife Matilda (Mawde), who died the year following, being commemorated by a funerary brass in the nave of St Gregory's.[176] It would be interesting to know how involved Agnes Reede and Mawde Westgate had been in planning and commissioning these rich textiles, and if, indeed, they oversaw the work in their own lifetimes. It is fortunate that both cloths survived the Reformation to be seen and recorded in the late eighteenth century, a testament both to their quality and the attachment felt to them by the parishioners.

Several aldermen-mercers chose St Gregory's church for burial, which may account for the extensive and ornately detailed wall-painting of a flamboyantly clad St George mounted on his richly caparisoned and prancing horse. Alderman John Wilby, merchant (d. 1444), and Matilda, his wife, chose burial in this church, Matilda, called Maude, having previously been married to John Dunston, 'mercator'.[177] Wilby was prominent in local government and he and Maude were co-founders in 1443 of the chapel of St Barbara in the Guildhall. Alderman John Pennyng, draper (d. 1459), and

[175] Blomefield, *History of Norfolk*, iv. 280, 284.
[176] NCC, reg. Godsalve, fos 277–80 (Mawde Westgate), 1539.
[177] NCC, reg. Wylbey, fos 5–6 (John Wilby, d. 1444), 13 (Maude Wilby, d. 1444).

Elene his wife, were named on a brass plate on the nave floor with a Latin inscription requesting prayers for their souls.[178] Such men and their wives took great pride in their membership of or association with the elite gild of St George, mercers, like the affluent drapers and goldsmiths, walking in the last but most prestigious rear groups of the annual gild procession.[179] Robert and Joan Toppes commissioned some finely carved dragons for the spandrels of their hall-showroom, demonstrating a similar corporate sense of pride in having arrived at the top of this gild's hierarchy and an eagerness to proclaim the fact.

Also in Wymer ward, St Margaret-over-Westwick, a parish favoured by many in the trades associated with dyeing and processing cloth, boasted a chapel of St Anne at the east end of the south aisle, its altar being dedicated to the Virgin. The tanners' gild, itself also dedicated to the Virgin, attended an annual celebration of the mass in this chapel. It is significant that in or near the chancel of St Margaret's church are buried or commemorated three Annes and one Hannah.[180]

There was also a chapel of St Anne at the Greyfriars, or Franciscans, which in view of the friars' accessibility and openness to female concerns, as well as their promotion of the holy kin, seems a natural choice of patron. The Franciscans had been especially supportive of Margery Kempe when she was shunned by fellow-travellers on pilgrimage in the Holy Land: her weeping and sobbing meant that she was ostracised and excluded from meals at Bethlehem, until she was taken into the hospitality of the Franciscan house.[181] Even on Mount Zion the friars seemed to have heard of her, asking her party 'yf that wer the woman of Inglond the which thei had herd seyd spak wyth God'.[182] In addition to several men, two women were involved in the early endowment in 1288 of Norwich Greyfriars: Mabel de la Canwet and Goda de Lodne.[183] The church of the Greyfriars was famously large, the nave alone measuring 150 feet in length by 80 feet in width. In 1431 Lady Margaret Carbonell, wife of Sir Richard, chose to be buried at Greyfriars, in St Anne's chapel.[184] Sir Richard, their son John and his wife Margery all followed Lady Margaret's example in opting for burial there.[185] The tradi-

---

[178] NCC, reg. Brosyard, fos 154–5 (John Pennyng, d. 1459).
[179] *RCN* ii. 230, 312.
[180] Blomefield, *History of Norfolk*, iv. 259.
[181] *Book of Margery Kempe*, i, ch. xxix, p. 73, lines 29–30.
[182] Ibid. lines 31–3.
[183] Blomefield, *History of Norfolk*, iv. 108. See also C. Harper-Bill and C. Rawcliffe, 'The religious houses', in Rawcliffe and Wilson, *Medieval Norwich*, 73–120.
[184] NCC, reg. Surflete, fo. 82 (Margaret Carbonell), 1431. Sir Richard's family had been in the service of Thomas Beaufort, half-brother to Henry IV, who had received the lordship of Castle Acre in 1398: H. Castor, 'The duchy of Lancaster and the rule of East Anglia, 1399–1440', in R. E. Archer (ed.), *Crown, government and people in the fifteenth century*, Stroud 1995, 53–78, esp. pp. 65–70.
[185] NCC, reg. Surflete, fo. 82 (John Carbonell), 1447.

tional allegiance of Sir Richard's family to the Lancastrian dynasty may have had a bearing on this choice: St Anne's iconography was sometimes interpreted as being emblematic of dynastic ambition, and was utilised by all interested if opposing parties during the Wars of the Roses.

Three churches still stand in a row in Oak Street, Coslany, Norwich, close to the riverside, as the name Coslany (river bank) suggests. Two of them, St Mary the Virgin and St Michael, possessed images of St Anne; and St Mary's, at least, had an altar dedicated to her. This was an area of staithes and warehouses, extensively developed by the mercantile entrepreneurs, many of whom were attached to these parishes through work or residence and requested burial there. At St Mary's, with its ancient round tower, were buried Alice and Gregory Draper, alderman, who in his will of 1464 left 26s. 8d. towards building the unfinished south transept, where they both lie.[186] In 1466 Alice Nyche, widow of Walter, directed that her legacy should be used to lead the roof of the newly-built vestry and requested burial next to her husband in this church.[187] This church's surviving roof timbers have been structured in an unusual way, the timbers in the crossing seeming to fan out around a central boss depicting the Virgin Assumptive crowned in glory.

Elizabeth Knowte, widow of John, died in 1493, and asked specifically to be buried by St Anne's altar, in the church of St Mary Coslany, beside her husband. She left £5 to make a silver foot to complete the cross already given by John, perhaps for use on this altar.[188] She also left the instruction that a priest was to sing mass at this altar for four years, the first year for her soul, the second for that of John Elys, her son, the third for Thomas Elys her former husband and, lastly, the fourth year for the soul of John Knowte, her most recent husband. This specificity is unusual, in that such prayers of intercession were normally inclusive of family, benefactors and 'all Christian souls', rather than personal to one nominee. Elizabeth's instructions, combined with an attachment to St Anne, signified by her desire to be buried, like her dead husband, next to St Anne's chapel, may give an indication of some of the complexities arising from multiple marriage that the saint's legend mediated for many whose marital experience mirrored hers.

It seems that St Anne's altar in the church of St Mary Coslany was in or near the Lady chapel, on the south side of the church, as were images and altars dedicated to St Mary Magdalen, the Virgin and a Virgin of Pity (or *pietà*), each with lights honouring them. Such a catalogue of people and their bequests highlights not only their concern for commemoration and demand for specific and familiar location for burial, but the attachment felt by these parishioners to their church and 'their' spiritual patrons and sponsors and the desire for 'customised' intercession. Most intriguing of all,

---

186 NCC, reg. Betyngs, fos 90–1 (Gregory Draper), 1464.
187 NCC, reg. Cobbalde, fos 90–1 (Alice Nyche), 1466.
188 NCC, reg. Aubry, fos 142–3 (Elizabeth Knowte), 1493.

Blomefield (without giving a source) writes that 'anciently, an anchoress called St Anne's anchoress resided in this churchyard', which would suggest an early female attachment to the saint here, either by the anchoress herself, or whoever was funding her, probably and usually in these circumstances a corporate activity.[189] It is difficult to assess how and if the men of St Mary's parish experienced a differently nuanced spiritual response to this imagery than their womenfolk, but their choice of location for burial is clear.

St Michael Coslany, the parish church a short walk away, is resplendent with expensive late fifteenth-century knapped flint and flushwork. Here were also honoured at least eight saints with lights, and probably altars, including the pre-eminent St Anne, together with SS Mary Magdalen, Margaret of Antioch, Katherine and Thomas. Aldermen father and son Gregory Clerk I and II, who sequentially owned an impressive house in Dial Yard, Coslany Street, and financed the building of the south porch and aisle, are buried here, as was Joan Clerk, wife of Gregory II.[190] A distinctly competitive edge is discernible in the building of chantry chapels in St Michael's. Very wealthy aldermen and their wives often undertook and remained involved with the rebuilding and remodelling of the church and its endowment during their lifetimes. Robert Thorp built and endowed a chapel dedicated to the Virgin at the east end of the south aisle, externally faced, as can still be seen, with freestone and black flints. This must have made an even more startling visual impact of dark and light stone when newly completed, before the brass plate proclaiming Thorp's standing as 'gentilman, Citizen, & Alderman of Norwich', was even read.[191] Effigies of him, his three wives and three sons and two daughters 'on stone', were visible in Blomefield's time, together with the plate commemorating them: 'Pray for the soul of Robert Thorp, gentilman, Citizen, & Alderman of Norwich. Founder of this chappyll and Ile, with a chantrie Prest, he to sing Perpetually for the soul of Robert Thorp, the souls of Elyzabeth, Emme and Agnes souls; the soul of John Thorp, his kyndred souls, and all Cristen sowls.'[192] Their names thus inscribed, the Thorps hoped to ensure that neither their posthumous sung commemoration, nor their names, should ever be forgotten in their parish.

How involved Agnes Thorp or her two predecessors had been in planning and arranging their memorial cannot be known for certain, but it cannot be assumed that Robert Thorp, or any other Norwich alderman, organised the family tomb without consulting his female next-of-kin. Agnes (d. 1503) certainly survived Robert, who was her second husband, leaving

189 Blomefield, *History of Norfolk*, iv. 491. See also Hill, 'Julian and her sisters', 165–88.
190 NCC, reg. Gylys, fos 102–3 (Clerk, d. 1518).
191 J. Finch, *Church monuments in Norfolk before 1850: an archaeology of commemoration*, Oxford 2000, 37–78 at p. 58. Finch also makes the point (pp. 55–7) that status labels on Norwich brasses of commemoration amounted to 74%, compared to the 52% current in the hinterlands.
192 Blomefield, *History of Norfolk*, iv. 494.

a will indicative of her own pious aspirations, so it may well have been that she was largely responsible for overseeing the memorial commissions. Aside from bequests to Carrow Priory for repairs to the house and for the prayers of the nuns, requesting that they kept Matins and Vespers of the Dead and a requiem mass for her and her friends' souls, Agnes left an annuity of half a mark (6s. 8d.) to a god-daughter who was a nun there.[193] She would have expected remembrance and intercession in return for the repairs and the annuity, as a supplement to the customary funerary prayers.

Significantly, Agnes demonstrated a keen interest in the Carthusians, marked by her legacy of 20s. to the prior and monks of the London Charterhouse. Again, she requested the community's prayers for the dead, but this time included the souls of both her husbands, who had not been mentioned previously. As with Carrow, she left 20s. for upkeep of the house, and half a mark to one of the monks, perhaps a godson or relative. Agnes claimed membership of the lay confraternity of the house (that is a share in its spiritual benefits) and asked that her letters of confraternity be returned to the monks. There was no charterhouse in East Anglia.[194] Back in Norwich, Agnes Thorp was among the 18 per cent, estimated by Norman Tanner in his analysis of surviving Norwich wills, who left money to anchorites, hermits and others living out religious vocations. She requested that a priest was to 'sing (mass) before' the anchoress at St Julian's parish church, for which she left a not insubstantial two marks (26s. 8d.), the implication being that he was to sing as many masses as he could, fortified by the intercession of the anchoress, until the money ran out.[195]

The burgeoning of memorial investment alone shows that Norwich's parish churches were the focus of much extravagant commemoration. The mercantile and civic elite with their wives were, in effect, appropriating the church buildings, despite the fact that these chapels were meant to benefit 'all Cristen sowls'.[196] It is unclear where the image of St Anne was actually positioned in the parish church of St Michael, the site of her altar there being unknown. That she stood in the metaphorical as well as the literal forefront, viewed by these affluent men and women as 'one of their own', is more than likely.[197]

---

[193] PCC, reg. Blamyr, fo. 26 (Agnes Thorpe), 1501/3. This reference is not included in Walter Rye's appendix of wills relating to Carrow.

[194] The Carthusians were noted for the asceticism of their spirituality; their prayers were, therefore, considered effective and desirable.

[195] The anchoress at this time was probably Elizabeth Scott: Gilchrist and Oliva, *Religious women*, 98.

[196] This is inscribed on the Thorp memorial in St Michael Coslany parish church.

[197] An apsidal chapel, dedicated to St Anne, on the east side of the north transept is identified in J. L'Estrange, 'Description of a chamber formerly adjoining the Jesus chapel of the cathedral', *NA* vi (1864), 177–85. J. R. Shinners suggests that it was built in 1330: 'The veneration of saints at Norwich cathedral in the fourteenth century', *NA* xl (1989), 133–44. William and Magdalen Bauchon commissioned a chaplain to say masses for him

A subject seldom touched upon, but which must often have been an area of great difficulty, was the tension resultant from the typical extended family situation exemplified in the Thorps's memorial.[198] Three wives meant at least three sets of family connections and often step-siblings and half-siblings, the wives themselves frequently having two or three other sets of family connections apiece. Complex issues of inheritance, displacement, resentment and jealousy or simple unresolved loss must lie hidden beneath many a pious inscription. How encouraging, then, to have an exemplar who had overcome such earthly problems, and, even more, had manipulated just such an extended family network, with all its potential pitfalls, to the eternal advantage of all humanity.[199] The multi-layered interpretations offered by the iconography of St Anne were all-important in fifteenth-century Norwich, as elsewhere. Her legend endorsed the dynastic ambitions of merchant and noble alike, while affirming the importance of the female line and marriage.[200] But however her suppliants might attempt to 'domesticate' their devotion to her it was her status as progenitrix that confirmed her place in the hierarchy of intercessors. An encouragement to women who did not easily conceive, as well as to the serially widowed, St Anne, in all her seeming-familiarity, remained, ultimately, the grandmother of God.

It would appear, then, that devotion to St Anne in Norwich and its environs attained immense popularity in the fifteenth century, especially among women of child-bearing years, and particularly, for different reasons, within the mercantile elite, both male and female. It functioned on several levels, with differing emphases at diverse times of need. The nobility, their supporters and clientage found in her cult validation of their claim to rule, even through the matrilineal line. The ambitious and wealthy public man may have seen approval of his desire to participate in government, or increase his family's influence, in depictions of St Anne as a solid and prosperous merchant's wife and matriarch of a highly successful and effective family of grandsons. The constant search for material security, even luxury, thereby found some justification, as did dynastic aspirations. John Cambridge's commitment of his loan-scheme to the chapel of St Anne in the city church of St Andrew could be interpreted in this light. Simultaneously, it was the means of earning constantly renewable spiritual merit. As

there in 1335/6: B. Dodwell, 'William Bauchon and his connection with the cathedral priory at Norwich', NA xxxvi/2 (1975), 111–18 at p. 115. Oblations to St Anne peaked at a recorded 2s. (Shinners, 'Veneration of saints', 138), so her cult in the cathedral church is not comparable to that later enjoyed in the city parish churches.

[198] M. Warner, *From the beast to the blonde: on fairy tales and their tellers*, London 1994, 218–40.

[199] Ibid. 81–95.

[200] There is an illumination of St Anne's three marriages in the Bedford hours, commissioned by John, duke of Bedford, on his marriage, his second, to Anne of Burgundy in 1434: *The Bedford hours*, 58, plate 47.

the inventories and painted glass of St Peter Mancroft show, richly decorated vestments, banners and altar frontals adorned with her image speak of high-level investment and thoughtful selection, under-girded by St Anne's association with the mass. The commissioning by individuals or groups, within this church alone, of skilled local silkwomen for the production of such fine embroidered textiles must have provided many opportunities for joint artistic endeavour in addition to considerable employment.[201] While the commissioned product advertised the status of the donors, it simultaneously proclaimed the worship accorded to St Anne. In a sense, the donors and the saint become mutually self-referential, each confirming the other's progress up the parallel hierarchies of earth and heaven.

For some women, Anne's cult was more subtle and complex, and its spiritual implications were potentially much more serious. The incarnation and the increasing emphasis placed by theologians in the Middle Ages on the matrilineal line had associations with conception and birth that elevated these carnal activities above the merely worldly and domestic.[202] With this process of female rehabilitation came the weighty responsibility for the spiritual nurture and ultimate salvation of the children of the family, and others, as advocated by the hugely popular *Liber celestis* of St Bridget of Sweden. The possibility of achieving a personal relationship with God, demonstrated by St Bridget along with other married mystics, such as Dorothea of Montau and Angela de Foligno, and their imitator, Margery Kempe, mirrored the married St Anne's incarnational role and its importance as a bridgehead to salvation. The spiritual and physical autonomy enjoyed by unregulated female households living to a rule of poverty and chastity may also have epitomised this direct and active kind of piety. St Anne had an *auctoritas* and status which attached to her devotees, often much-married women engaged in routine domestic and commercial activity, in addition to childbirth and the raising of children. This endowed them with an innate stature not always bestowed by the world, or by the law. Ultimately, the striking success of her cult in Norwich, as elsewhere, may rest on the multiple, indeed, interleaved layers of interpretation to which it was open.

Finally, a measure of the power of the cult of St Anne lies in reaction to the stripping of sites associated with her in the sixteenth century. So enmeshed was the power of belief that 'reforming' had to be enforced with some rigour and against popular opinion and then maintained only by lock and bar. The spa at Buxton in Derbyshire, for example, had become focused on the efficacy of St Anne as a healer and when it was stripped by an agent of Thomas Cromwell not only of her image but of people's votive offerings of 'cruchys, schertes and schetes, with wax', he reported that he had been obliged to 'lok ... upp and seal ... the bathys and welles ... that non schall

---

[201] Hope, 'Inventories', 196–7.
[202] *Life of St Anne*, 9, lines 328–36.

enter to washe them'.[203] Writing in the mid-eighteenth century of his own church at Fersfield, Norfolk, which had a chapel formerly dedicated to St Anne at the east end of the south aisle, Francis Blomefield noted that it had featured painted glass of some quality depicting Anne, the Virgin and the twelve Apostles.[204] This chapel had been associated with a gild of St Anne and had housed a 'famous' image of the saint; both gild and image had once been in receipt of widespread *post-mortem* benefactions from 'surrounding towns'.[205] A well or spring associated with the cult was still known in Blomefield's time as 'Tann's Well', a corruption of 'St Anne's well'.[206] Such popularity was dangerous and potentially subversive. St Anne had to go.

Adherence to local cults is, perhaps, not so surprising, when we consider that men such as Robert Codde, appointed by the crown to be Master of St Giles's Hospital, Norwich, in 1536, and lauded by visitation reports for his efficient charity to the indigent, was himself, by 1537, reluctantly involved with Robert Southwell in the demolition of the shrine of the Holy Rood at Bromholm Priory, north Norfolk.[207] It was possibly at this time that the hospital lost its own image of St Anne, which had stood in the chancel, next to, or on, an altar with lights dedicated to her. Since St Anne was a co-dedicatee of this hospital, it may be assumed that her cult was extremely important there.[208] In some areas, it may be that 'churchwardens dismantled their own churches in much the same fashion as vice-chancellors nowadays are dismantling their universities and hospital administrators the health service'.[209] But, where this was so, the oral traditions associated with well-loved feast days may not have been so easily packed away.

St Anne offered her suppliants security and success, and was an icon of infinite possibility. A construct more fluid than gendered, with appeal for all, she was invariably depicted as a woman past childbearing years, that is, in medieval terms, sexually inert. Once a sexually active and, eventually, fecund woman, St Anne arrives at the end of her story with the elevated status of a chaste votary. The saint's domestic appeal could mean something personal and empowering to a goodwife struggling to run a household and

---

[203] *Three chapters of letters relating to the suppression of the monasteries*, ed. T. Wright (Camden o.s. xxvi, 1843), 190, 143–4.

[204] Blomefield, *History of Norfolk*, i. 102–6.

[205] Ibid. i. 105. In 1476 John Byllyng of Fersfield gave the gild his best ram.

[206] Ibid. There was a separate chaplain who served here from its foundation to 1411, when it was united to the parish church. For St Anne's association with water see F. Sautman, 'St Anne in folk tradition: late medieval France', in Ashley and Sheingorn, *Interpreting cultural symbols*, 81–4.

[207] Rawcliffe, *Medicine for the soul*, 199.

[208] Ibid. 125, 130–1, 242.

[209] C. Richmond, 'The English gentry and religion, c. 1500', in C. Harper-Bill (ed.), *Religious belief and ecclesiastical careers in late medieval England*, Woodbridge 1991, 121–50. See p. 124 for evidence of the recitation of 'the legend' on feast days as part of *post-mortem* commemoration of deceased gild members.

manage her difficult and perhaps competitive sons and step-sons, while to her husband that devotion might validate a public life and the cultivation of patronage in gild and parish. But that is to simplify an appeal that transcended analysis in a period when salvation was no mere abstraction. The hope of heaven, so hard to achieve without grace, seemed, like so many things, ultimately to rest in every mother's hands: 'Now blessy seynt Anne, of thy gret goodness / With my trew hert I mekely beseche the / Here my prayer and do thy besynes: / Be mene for vs all with thy doughtres thre / To that most blyssyd Trynyte / Of hys gret mercy that we may be hys, / And when we dy to have eternall blys.' [210]

---

[210] *Life of St Anne*, 109, lines 652–8.

2

The Cult of St Margaret of Antioch

In pursuit of a pragmatic piety

To define the contrasts as well as the resonances between the medieval cults of St Anne and of St Margaret, it could be said that in the spiritual realm St Margaret was perceived as offering speedy protection in crisis, while St Anne's maternal iconography indicated the long haul. St Margaret, as helper-saint, offered to women in childbirth a more direct and immediate access to support, both physical and spiritual. The legendary St Margaret of Antioch, a virgin-martyr, was plainly popular with clerics and other celibate religious attracted by her spiritually potent body-denial, like Christ's, whose passion she mirrored, but it came at a high price. Her perceived power derived from her death-defying virginity and bloody martyrdom, and she was widely recognised, particularly by child-bearing women, as a crisis-management patron in childbirth and, in the event of maternal or infant death, an intercessor who expedited access to salvation. The young Margaret had taken control of her own body and thus her soul, an indication, it was believed, of her exceptional merit among the heavenly hierarchy. Ellen Ross has argued that the virgin-martyr, with her tortured and torn body, was a trope symbolising, indeed in a sense being, the broken body of Christ. Through her prolonged martyrdom, Margaret experienced Christ's bodily suffering, and thereby shared in his divine power to save by her direct intercession with God.[1] To the modern mind it is hard to engage with medieval thinking that made a self-sacrificing adolescent virgin a patron of childbirth. However, a reading of the contemporary verses and *legenda* reveal more subtle layers of meaning related to the carnal experience that was the lot of most women, willing or not, and with which they were medically and theologically identified.

Natural female sexuality and its bodily expression were not overtly countenanced except in sanctified or legalised categories governed by men. The 'ungoverned' female body had long been considered subversive to regulated society, as Margery Kempe's detractors bear witness. How should a young woman apprehend and define her natural instincts? This personal difficulty

---

[1] E. M. Ross, *The grief of God: images of the suffering Jesus in late medieval England*, Oxford 1997, 95–9. Like other legendary female virgin-martyrs, Margaret's martyrdom was lengthy and full of public sado-masochistic torture of her naked body by men, culminating in her beheading by a reluctant executioner.

is more than hinted at in the Old English version of Margaret's temptations and martyrdom:

> There came then out of the corner of the prison a most terrifying dragon of many different colours. His hair appeared golden, and his teeth were just like cut iron, and his eyes shone like strange gems, and from his nose there came a great amount of smoke, and his tongue breathed out and he caused a tremendous stench in the prison.[2]

The highly ambivalent language used in this early *Life* to describe the dragon confronting the martyred virgin makes it difficult for the reader to see the horror so much as to feel the overwhelming of the physical senses: the golden hair, the eyes shining like gems, the lascivious tongue breathing out the odour of perdition. But then St Margaret herself is explicit: she fears the size, power and uncontrolled energy of this creature: 'God Almighty, extinguish *the power* of this *huge dragon* and have mercy on me in my need and hardship and never let me perish, but *defend me against this wild beast.*'

The holy Margaret then grabbed the devil by the hair and threw him to the ground. She put out his right eye, shattered all his bones and set her right foot over his neck. Then, finally, she got to the heart of the matter: '*Leave my virginity alone*! Christ is helping me, for his name shines for all eternity.'[3] This very physical engagement with 'the dragon' and the injuries inflicted upon it mirror Margaret's own later destruction, and should perhaps be read as its spiritual precursor. Her internal battle becomes externalised and waged on the battleground of her own body: 'And yf also thyne eye offend the, plucke hym oute and caste hym from the.'[4]

Margaret was venerated possibly earlier than the eighth century, when her *passio* was recorded in a Latin text derived from the Greek.[5] This became the source of a number of vernacular accounts of the legend, including the Old English (Corpus Christi College, Cambridge, 303) version. Ninth-century manuscripts of the *Bibliotheca hagiographica latina*, no. 5303, are known, as are two eleventh-century versions, one of which was of Anglo-Saxon origin. Margaret was believed to have been a martyr of the Great Persecution (AD305–13), but the legend in its redactions lays no emphasis on the saint's historicity or date, perhaps because of its purpose as an allegory or parable. Its fantastical elements place it in another realm of meaning and power altogether. This Old English *Life* makes clear the nature of her battle: the devil to be overcome and which attempted to consume her was her vulnerability to the strength of her own sexual impulses. In this metaphorical battle her

---

[2] *The Old English Lives of St Margaret*, ed. M. Clayton and H. Magennis, Cambridge 1994, 12, 123.

[3] Ibid.

[4] Matt. xviii.9.

[5] *Lives of St Margaret*, 7. The most commonly found version of it comes from the Latin group and is known as BHL, no. 5303, version 1 (a).

virginity has become coterminous with her Christian faith, both of which she is required to lay aside by Olibrius, the Roman prefect, who offers her marriage: 'If you obey me and believe in my god … I will take you as my wife.' And, what is more, it would 'be as well for you as it is for me', which could be interpreted as an assurance of sexual satisfaction as much as a threat.[6] Olibrius has recognised Margaret's ambivalence, which is confirmed by her response to his sexual innuendo: 'I give my body to torments in order that my soul may rest with the righteous souls.' Margaret is the personifica-tion of the struggle that must exist between natural physical appetites and the cultivation of a highly developed spirituality that was the goal of the religious or the pious lay person.

The encounter with the devil-dragon, by which St Margaret is almost always identified in medieval iconography, occurs when Olibrius has her thrown into prison for resisting his advances. In this version she is 'swal-lowed' or overwhelmed by the dragon, whom she then causes to explode or burst open by making the sign of the cross, escaping from his ruptured belly entire and unscathed. Her power as a virgin martyr and, more particularly, her potency as the protector and patron of pregnant and labouring women who were not virgins, rested on this 'escape', or vanquishing of the devil. Margaret's deliverance from the belly of the dragon tells of her triumph over her 'lower nature'.[7] The vivid metaphor speaks of overwhelming evil liter-ally annihilated by dependence on Christ. The temptation is represented so dramatically because Margaret has pledged her virginity to a heavenly bridegroom. Spiritual deliverance through sexual integrity, and thus empow-erment of the female flesh, was a major theme of her legend. The devil in various forms represented her own sexual vulnerability and what was then understood as a typically female ambivalence to chastity, even though she was committed in mind and spirit to God.

While this legend superficially upheld the negative views of women expressed by the early Fathers of the Church, in particular about female lust-fulness and susceptibility to moral corruption, it could also be understood in a much broader and more ambiguous way as a means by which women could gain control over their own bodies and 'stand on the neck' of often life-threatening odds.[8] Whatever her status childbirth was the most dangerous time of any woman's life, jeopardising, as it did, not only her physical exist-ence but also her immortal soul if she died 'uncleansed', with the unbaptised

[6] *Lives of St Margaret*, 117.
[7] A letter of St Jerome to Eustochium, a consecrated virgin and daughter of his Roman disciple, the widow Paula, warned her to remember that she carried her worst enemy 'shut up inside herself'; her 'hot little body' should avoid certain foods and the risk of close male company: Brown, *Body and society*, 376. Brown remarks that, for Jerome, the human body remained a dark forest, 'filled with the roaring of wild beasts'.
[8] Ibid. 242. See also pp. 305–22 for the views of St John Chrysostom.

fruit of original sin still *in utero*.[9] And this was, for most women, a constantly recurring, often annual, danger, which did not diminish, but rather increased through repeated pregnancies.[10]

Adherence to the practice of denying burial in consecrated ground to women who died thus may have varied greatly over time and from place to place, but the underlying assumption that a woman in labour was potentially tainted was compounded by the instruction to midwives to remove the child from the mother's body if her death was imminent or had just occurred: 'Byd the mydwyf scho that hye / And yf the woman than dye / For to vndo hyre wyt a knyf, / And so to sawe the chyldys lyfe.'[11] *In extremis* the child was to be baptised by the midwife: 'And if the chyld be half bore / Hede and nec and no more / Byd hyre spare, neuer the latter, / To crysten yt and cast on water.'[12] While the imperative here is focused on the infant's baptism and consequent salvation, the secondary objective was removal of the baby from the mother's pelvis, alive or dead, so that she too might be released from the burden of original sin.[13]

In the context of parturition and the dangerous neo-natal period St Margaret's triumph over the devil could thus be understood on many levels. She offered an icon of physical protection, strengthening resistance to sexual surrender and, where that was not possible (or desirable), to the pain of childbirth, and, more subtly, represented the struggle for a higher integration of mind, body and intention. Her ability to burst out of the dragon's belly intact, and triumph over the congenital impulses of her 'lower nature', made her a predominant and powerful advocate of child-bearing and, therefore, women at risk, whose role in life as mothers and wives must constantly jeopardise their existence. The continuing popularity of bestowing her name on daughters at baptism – it was by far the most common name among female testators in Norwich between 1370 and 1532[14] –and the ubiquity of her name and image in Norwich and Norfolk churches show that, however men and women interpreted her cult, when little practical help was at hand she was embraced with some vigour as patron and intercessor.

---

[9] The foetus, being the product of sexual desire, occasioned by the Fall, was reckoned to be a spiritual pollutant. Galen had taught that sexual pleasure and ejaculation in the female were prerequisites of conception: ibid. 17–18.

[10] Women experiencing multiple pregnancy occasionally suffered spontaneous abortion, which, if not complete, could be life-threatening.

[11] *Mirk's instructions*, 180, lines 97–103.

[12] Ibid. lines 91–4.

[13] It should be noted that while a priest would be necessary to shrive the dying mother he was forbidden by the edicts of the Fourth Lateran Council, 1215, to involve himself in contact with blood either as a surgeon or in combat, still less when it contained the substance of concupiscence, which would, theoretically, have made him unfit to handle the sacrament.

[14] Tanner demonstrates that Margaret was far and away the most popular woman's name among testators in Norwich between 1370 and 1532: *Church in Norwich*, appendix 9 at p. 211.

The carnal theme is diffused throughout the early version of the saint's *Life*. When, in a vision, God speaks to Margaret through a dove, the connection is clear: '*you who through virginity* desired the eternal kingdom ... it will be granted to you with Abraham ... Isaac and Jacob [who were not virgins or martyrs]. Blessed are you, who have overcome the enemy'.[15] For a woman to vanquish her innate concupiscence under extreme temptation was reckoned to bestow superior standing among the spiritual elite and render her worthy of veneration. She had 'won her spurs', in that she had joined the celestial hierarchy as a woman who had become a spiritual 'male', escaping the highly dangerous threat, both physical and spiritual, of her own body.[16] Because of this Margaret became empowered in a way unknown even to the patriarchs, not least because of her resolute dependence on Christ, whom she praises as 'you who condescend to reveal to your servant that you are the one hope of all who believe in you'.[17] Even of women, perhaps especially of women, as this God had condescended to take on human flesh, with which the female sex was especially associated.[18]

The devil's confession to Margaret (a priestly function) and its conflation in this *vita* with involuntary human sexuality brings to mind Margery Kempe's dramatic opening to her book, when she describes the life-threatening birth of her first-born, and its aftermath, blamed by the author on her incomplete confession of sin, probably sexual sin.[19] All medieval women about to face giving birth confessed and received absolution 'for drede of paryll that may be-fall, / In ther trawallyng'.[20] Confession was considered essential to spiritual and physical health, and no woman beginning labour, including Margery Kempe, was unmindful of the inescapable risk of death: 'what for labowr sche had in chyldyng & for sekenesse goyng be-forn, sche dyspered of hyr lyfe, wenyng sche myghth not leuyn'.[21] Strong belief in the sacrament of confession as a means of redemption and healing for sinful flesh, especially that of women, is apparent in Margery's first chapter, where her own non-compliance resulted in what would now be understood as a florid and lasting post-partum psychosis with demonic hallucinations. Her eventual healing she attributed to the direct intervention of Christ, who appeared to her, and, significantly, sat on her bed. Immediately she began to feel better 'in alle hir spyritys'. [22] This experience led to her conversion and, ultimately, to a dedicated chastity. In her introduction, she describes how the

15 *Lives of St Margaret*, 15, at pp. 125, 127.
16 The mystic and theologian Jean Gerson (d.1429), writing against women teaching, said that 'they are easily seduced and determined seducers ... it is not proved that they are witnesses to divine grace': Bynum, *Jesus as mother*, 136 n. 85.
17 *Lives of St Margaret*, 15, 127.
18 Bynum, *Jesus as mother*, 110–25.
19 *Book of Margery Kempe*, i, ch. i, pp. 6–7.
20 *Mirk's instructions*, 179, lines 77–84.
21 *Book of Margery Kempe*, i, ch. i, p. 6, lines 29–32.
22 Ibid. i, ch. i, p. 8, line 19.

rewriting of her text (the definitive version of her *vita*) commenced the day after the feast of St Mary Magdalen.[23] That the priest, who had been unable to decipher the earlier transcription for four long years, is suddenly able to read it, as it 'was mech mor esy than it was a-for tyme', marks Margery's state of grace, and supplies a modest opening miracle for her attempt at personal hagiography.[24]

The Old English version of St Margaret's legend concludes its theme of salvation through renunciation of the flesh when her final ordeal and immersion in a cauldron of boiling water ends and she is summoned by God to her heavenly reward: 'Blessed are you who have *desired* virginity: *for this reason you are blessed in eternity.'*[25] Not, therefore, for her steadfastness or endurance, nor even for promulgating the faith to many thousands in the face of martyrdom, but for the desire for virginity, St Margaret gains her spiritual crown. Fleshly longing has been transformed into a spiritual desire that is only consummated in death. While this theologically sophisticated reading appealed to the aspirational Margery Kempe, was it how St Margaret was perceived by her pregnant medieval suppliants in and around Norwich? Or by those who eagerly watched the pageant of the gild of St George every April, where 'the Margaret', although splendidly accoutred and bejewelled, had become little more than a decorative and quiescent handmaid to the George and his dragon?[26] Clearly, devotion to the saint and the reasons that inspired it had evolved over time; East Anglian veneration of her cult was well established by the mid-eleventh century at both Cambridge and Bury St Edmunds, as liturgical manuscripts show;[27] the mid-sixteenth century saw her still represented in Norwich, an icon clothed in beautiful raiment, with new shoes and gloves, but now clearly relegated to a subordinate role in the city's civic pageantry as a passive recipient of George's gallantry, wearing his 'livery'.[28] Completely detached from her dragon and her personal battle, 'the Margaret' had by then transmuted into an eye-catching fashion accessory for the gild's victorious St George.

St Margaret and books: pearls, rubies and 'ful pore saks'

The *Life* of St Margaret written by Osbern Bokenham was begun, he says, on 7 September 1443, 'In the vigylye of the Natyuyte / Of hyr that is gemme of virgynyte', thus confirming Margaret's principle attribute, at least for the

---

[23] The feast day was 22 July, therefore it was begun on the 23 July.
[24] *Book of Margery Kempe*, 'Proem' and i, ch. i, pp. 5–7.
[25] *Lives of St Margaret*, 18, 131 (my italics).
[26] *Gild of St George*, 17.
[27] *Lives of St Margaret*, 75–7.
[28] *Gild of St George*, 140, 142. The accounts for 1537 show the George and the Margaret in matching velvet attire. In the following year, Margaret was provided with new shoes and gloves at the cost of 10*d*., and an attendant, 'oone ffoteman', who was hired for 8*d*.

male religious. That Bokenham describes the Virgin Mary as the '*gemme* of virgynyte' establishes an important link between the two saints: Margaret's name was often translated as 'pearl'.[29] Jewels also carried sexual connotations. Bokenham's contemporary John Lydgate (c. 1370–1450), monk-poet of Bury St Edmunds, used the metaphor more explicitly in his own legend of St Margaret to convey something sublime, hidden in a secret, sometimes foul place. 'A Royal Ruby in whiche ther is no lak, / May closed ben in a ful pore sak', offers a succinct, unsubtle description of the female body.[30] The records of the Norwich gild of St George note that as late as 1546 'the Margaret' in the gild procession was wearing a gold flower (a marguerite?) set with pearls, the 'concretisation' of her name and its meaning, possibly her rebus, or badge of identity.[31] Bokenham's legend was based on an earlier Latin redaction that he heard, he says, at 'mownt-Flask' in Italy, where the saint's body was reputedly enshrined. He thus took his inspiration from the source of her cult, thereby authenticating his own writing.[32]

Of the thirteen verse legends that Bokenham wrote, commissioned by a variety of patrons, many female, Margaret's *Life* appears first in the volume. It is his second longest at more than thirty pages and was apparently commissioned by his friend, Thomas Burgh, a friar living in Cambridge. Under Burgh's direction the completed manuscript was copied and thereafter presented to a convent of nuns there, as a postscript to the manuscript requests 'that thei shulde haue mynd on hym & of hys systyr Dame Betrice Burgh Of wych soulys ihesu haue mercy'.[33] Such a commission emphasises the contemporary perception of a virgin-martyr's *vita* as a means of engaging her protection and of securing intercession for the author and associated devotees. Writing a holy work was believed to be of great spiritual benefit to the author, and also to bestow considerable merit on the reader or patron commissioning it.[34] It was also a signal spiritual work of mercy, leading as it did to instruction in the faith and salvation, as well as being a source of hope and consolation to others. Even to own such a work was thought to be salvific, as St Margaret herself acknowledged in the unambiguous words of the Old English *vita*: 'I ask you further, Lord, that the person who makes a book of my martyrdom or has it in his house may have remission of all his sins, for we are flesh and blood and are always sinning and never ceasing.'[35]

---

[29] The description of the altar at the shrine of Our Lady of Walsingham, recorded by Robert Reynes, confirms the connection: the image of the Virgin Annunciate (that is, the newly-pregnant Mary) was accompanied by that of St Margaret, both in gold: Linnell, 'Commonplace book of Robert Reynes', 26.

[30] *Minor poems of John Lydgate*, ed. H. N. MacCracken (EETS e.s. cvii, 1962), 174, lines 13–14.

[31] *Gild of St George*, 17.

[32] *Hooly wummen*, prologus, p. 4, line 111; p. 6, lines 188–91.

[33] Ibid. note at the end of the manuscript, p. 289.

[34] Ibid. *Vita S. Margaretae*, 23, lines 834–40.

[35] Ibid.

It may be that men valued St Margaret for her virginal integrity and intercessory power, but women who were not virgins took from this legend something quite different: it was possible through vulnerability and suffering to
attain spiritual and perhaps even physical strength through a direct relationship with Christ. Add to this the intercession of St Margaret and the wages
of original sin were not inescapable for a woman in labour: 'if wummen in
trauayyng be / Oppressed wyth peyne & greuaunce, / And for helpe deuoutly
do preye to me, / Graunt hem sone good deliueraunce'.[36] The interconnec-
tion of St Margaret's passion with that of Christ, and thus the potential
for securing their joint protection, is demonstrated in the depiction of the
crucifixion on birth-girdles made of parchment, paper or cloth, and worn by
women in labour to ease their pain. In the last resort, it also became a kind
of spiritual passport, to help speed their souls to God.[37]

Margery Kempe, who in the early years of her vocation aspired to be
a bride of Christ, describes her three years of temptation, during which
she repeatedly encountered what she defined as the snares of lechery. It
may be indicative of the understanding that the laity in general had of the
iconography of St Margaret, but is certainly suggestive of Margery's, that she
describes her narrow escape from adultery as happening on St Margaret's
Eve. She recounts that, after a disturbing exchange with a man to whom
she felt attracted and who had propositioned her, they both went to hear
evensong, 'for her cherch was of Seynt Margaret'. It was thus the vigil of
her parish church's patronal festival, and Margery identified herself with the
plight of its patron and her name-saint, sorely tempted by the devil in her
own flesh. But feeling abandoned by God, Margery, unlike the virgin-martyr,
decided to succumb, only to be rejected and scorned, and thereby saved from
the repercussions of her fall from grace.[38]

In this appropriation of her patron's legend, Margery is presenting her
own problematic spiritual journey as a direct parallel, thus enhancing her
personal bid for sanctity. This is a recurring theme of her book, with the
saint changed to suit the stage of Margery's spiritual odyssey and the nature
of her pious aspirations. Whether she is emulating St Anne, St Bridget of
Sweden or St Mary Magdalen, non-virgins all, Margery competes with them
to stand first with Christ, with at least the status of a virgin-martyr. Margaret
is singular among Margery's saintly exemplars, signifying the virginity from
which Margery feels so distant after fourteen pregnancies and a self-confessed

---

[36] *Hooly wummen*, 23, lines 841–4.
[37] *Medical works of the fourteenth century: together with a list of plants recorded in contemporary writings*, ed. G. Henslow, London 1899, 32–3; T. Hunt (ed.), *Popular medicine in
thirteenth-century England: introduction and texts*, Cambridge 1990, 90, 98, 278; Rawcliffe,
'Women, childbirth and religion', 97, 107–8 n. 90.
[38] *Book of Margery Kempe*, i, ch. iv, p. 15.

troublesome predilection for conjugal sexual pleasure that in the early days of her conversion she felt would distance her from Christ.[39]

Screen panels, paintings, painted glass and purgatory

In Norfolk St Margaret was enormously popular, as elsewhere, as the first patron and protector of pregnant or labouring women. She survives now on only five painted screen panels in the county, but that these are in what were once the prosperous weaving hinterlands servicing Norwich may convey an idea of how ubiquitous she once was. She may also still be seen in several fifteenth-century windows, in wood-carvings and in glass.

At Filby All Saints she is pictured not with a simple cross-staff but with a crozier, symbol of episcopal authority, which she thrusts into the dragon. Significantly, she is placed on this finely painted screen between that great survivor of disaster, St Paul, and St Michael, assayer of souls. Sometimes she is represented with what appears to be a Tau cross-staff, reinforcing her role as a healing helper-saint.[40]

The churches of Ranworth St Helen and North Walsham St Nicholas each boast a St Margaret screen that was once of great beauty and of the highest quality, reflecting the investment and choice of parishioners and patrons, though who commissioned them is unknown. On the screen at North Walsham (then dedicated to the Virgin), St Margaret is grouped with St Barbara and St Mary Magdalen, reinforcing, through their eucharistic associations, her own standing as purveyor of divine power and conduit of spiritual redemption, rescue and resurrection (see plate 7).[41] Such attributes are clearly demonstrated too in an engraving of her in the centre of the late medieval silver paten of Felbrigg St Margaret. Margaret is simultaneously a representative of humankind and a triumphant advocate of humanity through suffering.[42] Such a close association with the eucharistic body seems to be indicated by this paten.[43]

[39] Ibid. i, ch. xxii, pp. 51–2.
[40] St Anthony, abbot, and St Francis of Assisi were both associated with the *tau* cross, as held by St Margaret on the St Peter Mancroft alabaster, as a token of their power to heal.
[41] Williamson, 'Saints on Norfolk rood-screens', 326, 342. This prosperous weaving community boasted a gild of St Margaret: Blomefield, *History of Norfolk*, xi. 79.
[42] Ross, *Grief of God*, 99; E. Robertson, 'The corporeality of female sanctity in the *Life* of St Margaret', in R. Blumenfeld-Kosinski and T. Szell (eds), *Images of sainthood in medieval Europe*, Ithaca, NY 1991, 268–87, esp. p. 272; Bynum, *Holy feast and holy fast*, 25. Sarah Salih points out that the pursuit of virginity by tortured martyrs reverses the effects of the Fall in that, like the prelapsarian Adam and Eve, they are naked and unashamed (i.e. asexual): *Versions of virginity in late medieval England*, Cambridge 2001, 85.
[43] The survival in Norfolk of this medieval paten depicting a female saint is unusual. Patens engraved with the Holy Name and the Vernicle, very fashionable in the fifteenth century, exist in some quantity and may be viewed in the treasury of the cathedral. Female

At Ranworth, in what might be termed a family context, St Margaret appears crowned, with the holy kin, on the south screen by the Lady altar (*see* plate 3). This iconography, showing the three Marys and their little sons, speaks of, and to, young women, their childbed experience and their small and vulnerable children. Both the holy kin and their female suppliants unite under the guardianship of the devil-defeating Margaret, who by associ-ation and merit shares the incarnational power of Christ's extended family.[44] According to the Old Testament, women in the *post-partum* period were considered ritually unclean for a period of thirty-three days following the birth of a male child, and sixty-six after that of a female.[45] By the late Middle Ages social responses to the ritual of purification had softened considerably, but a mother still found herself in some spiritual jeopardy should she sicken and die before ritual readmission to the community of the Church.[46] To such women, specifically, the screen seems to have offered a complex icon of support, protection and reassurance.

The ritual of purification – thanksgiving, cleansing and welcome back into the full fellowship of the parish – was resonant of Mary's Presentation at the Temple and the purification rites of Candlemas on 2 February.[47] A Candlemas ceremony was described with some emotion by Margery Kempe in her book, and may actually have taken place in St Margaret's, Lynn. During this ceremony Margery, like the beguine and mystic Marie d'Oignies before her, claimed, in 'hir gostly vndirstondyng', that is her meditative visualisation, to see Mary presenting Christ to Simeon in the Temple.[48] So overcome was she that she could barely offer up her candle to the priest, but went 'waueryng on eche syde as it had ben a dronkyn woman, wepyng & sobbyng', and, as usual, disturbing her fellow-worshippers and attracting unfavourable attention.[49] This parish church belonged to the Benedictine priory of Lynn, which was a cell of Norwich cathedral priory, and was the singular place of worship of the elite of Lynn, since it alone offered the full range of sacraments.[50] At St Peter Mancroft, in Norwich, the Candlemas

iconography on eucharistic vessels, however virginal, would not have found favour with the reformers.

[44] Williamson, 'Saints on Norfolk rood-screens', 336; Duffy, *Stripping of the altars*, 181.
[45] Leviticus xii.
[46] *Mirk's festial*, 57, lines 14–31. For the debate surrounding the late medieval attitude to purification see W. Coster, 'Purity, profanity and Puritanism: the churching of women, 1500–1700', in Sheils and Wood, *Women in the Church*, 377–87, and D. Cressy, 'Purifica-tion, thanksgiving and the churching of women in post-Reformation England', *Past & Present* cxxxxi (1993), 106–46. See also D. Cressy, *Birth, marriage and death: ritual, religion and life-cycle in Tudor and Stuart England*, Oxford 1997, 197–210.
[47] Luke ii.22–4.
[48] A Middle English life of Marie d'Oignies was in circulation and was read to Margery. See 'Prosalegenden: die legenden des MS Douce 114', ed. C. Horstmann, *Anglia* viii (1885), 173.
[49] *Book of Margery Kempe*, i, ch. lxxxii, p. 198, lines 15–17.
[50] Ibid. i, ch. xxv, pp. 58–60. See R. Swanson, 'Will the real Margery Kempe please stand

ritual would have exhibited an impressive array of silk copes, vestments and banners, as well as numerous lights sparkling on a treasury of silver utensils, to honour this feast.[51]

Screen images of St Margaret may also be seen at Walpole St Peter and an exceptionally fine example at Wiggenhall St Mary the Virgin, but as with St Anne, these few survivals do not reflect the great popularity of this saint, especially with women (*see* plate 8).[52]

A painted panel depicting St Margaret survives from only one standing city church, St Michael at Plea (*see* plate 9).[53] The regal image of the saint on a large panel measuring 101cm x 43.8 cm is no longer part of a screen, and is unlikely to have been so.[54] Painted in about 1420–30, perhaps originally part of a retable,[55] it shows an ermine-clad aristocrat of the spiritual hierarchy, who has won a sizeable martyr's crown of wrought gold.

Other images remain on walls and in glass, both in county and city. In Norwich, the saint appears with her dragon, though fast fading, painted in the western segment of the vault of the ante-reliquary chapel of Norwich cathedral, paired with St Katherine of Alexandria, her more bookish peer and fellow virgin-martyr, who was venerated as a protector from sudden death. They stand either side of the Virgin and Child.[56] The Virgin holds an apple to which the Infant extends his hand, emphasising this group's corporate role in the work of redemption made necessary by Eve's failure. [57]

At the ancient parish church of St Gregory in Norwich (which was undergoing a programme of rebuilding in the fifteenth century) 'the Margaret'

---

up!', in Wood, *Women and religion*, 141–55. Swanson suggests (p. 147) that Margery's book reflected some of the tensions felt by the mercantile elite during a time of major demographic shift. For further analysis of this interpretation see also K. Parker, 'Lynn and the making of a mystic', in K. Lewis and J. Arnold (eds), *A companion to the book of Margery Kempe*, Cambridge 2004, 55–73.

[51] Hope, 'Inventories', 160–2. White satin or blue worsted were two options for the vestments for 'Our Lady's Altar' (p. 161), decorated with orphreys and embroidered crowned 'M's.

[52] This dragon is curiously domestic, looking as if bred from a Gloucester Old Spot pig.

[53] Williamson, 'Saints on Norfolk rood-screens', 334.

[54] Ibid. 335.

[55] Lasko and Morgan, *Medieval art*, 40 (57). In this connection the fine Thornham Parva retable (dated 1310–20), featuring St Margaret, should also be mentioned (p. 26 [32]). See also Tristram, *English wall painting*, 301.

[56] A date of 1300–50 for this scheme is given in D. Park and H. Howard, 'The medieval polychromy', in I. Atherton and others (eds), *Norwich cathedral: church, city and diocese, 1096–1996*, London–Rio Grande 1996, 379–409 at p. 393.

[57] Tristram, *English wall painting*, 230, provides a good reference, but some dates have now been revised by more recent scholarship. For example, the retable in the Lady chapel, which Tristram dates at *c.* 1380 is now dated to *c.* 1420: Park and Howard, 'Medieval polychromy', fig. 142 at p. 395. Pamela Tudor-Craig, perhaps following Tristram, identifies the wall-painting in the ante-reliquary chapel as fourteenth-century Gothic: 'Painting in medieval England: the wall-to-wall message', in N. Saul (ed.), *The age of chivalry: art and society in late medieval England*, London 1995, 115 and n. 53.

features in the large and lively wall-painting of St George, who appears splendidly armoured, with a triple ostrich-feathered helm. He is mounted on a white horse, giving battle to the dragon, just as he might have been seen in the gild-day pageant in the 1520s.[58] But this Margaret, unlike the George, is immobile, a diminutive figure in the background, standing on a distant ledge with sheep, an image of resigned docility. She has become conflated with the rescued maiden-princess in George's legend, who is offered to the dragon, along with the last of the sacrificial sheep, as a ransom price for the town's physical security.[59] It is significant that Voragine defines the dragon in his legend of St George as a bearer of plague, conveyed by its foul breath, and therefore to be kept outside the city walls. The Maiden-Margaret is seen as a means of the dragon's 'containment' by her physical sacrifice. The association with the pascal lamb is obvious; that the maiden is a substitute for the sheep in Voragine's tale of St George suggests again the perception of St Margaret as a mirror and symbol of the passion.

An intact image of Margaret may still be seen in the glass of Martham St Mary, where each of two different panels at the north-east end, complete with vanquished dragon, shows a figure visibly pregnant with power. The less-frequently depicted pastoral guise of the saint as a beautiful young shepherdess and 'spinster', far removed from any city, just as outlined in the legend, also survives in a fine window panel at North Tuddenham church, in the Norwich hinterlands. A high-quality but dragon-less panel depicts the saint as a young and lovely aristocratic girl, complete with spindle and accompanying sheep, as first espied in the fields by Olibrius, and with whom he became instantly infatuated. This panel gives the impression of having been designed with the legend in hand. That this Margaret is remarkably well dressed for a workaday shepherdess may have been a compliment to women in this congregation, whose commercial success was dependent on wool and cloth, or may have been intended to indicate the saint's innate nobility, as described in the legend.[60] Her crown of leaves echoes the crown

---

[58] 'Item a sword covered with velvett with gilt harneys for the George ... a helm gilt with crest, and three ostreche fetheres ... a peyre of gloves gilt ... Item a dragon': *RCN* ii. 397–400, no. ccclxv. This entry, from an inventory thought to date from before 1420, shows the detailed attention to presentation and also substantial investment thought essential by the gild from an early date. The wall-painting also displays three ostrich feathers in George's headgear that is, perhaps, of a later date, and the fashion reflects Flemish/German influence. Tudor-Craig, on the other hand, judges the artist of this wall-painting as being a worthy parallel to the Veronese, Pisanello: 'The wall-to-wall message', 106–19 at p. 116.

[59] *Golden legend*, i. 58, p. 238. For ideas about the dragon as a communal danger rather than a personal nemesis see P. Horden, 'Disease, dragons and saints: the management of epidemics in the Dark Ages', in T. Ranger and P. Slack (eds), *Epidemics and ideas: essays on the historical perception of pestilence*, Cambridge 1992, 45–76.

[60] She is shown, significantly, spinning wool from a drop-spindle, a device which was reserved to spinners of long staple wool for the production of worsted cloth, the finer and more expensive end of the market.

of thorns of her Bridegroom, and the ram in the thicket proclaims her imminent sacrifice. In stark contrast, the church of Kimberley St Peter possesses a fourteenth-century glass panel of a stern-faced, mace-wielding Margaret of great distinction and tension. This dragon is still in his death throes but his writhing tail behind her leg and her expression of stoicism suggest that this is a battle that may have to be fought repeatedly.[61]

The finest of the wood-carvings depicting St Margaret must be that on a nave pew-end in St Helen's church at the St Giles's hospital, Norwich, later known as the Great Hospital, which bears the initials of hospital master, John Hecker (1519–32), who commissioned it shortly before the Dissolution.[62] The church also contains, in the Bishop Goldwell chantry chapel, a ceiling boss of Margaret placed like a 'satellite' of the Virgin's image which forms the climax of this scheme (see plate 10). The repeated image reminds that her intercession was intensely valued by both lay person and cleric.

Relatively little documentary evidence remains about bequests either for specific screen panels or windows, or to illuminate the factors governing a donor's choice of subject.[63] It is sometimes possible to arrive at a conjectural time scale by examining other, related bequests, as at North Walsham church. Here several legacies in the 1470s were devoted to ornamenting altars and providing painted decoration, suggesting a parish project, which may have included painting the screen.[64] To this dearth of documentation Alice Bishop and Alice Cannelles, who recorded their bequests to the screen at Marsham church (near Aylsham), offer welcome exceptions.[65] While Simon Cotton has shown that women were active in selecting rood-screens for their benefactions, this, as in the case of Alice Bishop, was often a work begun in life. Alice recorded clearly what she had paid and what remained outstanding, but many female donors may never have mentioned such projects in any last

---

[61] For this image see C. Hill, 'Some incarnational aspects of late medieval female piety in East Anglia', unpubl. MA diss. UEA 1999, plate 18 at p. 34. On balance, most representations of St Margaret's dragon show a creature still alive, if wounded, whereas St George's dragon (sometimes with female pudenda) is most often, if not always, dead. A local exception is the St George panel at Ranworth St Helen, where a very lively dragon is depicted engaging with a fashionably-clad George, which, like the image in the St Gregory wall-painting, would have been recognisable as 'the George' in the Norwich gild procession.

[62] Rawcliffe, Medicine for the soul, appendix 3 at p. 262.

[63] Cotton, 'Medieval roodscreens', 44–54. Few surviving wills that make such a bequest specify anything but general painting or gilding of the perke. This perhaps indicates that detailed specifications would often be finalised while the donor was living. For example, Alice Bishop of Marsham, in her will of 1501, left £3 to paint a panel of the screen 'where of I have payed with my owyn handde 33s 8d': ANC, reg. Bemond, fo. 25 (Bishop), 1501/3.

[64] NCC, reg. Paynot, fo. 3 (Robert Elmham), 1473; reg. Gelour, fo. 102 (William Oreed), 1475; reg. Aubry, fo. 5 (William Cook), 1478.

[65] ANC, reg. Bulwer, fo. 39 (Alice Cannelles), 1507.

will and testament.[66] Such an example may be found at the parish church of St Margaret, Upton, Norfolk, where the screen is inscribed for William and Agnes Wynne, both of whom died in 1505, but the screen is mentioned in neither will.[67] It is, therefore, difficult to present evidence which does more than hint at female preference or choice in commissions that have generally remained undocumented for male and female alike, or have, indeed, been lost. A singular exception in Norfolk is Margaret Davy of Lodden, who in 1503 left a bequest of 3s. 4d. to painting an image of St Christopher on the screen at her parish church.[68]

Fear of plague and other epidemic disease which had such a devastating effect on the population of Norwich (including the mercantile elite), in the second half of the fourteenth century may be an as yet unexplored aspect of the cult of St Margaret. Her legend emphasises her survival of her particular dragon by spiritual strength and endurance, rather than slaughter by the sword and lance chosen by the mounted St George in the protection of the plague-threatened city.[69] At this juncture in both their legends, they have each, in a sense, taken up the gendered role of the other: Margaret triumphing by becoming a 'spiritual male', and George by engaging with the bodily disposal of the dragon and its poisonous manifestations. In this light, the appropriation of her legend by the prestigious Norwich gild of St George takes on other, more subtle layers of meaning, including issues of control and subjugation.[70]

Many churches in Norfolk had altars or lights of St Margaret, usually signifying the possession of an image and a general attachment to her.[71] Blomefield notes that after 1349, when the parish church of St Margaret Newbridge united with that of St George Colegate, its principal image of St Margaret was transferred there, thus, in a very material way, foreshadowing

---

[66] Cotton, 'Medieval roodscreens', 44, 51.

[67] Ibid. 52. The same can be said of John and Clarice Miller at Thornham. He died in 1488 (NCC, reg. Wolman, fo. 43) but his will is devoid of such instructions.

[68] NCC, reg. Popy, fo. 351 (Margaret Davy), 1503.

[69] 'She thus had the victory/ Of hym, thorgh grace of God entere': Hooly wummen, 20, lines 715–16.

[70] Contemporary Bristol, which also had a thriving mercantile community, did not so favour St George's cult, but preferred that of St Katherine of Alexandria, whose veneration not only attracted a male clientele, but even outstripped that of the Virgin. St Katherine was venerated as patron of spinners and associated crafts: Adams, 'Religion, society, and godly women', 211–14. In striking contrast to Norwich's nine (including four dedicated to the Virgin and two to St Margaret) Bristol had only two parish churches dedicated to female saints (p. 209).

[71] The numerous dedications of churches to the saint in the diocese of Norwich attest to a long-term devotion. Many of these churches are of pre-Conquest foundation, such as Breckles, Hardwick, Hales, Hardley, Seething and Worthing, all these round-towered. Even now, hers is the fifth most frequently found dedication, with forty-seven parish churches or their remains known, of which four shared the dedication and five are redundant/ruined. These figures are calculated from The diocesan directory, 2006, Norwich 2006.

the incorporation of her legend in Norwich into the cult of St George.[72] Another image was to be found at St Michael Coslany, as is known from bequests for lights there.[73] According to her legend, lights in the saint's honour carried penitential significance. She petitioned God on behalf of her suppliants: 'if they … lyght or launpe fynde of deuocyoun / To me-ward: lord, for thy gret grace / Hem repentaunce graunte er they hens pace'.[74]

St Margaret will surely also have featured on many textiles used in parish churches, of which few records now remain. The inventories of St Peter Mancroft record the gift of Margaret and William Bacune, hosier, 'whos p(er) sons be peynted in it', of a banner cloth 'steyned' with the scenes from the life of St Peter, the patron of this parish.[75] The next item recorded on this folio is a similar banner, featuring principally St John the Baptist, together with the images of St Margaret, St William and St James 'in pendans peynted'.[76] As this second banner depicted the name-saints of the Bacunes they may have commissioned it as well. St William was patron of the gild of peltiers who had working connections with tailors and dealers in clothes, including hosiers, such as William Bacune.[77]

The parish of St Peter also possesses an important fifteenth-century alabaster featuring a group of nine female virgin-saints, local as well as legendary, with St Margaret and her dragon in the centre foreground, wielding a painted *Tau* cross, which she plunges into his throat.[78] Any specific connection with the women of the parish must, however, remain a matter of conjecture, although elsewhere portable alabasters of a similar size were hired out to aid the childbed of elite female parishioners.[79] It may be that Margaret's cult flourished here, however, simply because so many of the parishioners belonged to the gild of St George, which had appropriated 'the Margaret' for its own pageant: the men and women who worshipped at St Peter's dominated the hierarchy of this gild. It may be argued with some confidence,

---

[72] Blomefield, *History of Norfolk*, iv. 474.

[73] Ibid. iv. 499.

[74] *Hooly wummen*, 23, lines 836–40.

[75] Margaret's will survives, describing her as 'late wiff of William Bakon of Norwich': NCC, reg. Popy, fo. 44 (Bakon), 1501.

[76] Hope, 'Inventories', 221.

[77] E. Rutledge, 'Before the Black Death', in Rawcliffe and Wilson, *Medieval Norwich*, 257–88. Rutledge points out that trades associated with the cloth industry remained the one bright spot in the Norwich economy when other trades reflected a fall-off.

[78] *Tau* crosses were thought to offer protection against disease, especially plague: A. Hayum, *The Isenheim altarpiece: God's medicine and the painter's vision*, Princeton 1989, 37–9, fig. 23. St Jerome's concept of Christ as *verus medicus, solus medicus* (the true medicine, the only medicine) is central here.

[79] As Judith Middleton-Stewart has noted, alabasters in narrative groups of five or seven were often assembled in wooden frames to form a retable: *Inward purity*, 224–5 at n. 42 for Henry Totweye's gift of 6s. 8d. 'to the new alabaster table of the story of St Margaret' in 1457. This method of construction would have ensured the portability of individual panels.

though, that the actual survival of the alabaster is a testament to its importance in the life of the parish, and possibly of deep-seated attachment to
its central figure, St Margaret, as patron of safe childbirth.[80] The window
panels of the saint reinforce the impression of an active cult at this church.
The Epiphany alabaster of Long Melford church, featuring a Nativity aided
by a midwife, and a domestic Holy Family, similarly survives, owing to its
secret burial in the chancel through turbulent times of religious change and
iconoclasm. Attachment to both alabasters, and the incarnational piety that
they represent, was unquestionably strong enough to prompt concealment.[81]

The exceptional glass of St Peter Mancroft included the St Margaret series
of panels, commissioned by the wealthy businessman Alderman Toppes and
his wife.[82] In this particular case, though, the offer of spiritual and physical
aid implicit in the iconography of the saint's triumph may be overshadowed
by an overtly political interpretation. The commissioning and installation
of the St Margaret window, and perhaps the Elizabeth of Hungary series, was
perhaps timed to honour a pregnant Margaret of Anjou, queen of Henry VI,
who was visiting Norwich in 1453.[83] The gift of the glass in which these
saints appear could be construed as a deft political move by Toppes, his wife
and their fellow-parishioners. Such a reconciliatory gesture on behalf of the
previously disunited elite (a broken body politic indeed) was judged to bring
nothing but credit to the city of which the queen held the fee-farm.[84] Robert
Toppes had been mayor for the third time the previous year and was now
the leading alderman of the prestigious gild of St George.[85] The sponsorship
of this window, which complimented the queen by choosing her name-saint
and implicitly bestowed a blessing upon her first and only pregnancy,[86] might
have been read differently by supporters of the house of York. For them, the
queen needed not only divine intervention to successfully produce an heir to
the English throne after eight childless years of marriage to a feeble husband,
but also supernatural help in rising above her own alleged sexual misconduct

---

[80] As with the Long Melford alabaster, this, too, was buried, it is said in the churchyard
of St Peter Mancroft: Lasko and Morgan, *Medieval art*, 55–6.

[81] Middleton-Stewart, *Inward purity*, 224–5.

[82] Although the Toppes's glass was located in the north chancel chapel, and the St
Margaret glass was in the south chancel chapel, King has noted that the design of the
stone work of the east window of the latter chapel is in the same style as that of the
Toppes window. There are no extant documents to clarify who exactly commissioned
what, apart from the donor images: personal communication with David King.

[83] Margaret of Anjou's father was titular king of Hungary: D. King, 'A glazier from the
bishopric of Utrecht in fifteenth-century Norwich', *British Archaeological Association
Conference Transactions* xviii (1996), 220–3.

[84] Henry VI issued a new charter to the city in March 1451/2, granting the citizens their
liberties and customs, 'as in London': *RCN* i. 37–40, no. xxi.

[85] Toppes was mayor in 1435, 1440, 1452 and 1458, and MP in 1437, 1439–40, 1445–6,
1449, 1459 and 1461–2: J. C. Wedgwood and A. Holt, *History of parliament: biographies
of the members of the Commons House, 1439–1509*, London 1936, 863.

[86] King, *St Peter Mancroft*, pp. ccxxix–ccxxx, and 'A glazier' 220.

with the duke of Somerset.[87] It was, in the circumstances, fortunate that she was delivered of a healthy son later that year. The advent of the new prince was also, in a sense, to Norfolk's credit, since the less cynical could attribute his conception and birth to the patronage of Our Lady of Walsingham, to whom Queen Margaret had made sumptuous oblations whilst on pilgrimage.

From childbed to chaste widowhood: the iconography of St Margaret and St Jerome

What links may be established between the cult of the virgin-martyr St Margaret and that of St Jerome? The city church of St Gregory which contains the wall-painting of St George with a diminutive St Margaret also possesses the remains of other fine wall-paintings featuring the Church Fathers, including Jerome, high up on the south side, above what once was the chapel of St Thomas Becket with its altar dedicated to St Anne and St Thomas.[88] Are Jerome and Margaret connected by ties other than their assumed contemporaneity? The theme of Margaret's legend and the emphasis of much of the writing of Jerome combine in their mutual elevation of virginity, and sexual continence in general, as a means of preserving spiritual integrity and thereby obtaining union with God.

For women of the eastern Mediterranean in the fourth and fifth centuries (including the putative young St Margaret and her peers), raised in an Aristotelian culture that defined women as morally weak and sexually voracious, virginity or abstinence offered a measure of control and personal freedom, in addition to liberation from the dangers of childbirth.[89] The cults of these two saints, as revealed in Norfolk iconography of the fifteenth century, perhaps reflect women's aspiration towards an element of autonomy in their challenging and often dangerous lives: St Margaret for the childbearing wife, and St Jerome, that 'louer of widows', for the often much-married widow now free to pursue a sworn chastity in order to retain her material and spiritual autonomy. Jerome's teaching could be interpreted as encouraging a more single-minded pursuit of penitential devotion among those now free to follow such a vocation: widows who aspired to be, in spiritual terms, 'born-again virgins', or, more pragmatically, 'career widows'. Like their sisters devoted to

---

[87] Prospero di Camulio, Milanese ambassador to the court of France, later reported the wild rumour that Queen Margaret had poisoned Henry VI and planned to marry Somerset: J. R. Lander, *The Wars of the Roses* (1965), Stroud 2000, 98.

[88] Their images were displayed in wall niches by the altar: Blomefield, *History of Norfolk*, iv. 273.

[89] Brown, *Body and society*, 264–7.

the Magdalen, their pursuit of a contemplative spirituality also encouraged a commitment to charity in the practice of the comfortable works.[90]

Such a one was Margaret Purdans, pious widow of alderman Richard Purdans of St Giles, Norwich, with her extensive network of mainly well-connected female friends in Norwich. In a real sense, members of this group of women were disciples of their own Jerome, in the person of the Norwich hermit and priest Richard Fernys (d.1464), who may well have acted as their spiritual director.[91] On the evidence of his and their wills, he certainly stood at the centre of this circle.[92] The 'reading' of the cult of St Jerome espied through such an interpretive glass may reveal more of those women who, through their lifetimes, as their circumstances evolved, progressed through one devotion to others, assuming different priorities.

The four doctors

The trend for choosing Jerome, Ambrose, Augustine and Gregory as inter-cessory patrons on screens, especially in a personalised context, is an interesting development, and may reflect more than conformity to traditional patriarchal orthodoxy. The four Latin doctors may have been favoured by parishioners as a mark of fidelity to orthodox Catholic teaching at a time when radical changes were being made and dissent was in the air.[93] But other layers of meaning might offer nuances of interpretation not quite so obvious. St Jerome (d. 420), for example, had a particular place in Brigettine piety. The priest Symon Wynter of Syon composed Jerome's *vita* at this prestigious eponymous foundation (between the 1420s and 1444) for Margaret, duchess of Clarence, formerly widow of John Beaufort.[94] Drawing upon Dominican sources, it recounts St Bridget's revelation from the Virgin, who affirms Jerome's unimpeachable spiritual credentials:

---

[90] At Combs church, in Suffolk, two panels of glass remain depicting the seven comfort-able works, as well as five scenes from a life of St Margaret window: Woodforde, *Norwich school of glass painting*, 59.

[91] Margaret Purdans seems to have inspired a lasting affection and spiritual attachment in men and women of her acquaintance. John Baret (d.1463), wealthy and very pious merchant of Bury St Edmunds, like Margaret, left 20s. to Julian Lampet and gifts to her servants in his will, and bequests to Margaret, including symbolic jewellery, with an affectionate testament to their long-standing friendship.

[92] Examples are NCC, reg. Jekkys, fos 15–16 (Fernys), 1464, and reg. Multon, fos 89–91 (Katherine Kerre, formerly Moryell), 1498. Katherine's sister, Christine Veyl, held a particular place in the estimation of Fernys.

[93] Duffy, 'Parish, piety and patronage', 150.

[94] G. R. Keiser, 'St Jerome and the Brigettines: visions of the afterlife in fifteenth-century England', in D. Williams (ed.), *England in the fifteenth century: proceedings of the 1986 Harlaxton symposium*, Woodbridge 1987, 143–52 at p. 143.

Doughtir, haue thou in mynde how I toolde the that Ierome was a lovere of wydous, a folewer of parfyt monkis and an auctour and defensour of trouthe that gate the by his meritis that prayere that thou saydest? And now I adde to and say that Ierome was a trompe by whiche the Hooly Gooste spake. He was also a flaume inflaumyd by that fyre that come vppon me, and vppon the appostelis on Pentecost day. And therfor blessid are thay that here (t)his trompe and floew therafter.[95]

Jerome's *vita* is notable for its visions of purgatory. Like the early fourteenth-century *Gast of Gy*, which also uses Dominican sources, the *vita* was not simply a description of purgatory as a physical place, a 'last chance saloon'. It dwells in graphic detail upon specific and highly individual punishments, with a view to eliciting the readers'/listeners' repentance and, therefore, salvation. This goal was promoted by St Bridget as the distinct and primary responsibility of mothers. Margery Kempe's understanding of this precept was demonstrated in her uncompromising, some would say ruthless, approach in bringing her sick son to repentance and confession.[96] The portrait of the eldest Bacon son in surplice and rosary on the Fritton St Catherine church screen may well be meant to signal his mother's performance of this Briget-tine duty. The reputed miracles of Jerome, his being a 'louer of widows' and 'a tendir trumpe that the holigost spake in', together with his visions and voca-tion to warn, combined to make him a popular choice of patron saint among anxious Christians facing death and judgement. Jerome was well known, even by those who could not read, because of his appearance as a prophet of warning in fifteenth-century sermons: 'for Seynt Ierome seith whethur that he eat, drynke, or slepe, or what-euer els that he dothe, it semeth hym, seith he, that the angels trompe sowneth in is eere seyinge thus, "Ryse, ye dede men, and com to the Dome"'.[97]

At Ludham St Catherine the screen bears an inscription recording the princely contribution in 1493 of John and Cicely Salmon 'that gave forten pounds', which had perhaps enabled the planning of a single *schema*, if not its complete execution.[98] In his will, proved in 1487, John left a double bequest of 20s. to the maintenance of the roodloft and a further 20s. for its painting, though whether this was in addition to the £14 or was the completion of that sum remains unknown. Although the screen is dated 1493, John's grave marker nearby indicates that he died in 1486. It may be assumed, therefore, that Cicely had some say in the work undertaken on the screen during the seven years between John's death and its completion. This

---

[95] Ibid. See also 'Symon Wynter: the *Life* of St Jerome', ed. C. Waters, in A. C. Bartlett and T. H. Bestul (eds), *Cultures of piety: medieval English devotional literature in translation*, Ithaca 1999, appendix at p. 249.
[96] *Book of Margery Kempe*, ii, ch. i, p. 221–2 lines 30–4.
[97] *Middle English sermons*, ed. W. O. Ross, Oxford 1960, (4), 18.
[98] NCC, reg. Caston, fo. 288 (Salmon), 1487; Cotton, 'Medieval roodscreens', 49.

would also have allowed time for the parish to accumulate further funding for the project, as needed.

What might reasonably be termed the Salmon screen comprises a fashionable amalgamation of saints, reflecting the aspirations of the parishioners, and perhaps even their reading (or listening) habits and political affiliations. It features the four doctors of the Church: Augustine, Ambrose, Gregory and the ever-popular hermit and cardinal, Jerome; three saintly English kings: the 'martyred' Edmund, king of East Anglia, Edward the Confessor and Henry VI; a revered nobly-born local saint who espoused poverty, St Wulstan of Bawburgh; and two martyred deacons, Stephen and Laurence, together flanked by St Mary Magdalen in the northern-most panel, and the helper-saint, St Apollonia, on the southern-most.[99] High-born saints predominate. Doubtless, Cicely had her say, but neither she nor John opted to sponsor a name-saint, as major benefactors frequently did. It may be that the consensus of parish opinion, led by the wardens, decided otherwise, or that these are Cecily's preferred saints. Since screens were most often painted piecemeal, as and when funding became available, either from the living or the dead, it is implausible that wives and widows did not make their views known.

Widows, indeed, were free to make their own decisions and often did so. In the parish of St Peter Mancroft, Elizabeth Drake (d.1504), widow of William Davy, vintner, her first husband, then of John Carleton, mercer, thirdly of John Jowell, alderman and bedweaver, fourthly of William Drake, esquire, and, at the time of her death, wife of her fifth husband, Robert Gardener, alderman and mercer, gave a generous £5 to gild the roodloft between the chancel and the chapel.[100] It seems likely that Elizabeth maintained some control of her considerable fortune which accumulated throughout her remarkable marital career. John Jowell, the third of her five husbands, instructed in his will of 1499 that she should have all the goods and movables she had brought to the marriage: 'that cam to me by hir'.[101] Likewise, in 1529, Alice, widow of Thomas Rudkyn, left an impressive £10 to the church of St Laurence, Norwich, to make 'a perke' or roodloft in the north aisle.[102] Across the city, Margaret, widow of Henry Larke, a smith, who died in 1532 and was buried in the churchyard of All Saints, Norwich, similarly left a legacy towards gilding the 'rodeloft' of this church.[103]

---

[99] This is an interesting pairing: the Magdalen with the proto-martyr Stephen, who, as the first in the New Testament to mirror Christ's passion, could be, in a sense, his spiritual heir.

[100] NCC, reg. Spyltymber, fos 66–70 (Elizabeth Drake) w.1503, probate 1508.

[101] PCC, reg. Moone, fo. 2 (Jowell), 1499. Among this group of the much-married, Isabella Swayn (d.1495), Elizabeth Thursby (d. 1519) and Katherine Tilles (d. 1526/7) each had three husbands, and each woman left a will which is extant. Likewise, two known aldermen had four wives each: William London (d. 1494) and Edward Rede: Frost, 'Aldermen', 141.

[102] NCC, reg. Haywarde, fos 142–3 (Alice Rudkyn), 1529.

[103] NCC, reg. Alpe, fos 173–5 (Margaret Larke), 1532.

Aside from honouring a saint, such as Margaret, and securing remembrance in prayer among one's friends, colleagues and neighbours, having a panel painted or gilded was a very effective way of promoting a person or a family in a visible and communicable medium. It was also a means of advertising commercial success and prosperity. The practice of depicting the donor(s) in the act of supplicating the saint on the screen panel is apparent in Norfolk, though was never common.[104] Portraits of female donors are of interest because one could argue that they are depicted as they wished to be remembered, displaying characteristics that they considered admirable and with saintly patrons of their choice. The diminutive but carefully painted Baymonts each occupy the left-hand corner of a panel with their chosen saints, Jerome and Ambrose, on what was once a high-quality screen at Foxley church, Norfolk (see plate 11). Anne Baymont is depicted with a wholesome colour and looks the picture of good health, while her husband, John, seems grey and haggard of face, perhaps suggesting the imminence of his death and hinting that his wife was the executrix of this work (see plate 12).[105] Of greater interest, however, is the fact that the widow, Anne, kneels at the feet of a youthful St Jerome, looking appealing in his cardinal's red, while her sickly husband supplicates St Ambrose.

More boldly, John Bacon (d.1510) and his wife and children are portrayed on two panels at Fritton St Catherine, south of Norwich, the self-assured couple assuming the same size and stature as the saints in the other panels. Marshalled behind their parents, the more diminutive Bacon children face toward the right and the empanelled saints.[106] Again, like the Baymonts, this couple favoured the Doctors of the Church. The Bacons' foremost son, in a group of eleven siblings, seems to wear a surplice, perhaps being in holy orders, and he prays with a heavy rosary, as do his parents and one of his three sisters.[107]

This focus on the Doctors of the Church is also apparent at St Margaret's, Burnham Norton, where the 1450 pulpit displays portraits of John and Katherine Goldale, the donors, alongside the four Latin Doctors. As can be

[104] Duffy, 'Parish, piety and patronage', 133–63 at pp. 144–5.

[105] John Baymont made his will in 1485, leaving 5 marks (£3 8s. 4d.) towards the painting of this screen, which could not have paid for much more than a single panel. He may have made some contributions while he lived, or arranged with his wife to finalise matters from his estate. The family continued as benefactors of this church; as late as 1543 Joan Baymont, widow, left a selection of gifts to it, including altar cloths, a surplice and £6 for a new cope: NCC, reg. Attmere, fo. 373; Duffy, 'Parish, piety and patronage', 142–3.

[106] This is Fritton St Catherine, near Hempnall, not to be confused with Fritton St Edmund, near Reedham.

[107] Duffy, *Stripping of the altars*, plate 125. Of similar date, John Chapman of Swaffham and his wife are depicted carved on an elaborate pew-end in their parish church, the wife taking the upper, prominent position. Similarly, the rosary is a dominant design feature, and could be read as a very literal request for intercession. The Chapmans were generous benefactors of the parish.

clearly seen, Katherine's large and lively figure is placed next to that of St Jerome, and her name is painted beneath his image. Is the appearance of these images on the pulpit redolent of orthodoxy, authority and teaching? Or is it also telling us something about the Goldales? Katherine's portrait has survived in better condition than that of her patron, St Jerome.[108] Simon Cotton has also noted that the rood-screen at this church bore an inscription stating that it was donated by William and Joan Groom in 1458, and that it contained their portraits.[109] For a time they alone escaped the depredations of iconoclasts. H. M. Cautley observed that previously the figures of the Virgin, St Ethelbert and St Gregory accompanied them. Ironically, the lay status of William, Joan and their children had, as with the Goldales, ensured their preservation.[110]

These screen panels may also reflect the wide circulation and influence of Brigettine-inspired vernacular texts. Symon Wynter composed his *vita* around the time that 'A Revelacyone schewed to an holy woman' was written.[111] Such texts warned of the dangers awaiting all men and women, professed and lay alike, and undoubtedly influenced the choice of subjects in screen painting among those who heard or read them. Margery Kempe described her visit to the tomb of St Jerome (in the basilica of Santa Maria Maggiore) whilst on pilgrimage to Rome, and the vision of him given to her 'gostly sygth'. He praised her burdensome gift of tears, 'for many shal be sauyd therby. And, dowtyr, drede the nowt, for it is a synguler & a specyal yyft that God hath youyn the – a welle of teerys the whech shal neuer man take fro the'.[112] Aside from being comforted by his personal valida-tion, Margery clearly understood the wider significance of St Jerome as a messenger of warning and the necessity for contrition, indeed, to the point where she took this role upon herself as a God-given mission.[113]

It may be significant that Norfolk donors appear on the panels depicting Doctors of the Church but are never found on those that honour virgin martyrs, actual or legendary, such as St Margaret. Choosing the Doctors would indeed seem to be a very public, perhaps even corporate, statement of affiliation, a decision reached collectively by the parish. St Margaret's iconography was, in a sense, made more powerful by her ability to tran-scend female flesh, and may not have been perceived or utilised in the same way. Again, caution must be observed in any inference drawn about the few

---

[108] The image of Katherine shows her in an attitude of adoration, hands apart, wrists turned out, typical of Norfolk funerary brass depiction.

[109] Cotton, 'Medieval roodscreens', 44–54 at p. 47.

[110] Williamson 'Saints on medieval rood-screens', 322; H. M. Cautley, *Norfolk churches*, Ipswich 1949, 182–3. Fragments of the donor inscription remain.

[111] Keiser, 'St Jerome', 146.

[112] *Book of Margery Kempe*, i, ch. xli, p. 99, lines 13–24.

[113] Ibid. i, ch. vii, p. 20, lines 10–17.

survivors of iconoclasm and changing fashions of worship.[114] It is, however, very striking that surviving female images on panels are generally more muti-lated than male, unless the latter bear, for example, papal emblems, such as Jerome's cardinal's hat.[115]

St Margaret's main attraction, ultimately, reposed in her offer of personal empowerment to women in the time of their greatest physical and spiritual vulnerability: childbirth. Such specialised protection was perceived in terms of a contract that could be entered into at need, as the pregnant Margaret Paston indicated when, in 1441, she requested her absent husband to wear the ring that she had given him, bearing an image of the saint, her patron and namesake.[116] It was more than a mere love-token. By wearing it John also became a suppliant and client of St Margaret and a party to his wife's ante-natal care. Encouragement and confidence were benefits of Margaret's cult that were to be found, too, in the cult of St Anne. Similarly, both saints were invoked for help to overcome infertility. Among the fifteenth-century followers of St Jerome were likely to be those same women whose repeated experience of marriage had, earlier in their lives, found affirmation and inspi-ration in the apocryphal life of St Anne and her *trinubium*. Anne had shown that marriage and motherhood were not incompatible with female piety and chastity, nor even dynastic ambition. For the nubile and fecund woman, the virgin-martyr St Margaret had other attractions.

Interpreting St Margaret

Jacobus de Voragine's *Golden legend* assigns to St Margaret the attributes of the pearl: shining white, small and potent: 'white by her virginity, small by humility, and powerful in the performance of miracles'.[117] As the gem was said to be effective against bleeding and 'passions of the heart', so to Margaret was accorded the ability to control effusions of blood, including her own. Such power was sought by women, pregnant or not, but especially before, during and after parturition. The capacity to prevent haemorrhage could also

---

[114] In Norfolk, eighty screens bearing images survive; in Suffolk, thirty-nine: Duffy 'Parish, piety and patronage', 134.

[115] The screen at Ludham shows just such selective destruction. The St Gregory's papal tiara and the St Jerome's cardinal's hat are damaged.

[116] 'I pre yow that ye wyl were the ryng wyth the emage of Seynt Margete that I sent yow for a rememrav(n)se tyl ye come hom': *Paston letters*, i. 125, letter. 217, lines 28–9. To 'remember' is to pray.

[117] *Golden legend*, i. 368. The anonymous poem, 'Pearl', written by c. 1400, with its emphasis on sexual purity, should be considered in this context. Some scholars believe that it may have been written as an elegy on the death of Margaret, daughter of John Hastings, earl of Pembroke, and granddaughter of Edward III: J. M. Bowers, *The politics of Pearl: court poetry in the age of Richard II*, Cambridge 2001, 9.

be understood to include the ability to control menstruation. This is implicit rather than explicit in her legend. Female health, according to humoral theory, depended on a proper balance obtained by regular, but not excessive, menstruation.[118] This theory was the basis of practical measures undertaken in preparation for successful conception which required a personal *regimen* for good health, an activity well within St Margaret's provenance.

In view of the limited options available to a medieval woman experiencing a complicated, dangerous birth, support from a heavenly patron might be the only accessible aid or hope.[119] Women in labour understandably identified very readily with a female icon of transcendent physical endurance. At another level St Margaret's tortured and bloody body was perceived as a mirror or text of Christ's passion, like him being 'fecund' in bearing and saving the world. 'I ask you', she says to the onlookers in her final minutes, 'in the name of our Lord and Saviour Christ that he give you forgiveness of your sins and bring it about that you reign in the kingdom of heaven.'[120] After her martyrdom, the angels reassure Margaret about the fate of her fragmented remains: 'do not be sorrowful concerning your holy body … [for] whoever touches your relics or your bones will have *their sins wiped out at that moment* and their name written in the book of life'.[121] Redemption through sanctified, if broken, female flesh, as well as through Christ's passion, is clearly signalled here.

A concern with female well-being and fertility, it could be argued, inverts the general perception of Margaret's chastity. But does it? The thrust, so to speak, of her legend is that a virgin who refused to surrender to either her own sexual nature or that of one in authority over her, and, as a consequence, suffered in imitation of Christ, elected to intercede for women who had done none of these things. Her inviolate, devil-denying virginity gave her the power to do so. But St Margaret of Antioch was never a one-dimensional icon to her pragmatic medieval female clients. Thus, in Lydgate's words, she petitioned God: 'Suffre no myschief tho wymmen, lorde, assaile / That

---

[118] *The Trotula: a medieval compendium of women's medicine*, ed. M. H. Green, Philadelphia 2001, 90 (136), 'On immoderate menstruation'. This remedy recommends a fumigant made of a mixture of old soles of shoes, penny royal and laurel leaves, used in conjunction with a pessary made of hot ashes and hot red wine wrapped in clean linen. According to the humoral imbalance thought to be causing the haemorrhage, such as excess of black bile or phlegm, so was the remedy selected. Juicy violets, prickly lettuce, pomegranate, oak apples, nutmeg, eglantine, brambles, agrimony were among the ingredients used. See also pp. 69–7. Fumigants were also popular to aid a difficult birth, as were scented baths and the anointing of the affected parts with rose or violet oil (pp. 79–81).

[119] It should be noted that even a woman of the standing of Margaret Paston was dependent on a midwife disabled by sciatica. This may in part account for her 'commissioning' of St Margaret.

[120] *Life of St Margaret*, 135.

[121] Ibid. 137 (my italics).

calle to me for helpe in theire greuaunce, / But for my sake save hem fro myschaunce.'[122]

Margaret offered practical help and spiritual protection to child-bearing women and their infants: the former during parturition and the neo-natal period, the latter to those who died, in or after childbirth. 'Now, gloryous lady, lete thy pyte habounde, / *Oure soulys to brynge wher thy soule ys*', writes Bokenham in his supplication to the saint.[123] The promise of heaven was much more than any earthly *accoucheur*, or perhaps even the parish priest, distanced by taint of parturition blood, could hope to offer.

---

[122] 'The legend of Seynt Margarete': *Minor poems of John Lydgate*, 90, lines 466–9.
[123] *Hooly wummen*, 24, lines 864–5 (my italics).

3

The Cult of St Mary Magdalen

The return to Eden

The local investment of devotion and material wealth in the popular medieval cults of St Anne, St Margaret and now St Mary Magdalen invites many questions. The cults of SS Anne and Margaret offered routes for spiritual and temporal aspiration, perhaps even survival, but they also facilitated more subtle codes of self-expression. The cult of the Magdalen arguably demonstrates this point more than any other. Like the *legenda* of the virgin-martyr Margaret, Mary Magdalen's story is rooted in the fleshly battle perceived as peculiar to female concupiscence, which Margaret triumphantly wins but which the Magdalen initially loses. United by her non-virginity with the legendary much-married St Anne, but distanced by the perception of her early promiscuity, her 'fallen' status as a single woman identified her as transgressive and dangerous, requiring Christ's direct physical intervention to 'turn[ed] them to worshyppe'.[1] It is no coincidence that Margery Kempe, in emulation of her heroine and role model, required a similar personal intervention from Christ to vanquish her own *post-partum* demons in her quest for spiritual liberation and conversion.[2] The wide spectrum of experience covered by the Magdalen's legend, from high-born whore by way of Apostle, preacher and teacher to 'friend of God', to arrive, ultimately, at the heavenly high table, appealed greatly to professed religious, as well as to the spiritually aspirational woman. Significantly, it is the image of the repentant harlot that has continued to inspire many artists throughout the centuries, rather than her *persona* as an authoritative preacher and desert hermit, and it is this, for some a disturbing characterisation, that perhaps still captures the imagination.

The name and sometimes the image of the Magdalen linger on, be it in hospital, *patisserie* or women's reformatory.[3] In recent decades the saint and her long-term utility as an icon and complex metaphor have again become the focus of international scholarly endeavour, and her life, legend and role in late medieval preaching and popular devotion have been reinterpreted and redefined.[4] None of this, however, has explored a local or regional

---

[1] Julian of Norwich, *Showings*, pt II, ch. xxxviii, p. 446, line 18.
[2] *Book of Margery Kempe*, i, ch. i, p. 8, lines 12–21.
[3] At the time of writing there is in Norwich a centre for the support of female sex workers called the Magdalen Group.
[4] See V. Saxer, *Le Culte de Marie Madeleine en occident des origines à la fin du moyen âge*, Auxerre–Paris 1959; S. Haskins, *Mary Magdalen: myth and metaphor*, London 1993; and

medieval view, which is only possible through a study firmly rooted in the archives, literature and material culture of the region in question. In East Anglia surviving fifteenth-century texts, especially Osbern Bokenham's *vita* of St Mary Magdalen, his longest, and the mini-plays concerned with the saint subsumed in the *N-town play*, as well as two more about her in the *Digby plays*, may help to illumine local attachment and highlight its significance.[5]

The genesis of the myth of the Magdalen, one of international status and extraordinary resilience, lies in the Gospels, even a cursory reading of which makes clear that a conflation has taken place of at least three, maybe several, named and unnamed women. Mary of Magdala, a leading figure among a group of female followers of Jesus, exorcised of seven demons, who accompanied him and his male disciples from Galilee, has become identified with Mary of Bethany, contemplative sister of Lazarus and Martha; with the woman at the house of Simon the leper, in Bethany, who came with spikenard to anoint Christ's feet (St John's Gospel names her as Mary, sister of Lazarus); and with the anonymous sinful woman who washed Christ's feet with her tears and anointed them.[6] These different reports may tell of one woman, or, more probably, of at least two, but the association of the woman called Mary Magdalen with the broken and crucified body of Jesus is clear and unambiguous, as is her faithful presence at his death.[7] By the Middle Ages her encounter with the resurrected Christ, narrated by all four Gospels, had endowed her with the title 'Apostle to the Apostles', placing her second only to the Virgin in an otherwise extremely patriarchal hierarchy of intercessors. A woman who had originally been (albeit obliquely) reported in the Gospels as a dynamic and resourceful presence among Jesus of Nazareth's peripatetic female supporters was later interpreted (by male clerics) as a personal model for relationship, even union, with God. This was powerfully reinforced by her remarkable transformation, reported as exorcism. This reading of the text was thought appropriate for women in need of rehabilitation from their innately lustful nature. The sermon for the Magdalen's feast day in the fifteenth-century *Speculum sacerdotale* emphasises this point: 'In syche day ye schull have the feste of Marye Magdalene, whiche was the *synneful woman and servyd to hure fleschely desires*, and to

---

K. L. Jansen, *The making of the Magdalen: preaching and popular devotion in the late Middle Ages*, Princeton 2000.

5   *Hooly wummen*, 136–72: this *Life* includes a prolocutory and a prologue; *N-town play*: 'The raising of Lazarus', 230–45; 'The announcement to the three Marys', 359–65; 'The appearance to Mary Magdalene', 365–9; *Digby plays*, 'Mary Magdalene', pts I, II, 55–136. For an East Anglian provenance for the Digby plays see T. Coletti, '*Paupertas est donum die*: hagiography, lay religion, and the economics of salvation in the Digby *Mary Magdalene*', *Speculum* lxxvi (2001), 337–78 at p. 337. See also G. M. Gibson, 'Bury St Edmunds, Lydgate and the *N-town cycle*', *Speculum* lxvi (1981), 56–90, esp. pp. 62 (*Digby plays*), 57–74 (*N-town*).

6   Luke viii.1–3; Mark xiv.3–9; Luke vii.37–48; John xii.3–8.

7   She is named in Matthew xxvii.56; Mark xv.40; and John xix.25.

whome God afterward gave syche grace that sche servyd forgeveness of here synnes.'[8]

It is apparent that the solitaries and their followers who were attracted to the cult of the Magdalen found the immediacy of her relationship with God incarnate inspirational.[9] Despite the misogyny of some mendicant devotees of the *cultus* who had, through their negative view of women, made the cult of extreme penitence necessary, the Magdalen's iconic status was clearly more complex than simply that of a redeemed sinner.[10]

Here is a woman's voice from almost six hundred years before Bokenham:

> Accept this spring of tears
> You who empty sea water from the clouds
> Bend to the pain in my heart, you
> Who made the sky bend to your secret Incarnation
> Which emptied the heavens.
> I will kiss your feet, wash them,
> Dry them with the hair of my head, those feet whose steps
> Eve heard at dusk
> In Paradise and hid in terror ...
> Do not overlook me, your slave,
> In your measureless mercy.[11]

This hymn, written after AD 843 by a poet-turned-nun in Constantinople, exemplifies the penitence and humility with which Mary Magdalen has traditionally been associated, and indeed, promoted. But it is characterised, too, by physicality, a charge of sexual energy that also marks the Gospel story of the woman who throws herself at Christ's feet, lays her tear-stained cheeks on them, strokes them with her hair and then massages them with expensive aromatic spikenard. This aspect of her behaviour is tacitly acknowledged, too, by Jesus, enacted in the *Digby plays* text, when he says of her: 'this woman in al wyse, / How she with teres of hyr better wepyng / She wassheth my fete, and dothe me servyse, / And anoy[n]tyt hem with onymentes, lowly knelyng, & with her her, fayer and brygth shynnyng, / She wypeth hem agayn with good In entent'.[12] Of particular significance in the Middle Ages was the Magdalen's legendary association with female sexuality. Yet she was absolved by Christ: 'I for-geyffe the thi wrecchednesse / And hol in sowle be thou made

---

[8]   Quoted by Haskins, *Mary Magdalen*, 429 n. 36 (my italics).
[9]   Julian of Norwich is an example of this. Margery Kempe, though not a solitary, felt the same identification.
[10] Haskins, *Mary Magdalen*, 148–51.
[11] Kassiane, nun of Constantinople, was writing hymns in about the 850s. This hymn was incorporated into the holy week liturgy. There is a translation by A. Barnstone in S. Cahill, *Wise women: over two thousand years of spiritual writing by women*, New York–London 1996, 57.
[12] *Digby plays*, 'Mary Magdalene', pt I, 80, lines 665–70.

therby!'[13] Of her it was written in the Gospel: 'many synnes are forgeven her, because she loved moche'.[14] This was undoubtedly an appealing statement to those who contemplated purgatory with the trepidation born of certainty.

Mary Magdalen's physical closeness to Christ raised her to be the first among the women who 'ministred unto hym of their substaunce'.[15] Her 'substaunce' was reckoned to be based on royal wealth according to Voragine's thirteenth-century *Golden legend*, again an affirmation, to those in need of it, that wealth of itself constituted no bar to salvation, so long as it was shared in humility by a penitent benefactor with those who represented the suffering body of Christ on earth, the poor. The persistent perception of the Magdalen was as a deeply sinful female penitent risen to a position of unrivalled holiness among the saints. This made her an extremely potent icon and protector, particularly during times of anxiety about sudden and unshriven death. John Dalton, wealthy merchant of Hull, reflected such a preoccupation in a lengthy and *angst*-riddled preamble to his will of 1487:

> the daies of men in this mortall lyfe be bot short, and the houre of deith is in the hand of Almighty God; and that He ordeyned the termes that no man may passe: remembryng also that God hath ordeyned men to dye, and ther is no thing more certayne than deth, and nothing more uncertayn then the houre of deth … and (th)at deth giffes noo respit certayn to levyng creature, but takis thaym sodaynly.[16]

The cultural acceptance that female flesh might stand in particular need of rehabilitation would not have surprised anyone in the late Middle Ages, and should not surprise anyone who reads a tabloid newspaper in the twenty-first century. Promoted as a humble penitent, who was, in fifteenth-century eyes, a reformed harlot, the Magdalen was endowed by her proximity to the wounds of crucifixion with the redemptive power of the eucharist, highly desirable in an intercessor and advocate. 'In how litill space how many woundes bee! …/ To see his tendere fleshe thus rewfully arayed …/ I feyll my harte wax cold / Thes blessite fete thus bludy to be-hold / Whom I weshid with teres manifold / And wyped with my heare', cries Mawdleyn, in the *Digby plays*.[17]

This affinity hints at the Magdalen's other *personae*, which were largely overshadowed by the focus on her sexual promiscuity: she was the leading woman, indeed the only woman not kin, who remained by the crucified Christ (with John) till the end, when all the male Apostles had fled.[18] Even

---

13 Ibid. lines 676–7.
14 Luke vii.47.
15 Luke viii.2–3.
16 *Testamenta eboracencia*, 4, 21–2.
17 *Digby plays*, 'The burial of Christ', 174–5, lines 90, 94, 97–100. There is a sense in which the anointing of Christ's feet, and their wiping with the Magdalen's unbound hair, anointed her head too, blessing her penitential gift of herself to God and healing her perceived waywardness which was represented by her wild and abundant hair.
18 Matt. xxvii.56; Mark xiv.50; John xix.25.

in the Gospels she is tacitly regarded as a figure of standing and authority, having more than parity with the Apostles, because of her constancy and immediate receptivity to the resurrected Christ.

The Magdalen's continuing involvement with the physical body of Christ through the preparation of his corpse for burial intensified her later association with the eucharist, as did widespread depictions in which she was identified by her proximity to his wounded feet in death, as she had been in life:[19] 'Thes are the swete fete I wipet with heris / And kissid so deuowtlye / And now to see tham thyrlite (pierced) with a nayle / How shulde my sorowfull harte bot fayle / And mowrn continually?'[20] The feet of the *Christos* were of course emblematic of his true humanity, his incarnation, and they figure as such in representations of the adult Christ, much as did his genitals in many paintings of him as infant. In this context, the Magdalen's physical and spiritual veneration of the feet, living, wounded or dead, takes on a profound, almost sacramental significance, particularly to those (especially women) devoted to the practical, often very personal, tasks involved in the accomplishment of the corporal works of mercy. Like Richard Rolle before her, and Marguerite of Oingt before him, Julian of Norwich understood the attachment to Christ's wounds as redemptive. In her *Showing* of the passion she describes Christ's body: 'The hote blode ranne out so plenteously that ther was neyther seen skynne ne wounde, but as it were *all blode*', that is, all sacrament.[21] The perception of Christ's passion as the ultimate charitable act meant that related acts of charity, such as the seven comfortable works, were seen as similarly redemptive, being somehow associated with his sacrifice and the act of self-giving.[22] Religious gilds were but one expression of this. Julian goes on to explore the wider meaning of her vision with its emphasis on Christ's gift of himself, but with an awareness of context that made her know that a wider, more inclusive message was being opened to her: 'This [blood] was so plenteous to my sight that me thought if it had ben so in kynde and substance, for that tyme it shulde haue made the bedde all on bloude, and haue passyde over all about.'[23] Gravely ill, she knows well enough that her bed and room are not covered in blood, but that the revealed message is as dramatically vital. Julian's parallel between 'waters plenteous in erth to our servys, and to our bodily eese', and Christ's other gift of his blood, 'to wassch us of synne; for ther is no lycour that is made that lyketh hym so wele to yeue us ... plenteous as it is most precious ... it is our own kynde, and blessydfully ovyr flowyth vs by the virtu of his precious loue', forever links the material world and physicality with spiritual, even universal, wholeness

---

[19] Luke xxiv.55–6; Mark xvi.1.
[20] *Digby plays*, 'The burial of Christ', 180, lines 265–70.
[21] Julian of Norwich, *Showings*, pt II, ch. xii, p. 342, lines 6–7.
[22] Duffy, *Stripping of the altars*, 131–54.
[23] Julian of Norwich, *Showings*, pt II, ch. xii, p. 343, lines 9–12.

and salvation.[24] Julian's imagery has very Magdalen-like resonances because of Mary's association with the wounded and bloody body of Christ and also her own spiritual wounds which acknowledged him as 'our own kynde'.

Julian's theology also developed at some length the necessity of spiritual failure before repentance and absolution could lead, by grace, to renewal, growth and redemption. It is not, therefore, surprising to find Mary Magdalen topping Julian's list of sinners who became what might be termed premier saints specifically because of their flawed humanity: 'in the new lawe he brought to my mynde furst Magdaleyne', she says, 'how they be knowen in the chyrch on erth with ther synnes, and it is to them no chame, but alle is turned them to worshyppe'.[25] Margery Kempe, attracted by such theology, and with concerns about her own sexual vulnerability, like Julian, placed the Magdalen at the head of a list of sinner-saints when meditating. It was then that God said to her: 'Haue mend, dowtyr, what Mary Mawdelyn was, Mary Eypcyan, Seynt Powyl, & many other seyntys (saints) that arn now in Hevyn, for of vnworthy I make worthy, & of synful I make rytful.'[26]

Mary Magdalen's unique and symbolic role derived from her status as one who had daily served, then accompanied, Christ on his journey from one world to the next, from earth-bound teacher to heavenly lord. Her relationship to him, therefore, became an outward expression of her own transition from a sinful life in the flesh to that of the interior world of the spirit and thus to penitence and the redemption of that same body and spirit. Just as the Annunciation to the Virgin was about the reception of the spirit of God in Everyman and Everywoman, so the spiritual 'rags to riches' experience of the Magdalen was the prize offered to all sinners who were penitent and 'loved much'.

The ninth-century nun's hymn draws parallels between Mary Magdalen's penitent tears and the waters of ocean and cloud, that is to say the waters of creation. Her tears, it is implicitly signalled, are an aspect of divinity that she shared with a God whose incarnation had emptied the heavens. Not for nothing did Margery Kempe wear her gift of tears like a livery of Christ. As she outran the Virgin in the handmaid stakes, so she out-wept the Magdalen, not only over Christ's passion, but over every person, child or man, whom she saw who could be in some way associated with his vulnerability and pain.[27] Significantly, Margery in her book marks the beginning of her spiritual climb to penitence and conversion with her Magdalen-like fall from grace in her consent to illicit sex on the eve of the feast of St Margaret of Antioch, her name-saint and parochial patron.[28] Margery (or

---

[24] Ibid. lines 13–19.
[25] See n. 1 above, and Paul, whom she also lists: Romans vii.8–11.
[26] *Book of Margery Kempe*, i, ch.xxi, p. 49, lines 23–6.
[27] Ibid. i, ch. xxviii, p. 69, lines 32–9.
[28] Ibid. i, ch. iv, pp. 14–15.

her editor/scribe) was consciously using a recognisable hagiographic model.[29] The potency of St Margaret's legend was based on her triumph over her own sexuality and her dependence on Christ to achieve physical and spiritual integrity.[30] But Margaret was a virgin. Margery, like the Magdalen, was not, and desperately sought to overcome her *post-gravida* status to achieve a similar neo-virginal intimacy with Christ.

The imagery employed by Margery in her description of the joyful spiritual affinity she experiences with Christ resonates strongly with the symbolic physicality in the writings of Mechtild de Magdeburg (d.c. 1280), and those of the thirteenth-century Flemish beguine Hadewijch of Brabant: 'Whan thu art in thi bed, take me to the as for thi weddyd husband ... boldly take me in the armys of thi sowle & kyssen my mowth, myn hed, *& my feet* as swetly as thow wylt', says Christ to Margery.[31] It may be argued that use of sensual, even erotic language by the visionary was inculcated by what might be termed a Magdalen-esque piety in its aspiration toward contemplation and the interior life.[32] The feet of Christ, which in her meditation he bids her kiss, tell us exactly where Margery's aspirations lie.

Acknowledged as patron of the penitent and the hermit, the Magdalen achieved an unassailable status as *apostola apostolorum*. This placed her high above all subsequent martyrs, virgin or otherwise, and in many respects superior to the male Apostles.[33] In a real sense Mary Magdalen personified the marginal and subversive, her turbulent body and spirit needing the direct exorcism of God incarnate before she could begin her 'return journey'. The seven demons of which she was exorcised were identified by medieval theologians as the seven deadly sins.[34] These, they argued, were replaced by her patronage of the seven corporal works of mercy, an appropriate transition

---

[29] S. Fanous, 'Measuring the pilgrim's progress: internal emphases in *The book of Margery Kempe*', in D. Renevey and C. Whitehead (eds), *Writing religious women: female spiritual and textual practices in late medieval England*, Cardiff 2000, 168–70. See also *The book of Margery Kempe: an abridged translation*, ed. L. H. McAvoy, Cambridge 2003, 13–14.

[30] 'You cannot overcome a chaste virgin. Christ himself has blessed my body, and to my soul he will give a crown of glory': *Lives of St Margaret*, 129.

[31] *Book of Margery Kempe*, i, ch. xxxvi, p. 90, lines 19–26. For Mechthild and Hadewijch see *Medieval women's visionary literature*, ed. E. Petroff, Oxford 1986, 16, 23 and 15 n. 47 respectively.

[32] The experience of the visionary Angela of Foligno (1248–1309), Franciscan tertiary, confirms this focus. She heard Christ say: 'Daughter and my sweet bride ... since I have entered you and rested in you, you may now enter me and rest in me. I was with the Apostles, and they saw with the eyes of the body, and they did not feel me as you feel me': Petroff, *Visionary literature*, 17 n. 51.

[33] Mark xvi.9; Luke xxiv.10. The Magdalen is described as 'Apostle to the Apostles' in an office written for her in the thirteenth century: Saxer, *Culte de Marie Madeleine*, 324–5. See also Haskins, *Mary Magdalen*, 135 n. 5.

[34] Luke viii.2. According to Luke, not only Mary Magdalen but also Joanna and Susannah had been cured of demons and infirmities before they began their life ministering to Christ 'of their substance', but Mary occupied a special place of leadership. Significantly, these women had to be 'transformed' in order to be capable of sacrificial service, whereas

for one who had tended Christ's body on earth.[35] In her legend this practice extended to include an unofficial eighth work, education, characterised by preaching and teaching, which were spiritual works of mercy largely
reserved to the priesthood. Christ's broken body as a text is central to this
concept, a text of which the Magdalen was the foremost exponent: 'How
many bludy letters beyn writen in this buke / Small margente her is', she says,
summoning Joseph of Aramathea to view the corpse.[36] It was for this reason
that the Magdalen's appeal extended beyond mystics and the mendicants to
exert a powerful influence in English urban society, both male and female.
Thomas Salter, priest, educated as a small boy by a sister of St Paul's hospital,
Norwich, reflects exactly this broader and subtler appeal.[37]

The Magdalen in Norfolk

How can the significance of such a cult in fifteenth-century Norwich be
recognised and understood now? The physical attributes of the Magdalen,
her abundant and unruly hair and her pot of costly ointment, in addition to
the widespread dissemination of her apocryphal legend, rendered her depictions, as well as her *vita*, an easy and primary target of agents of iconoclasm.[38]
She may have aroused particular antagonism among those incensed by the
apparent 'feminisation' of the catholic faith.[39] A single trace of a medieval
image survives in the city of Norwich in a fourteenth-century painted panel
currently in the St Andrew chapel of the cathedral (*see* plate 13), though
in the mid-eighteenth century Blomefield was able to convey something of
her medieval ubiquity.[40]

On the south-west side of the French Market and close to St Peter
Mancroft, St Stephen's, the parish church of many of Norwich's ruling elite,
once contained a substantial chapel of the Magdalen in the south chancel
aisle.[41] Its altar was jointly dedicated to her and to St John the Evangelist, with whom she had been present at the crucifixion.[42] It was patronised

---

the Gospels record no such necessity for their fellow male disciples, despite some clear
character defects.

[35] For fifteenth-century manuals on these topics, designed for confessional use and as a
tool for private devotion and self-examination, see Hughes, *Pastors and visionaries*, 196–7,
and *The religious life of Richard III: piety and prayer in the north of England*, Stroud 1997,
104–53.

[36] *Digby plays*, 'The burial of Christ', 180, lines 272–3.

[37] See chapter 5 below.

[38] While arguing for her post-Reformation retention as an icon of penitence, if stripped
of most of her attributes, Christine Peters notes that the Magdalen was omitted from
saints' days honoured in the 1552 Prayer Book: *Patterns of piety*, 234 and n. 81.

[39] Richmond, 'The English gentry and religion', 140–2.

[40] This panel is dated at 1380–1400: Lasko and Morgan, *Medieval art*, 37.

[41] Blomefield, *History of Norfolk*, iv. 152.

[42] Ibid. iv. 153; John xix.25–7.

by men and women of the Danyel family, who founded a chantry there.[43] Undoubtedly this chapel possessed an image of the saint with lights, as did other city churches, such as St Michael Coslany, and its neighbour, St Mary Coslany.[44] The latter, dedicated to the Virgin, also boasted a window of the Magdalen on its south side, which, together with the image, may betoken a special devotion here. It is seldom that such architectural detail is mentioned in a will but it is worth noting that this was the parish church of the glazier Helen Moundeforde, who was buried there in 1458, as was her glazier husband William 'the Dutchman' twenty years later.[45]

Seven painted rood-screen panels depicting the Magdalen survive across the county of Norfolk.[46] The inclusion among other female saints of a finely-drawn and beautiful Magdalen on the screen at Wiggenhall St Mary the Virgin is given special endorsement by her full-length representation, bearing a pot of unguent, on a carved pew-end in the north side of the nave in this church. Her prominence in the iconography of this church may be especially signifi-cant in view of the association of the parish with the community of nuns at Crabhouse Priory nearby. The relationship is emphasised by the surprising abundance of pew carvings of nuns, novices and perhaps vowesses, as well as the virgin martyr, St Agatha (a cleaver slicing through her right breast) and other, unnamed female saints. This demonstrates in a very tangible form the pious aspirations of women, lay as well as professed, exemplified in Norwich by Margaret Purdans, her friends and legatees, some of whom were nuns (in her will she bequeathed a book in English to Carrow Priory), hospital sisters (Alice Sowe, a sister at St Giles's hospital, received 6s. 8d.) and solitaries (Julian Lampet was to receive 20s. and Katherine Forster 5s. by which to remember her).[47] The screen at Thornham All Saints, north Norfolk, is unique in that it features the Magdalen occupying a panel next to that of

---

[43] Although documentary evidence is not abundant, Blomefield records that the chantry priest was commissioned to 'sing for the souls' of Maud (a diminutive of Magdalen) and Emma Danyel, wives of the founder John (mayor 1406, 1417), as well as those of his parents, Roger and Christian Danyel, and his brother, Walter and sister-in-law, Joan Danyel. These brothers also provided in their unusual joint will (1418) for the mainte-nance of almshouses that they founded in the parishes of St Stephen and St Catherine. Residents of the almshouses would also have been expected to pray for the Danyel family. The cult of the Magdalen was central to the performance of the seven comfortable works, and the provision of almshouses covered most, if not all, of them. The lack of subsequent documentary evidence implies that the Danyels's almshouses were short-lived: NCC, reg. Hyrnyng, fo. 32 (Daniel), 1418. See also C. Rawcliffe, *The hospitals of medieval Norwich*, Norwich 1995, 148.

[44] Blomefield, *History of Norfolk*, iv. 449, 490. See also the will of Geffrey Whitlake, barker, NCC, reg. Ryxe, fo. 262 (Whitlake), 1505.

[45] NCC, reg. Gelour, fo. 20 (Mounford), 1478.

[46] Williamson, 'Saints on Norfolk rood-screens', 305. They are at Garboldisham, Ludham, Oxborough, Thornham, Walpole St Peter, North Walsham St Nicholas and Wiggenhall St Mary the Virgin.

[47] NCC, reg. Caston, fos 163–5 (Purdans), 1481/3.

her legendary brother, Lazarus, who, according to the Gospel of John, was raised by Christ from the dead (*see* plate 14).[48] The pair together represent a complex iconography of resurrection,[49] in particular making a very strong statement about sin, the death of the flesh and trust in the redeeming merits of the passion to overcome both. 'I am the resurreccion and lyfe. Whosoever beleveth on me: ye though he were deed, yet shall he live', says Christ to Lazarus' sister, Martha.[50] John and Clarice Miller, the donors, whose names were inscribed on the screen, had lived through several major epidemics of the plague.[51]

It is no doubt significant that this particular screen is dominated by twelve Old Testament prophets (heralds of Christ), who are flanked by St Barbara (alongside the redeemed sinner St Paul) on the north side and the Magdalen on the south; Barbara was doubtless chosen as a protector from sudden death, and the Magdalen because of her close association with the redeeming wounds of Christ. Mary's image turns toward that of Lazarus, holding up a gilded and crocketed jar in her right hand and (unique among surviving Norfolk screens) proffering a lock of her golden hair in the left, both symbols of her acknowledgement of Christ's godhead and her service to him. It reminds, too, that in anointing Christ's feet and wiping them with her hair, Mary was herself receiving the same sacramental anointing, mutuality making the blessing reciprocal. But the risen Lazarus, depicted here in rich golden brocade and all the glittering magnificence of his spiritual resurrection, had, inevitably, like the rest of mankind, eventually to die. His scroll bears words declaring his (and the Millers') continued dependence on Christ: 'Propter me multi crediderunt in Jesum.'[52]

East Anglian texts: plays and players

Some fifteenth-century texts of local and regional provenance, notably the *N-town play*, Bokenham's *Lyf of Mary Maudelyn* and the *Digby plays*, demonstrate the appeal of the Magdalen to popular piety at different levels of society. The *N-town* cycle incorporates three plays that promote the significance and centrality of her role in disseminating the news of Christ's resur-

[48] John xi.1–44.

[49] This, and other painted panels mentioned in this section, may be seen in Hill, 'Incarnational piety', passim.

[50] John xi.25.

[51] NCC, reg. Wolman, fo. 43 (Miller), 1488. No mention is made of the screen in his will. There is a small commemorative brass in the nave which records that John died in 1488.

[52] See also the Magdalen with St Barbara and St Margaret on the screen at North Walsham St Nicholas.

rection: 'The raising of Lazarus', 'The announcement to the three Marys' and 'The appearance to Mary Magdalene'.[53]

Mary appears in the first play at her brother's side as he dies, prefiguring her relation to the crucified Christ; she becomes mad with grief, then takes the stage as witness to Lazarus' resurrection. In the next play in which she features, she is a co-recipient of the angelic message that Christ, too, has left the grave. Her final and most important appearance is as the first solitary witness of the resurrected Christ and as his primary messenger; that is, she is the first to receive him and the first to proclaim his resurrection. She describes him as: 'Qwyk and Qwethynge, of flesch and felle'; that is alive, able to speak, whole of body. The Magdalen perceives in her revelation yet another return journey, Christ's. Then, for the first time in the play she comprehends the significance of her own spiritual quest. 'So grett a joy nevyr wyff had non', she says, thereby proclaiming the supremacy of her new spiritual integrity over her former carnal passions.[54]

Lepers: the cursed and blessed

It is essential in this context to be mindful of the indivisibility of body and soul in the pre-Cartesian thought of medieval theology.[55] The human being was a conjoint whole, and disease was believed to be an expression of physical and spiritual imbalance or malaise. Spiritual and moral failings were expected to manifest appropriate visible physical signs; thus leprosy was often (but not always) believed to be the result of sexual misdemeanour or pride, the two, in a sense, being interchangeable.[56] Thus Margery Kempe describes her errant son as looking like a leper, covered in spots and lumps, while Julian's shocking vision of a violent personal devil reveals a tile-red skin with 'blacke spottes ... lyke frakylles', an image redolent of septicaemic plague or decomposition.[57]

The disfigurement of the flesh by disease mirrored, it was believed, a soul spotted by sin, and true relief for both was only available through penitence, confession and absolution.[58] The dramatic depiction of the scourged

[53] *N-town play*, i, plays 25, 36, 37. It is perhaps not coincidental that the play 'The woman taken in adultery' precedes 'The raising of Lazarus'.

[54] Ibid. i. 368, play 37, line 73.

[55] K. Park, 'Medicine and society in medieval Europe, 500–1500', in A. Wear (ed.), *Medicine in society: historical essays*, Cambridge 1992, 59–90.

[56] S. N. Brody, *The disease of the soul: leprosy in medieval literature*, Ithaca, NY 1974, 125–7.

[57] *Book of Margery Kempe*, ii, ch. i, p. 222, lines 11–12; Julian of Norwich, *Showings*, pt II, ch. lxvii, p. 635, lines 5–6.

[58] The canons of the Fourth Lateran Council of 1215 required confession and absolution before medical treatment: D. W. Amundsen, 'Medieval canon law on medical and surgical practice by the clergy', *Bulletin of the History of Medicine* lii (1978), 22–43.

or crucified Christ as a leper, that is as one who in humility took upon himself the most despised of human flesh, derives from St Jerome's commentaries on Isaiah.[59] It is also closely connected with the promotion of penitence inherent in the cult of the Magdalen: 'Woman, in contrysson thou art expert', says Jesus to Mary in the *Digby plays*, just before exorcising her demons.[60] Contrition is also exemplified in the iconography of the fifteenth-century *pietà*, or Virgin of Pity window, at Long Melford church, which also features a tiny donor kneeling at the feet of the leprous, moribund Christ who rests on his mother's lap. This bearded Christ-figure is diminutive, eyes wide open and connecting with the Virgin's tearful gaze, his right hand reaching for her right breast, thumb extended. She clearly now feels the pain that the Church taught was spared her at his birth. His body, speckled by black lesions, ostensibly congealed blood from his scourging, must have been instantly associated in the minds of many contemporary viewers with the visible signs of septicaemic plague, as well as leprosy. Multiple haemorrhages under the skin produced this deadly effect, and both diseases were widely believed to be the result of mankind's moral bankruptcy. As an anonymous poet of the fourteenth century succinctly put it, 'The people stained by sin, quake with grief ... vice rules unchallenged here'. [61] The city parish church of St Giles possessed a venerated *pietá* near the west end of the nave, before the altar of which Thomas (d.1458) and Joan Colchester requested burial, and to the honour of which many parishioners bequeathed lights.[62]

Leprosaria or 'lazar houses' were to be found on the margins of many cities. It was believed that Mary Magdalen's brother was not only Lazarus of Bethany, but also the leper of the same name in Christ's story.[63] He had become conflated with the beggar 'full of sores' in the long parable about the responsibilities of the affluent toward the sick poor, and their punishment should they fail in them. The beggar Lazarus was rewarded with heaven after death, because he had expiated his sins by suffering in life.[64] This connection

---

[59] *PL* xxiv.506–7. This is discussed in C. Rawcliffe, 'Learning to love the leper: aspects of institutional charity in Anglo-Saxon England', in J. Gillingham (ed.), *Anglo-Norman Studies*, XXIII: *Proceedings of the Battle conference, 2000*, Woodbridge 2000, 231–50.

[60] *Digby plays*: 'Mary Magdalene', scene 14, p. 81, line 686.

[61] R. Horrox, *The Black Death*, Manchester 1994, 126. See also pp. 130–4, where the plague is attributed to divine disapproval of tournaments, as well as to indecent clothing: 'women ... wearing clothes that were so tight that they wore a foxtail hanging down inside their skirts at the back, to hide their arses ... (which) must surely bring down misfortune in the future'.

[62] Blomfield, *History of Norfolk*, iv. 239–40. A gild of the Blessed Virgin Mary met before this image, though whether it was of stone, wood, glass or painted plaster is uncertain. One may speculate whether this was the *pietà* before which Margery Kempe wept and was admonished by the priest, upon whom she rounded full of righteous indignation before being taken home and given hospitality by a supportive woman parishioner: *Book of Margery Kempe*, i, ch. lx, p. 148.

[63] Luke xvi.

[64] Luke xvi.25.

reinforced Mary's association with redemption and resurrection on the one hand, and her patronage of lepers on the other. That lepers were afflicted by an inflamed sexual appetite, which the legendary saint had herself overcome with Christ's help, was another link.

Norwich had six extra-mural hospitals for the care of lepers, of which the first, reputedly founded by Bishop Herbert de Losinga (d.1119), one of the earliest in England, was dedicated to St Mary Magdalen, and still stands at Sprowston, on the periphery of the city.[65] Situated a mile to the north of the Magdalen Gates, in the fifteenth century this hospital became a focus of contention between the prior and the city regarding contested liberties and the annual July fair. In 1441 the mayor became involved in a violent fracas during the fair, resulting in the arrest and indictment of a clerk and the eruption of the ever-simmering dispute between the monks and the city. The situation at the hospital had degenerated from that of the 1140s when Lady Legarda, wife of the prominent Norman official William of Apulia, nursed the sick there. As Thomas of Monmouth records, she lived 'hard by' as a beggar, 'for the salvation of her soul', helping the sick to celebrate the opus dei.[66] The search for holy poverty by women of gentle birth clearly had a precursor in Norwich long before Clare of Assisi (c. 1194–1253) and Elizabeth of Hungary (1207–31) pursued their vocations among the sick poor.[67] Appropriately, the hospital possessed an image of the Magdalen to grace its lectern.[68] In this visible synthesis of her image and the authoritative book, penitence and the redemptive power of the Gospels join together, as they did in her legendary role as preacher and teacher.

Lepers and unfortunates with skins disfigured by disease were required by some city corporations in the later Middle Ages to live in such establishments, while yet others chose to; lepers at least had to limit their contact with foodstuffs whilst shopping in the market and in Norwich were required to select produce with a stick rather than their limbs. Their breath was commonly thought to transmit contagion in the same way as miasmas were transmitters of plague. They were, therefore, if without means or immobile through advanced disease, dependent on begging and money derived from the gifts of testators. Between 1370 and 1532 two out of five Norwich testators made small gifts to the five sick-houses at the gates.[69] The city is, perhaps, notable in that its leprosaria and their occupants attracted markedly

---

[65] Unlike the other five city leper hospitals, it did not attract a widespread level of benefaction, largely because of its links with the cathedral priory: Rawcliffe, Hospitals, 46–7.

[66] The life and miracles of St William of Norwich by Thomas of Monmouth, ed. A. Jessop and M. R. James, Cambridge 1896, 31.

[67] According to this tradition, the countess of Lincoln allegedly founded one of Norwich's leper houses, outside St Augustine's Gate: NRO, Misc 1/5.

[68] Archdeaconry of Norwich: inventory of church goods temp. Edward III, ed. A. Watkin (NRS xix/1, 2, 1947–8), ii, p. xix n. 18.

[69] Tanner, Church in Norwich, 133; appendix 12 at p. 223.

more support than its prisons. So acute was their miserable physical condition that they were believed, like Lazarus, to have by-passed any need for *post-mortem* purgation. Their mental and physical suffering was understood to be so great as to merit an immediate transit to heaven. Their spiritual standing with God, therefore, made charitable provision for their sustenance especially meritorious, as were their reciprocal prayers.[70] In what was, metaphorically at least, their penitential isolation, life imitated legend, since the Magdalen had sought the solitary desert experience for thirty years: 'In wych place was growyng no tre / ner herbe, ner watyr, ner no solace / To hyr bodyly counfort in no degre', says Bokenham, demonstrating an almost unsustainable level of body-denial.[71]

The *leprosarium* of St Mary Magdalen, on the Gaywood Causeway outside Lynn, may well have been the place visited by Margery Kempe in order to fulfil her desire, in imitation of Marie d'Oignies, and of St Catherine of Siena, to kiss lepers. She describes in her text the revulsion she formerly felt when, 'in the yerys of wordly prosperite ... ther was no-thyng mor lothful ne mor abhomynabyl to hir ... than to seen er beheldyn a lazer'.[72] It is clear that she connected her earlier affluence with her lack of compassion, indeed contempt for such suffering. She regards it as a matter of grace that she has undergone such a complete conversion, and sets off, having gained her confessor's consent to this activity, on the clear understanding that 'sche shulde kyssen no men'.[73] It is no coincidence that this episode is preceded by her conversation with Christ about the comparative merits of the Magdalen, patron saint of lepers, and herself in his affections. Hospital regulations, however, sometimes stated the necessity for humility and the avoidance of pride, and those of Gaywood (confirmed before 1313) included a specific warning against this spiritual danger. The lepers' conduct should reflect humility, chastity and patience at all times.[74]

A model for the elite?

Resolving to commission Osbern Bokenham to write a verse life of the Magdalen, Lady Isabelle Bourgchier, countess of Eu, sister to Richard, duke of York, and aunt to two future Yorkist kings,[75] at a Twelfth Night party in 1445 made plain that Elizabeth de Vere, countess of Oxford, was not going

---

[70] Rawcliffe, *Medicine for the soul*, 203.

[71] *Hooly wummen*, 168, lines 6158–60.

[72] *Book of Margery Kempe*, i, ch. lxxiv, pp. 176–7, lines 35–7.

[73] Ibid. i, ch. lxxiv, p. 177, line 6.

[74] *The making of King's Lynn: a documentary survey*, ed. D. M. Owen, London 1984, 215, 260. In 1389, when Margery was sixteen, a committee of inquiry into provision for lepers was elected. The twelve included her father, John Brunham.

[75] These were Edward IV and Richard III: *Hooly wummen*, p. xxi.

to gain the literary ascendancy through her commissioning him to write a *Life* of St Elizabeth of Hungary. Such was her insistence that he incorporated the exchange into the prolocutory of the *Life*: 'I haue' quod she 'of pure affeccyon / Ful longe tym had a synguler deuocyoun / To that holy wumman, wych, as I gesse, / Is clepyd of apostyls the aposttllesse.'[76] Lady Bourgchier's promotion of the Magdalen to the front of the heavenly queue, ahead of St Elizabeth, conveyed to Bokenham her own priority, and what she thought should be his too, despite his other commitments. It was a command that Bokenham felt he could not refuse. Singular devotion might command singular grace, as Margery Kempe continually reminds us in her text, as well for the scribe as for the devotee.[77] The rehabilitation of 'fallen' female flesh to an elevated spiritual status above and beyond the male Apostles resonated well with what was to become a Yorkist preoccupation with claims of succession through the female line.[78] The cult of St Anne too may also have owed some of its popularity in England to its appeal to a dynasty which claimed the throne through the female line. That the Magdalen should rise above St Elizabeth in this metaphorical battle for precedence between two noblewomen may also say something about Bokenham's own elevation of contemplative and penitential piety (of an implied intellectual elite) above the more lowly (and feminine) practical execution of the comfortable works, though the Magdalen, too, is associated with such deeds.

Bokenham's *Life* confirms the Magdalen's status and affinity to Christ as described in the Gospels, but also portrays her during her legendary exile in Marseilles as a powerful preacher and evangelist, the undoubted leader of her Christian expatriate community.[79] This more political aspect of the saint's legend might, arguably, hold a more potent appeal for women such as Lady Bourgchier than the tale of the penitent whore, royal though she might have been. The unusual Magdalen screen panel at the parish church of Bramfield St Andrew in Suffolk shows such a regal and commanding young woman, almost a Florentine Medici in her apparel and ornate head-dress, and her alluring heavily-hooded but down-cast eyes (*see* plate 15).[80]

There was an acknowledged cult of the 'good rood' at Bramfield, the material remains of which are still visible on the north nave wall (*see* plate 16).[81] The scrolls displayed by barely visible angels once bore the words 'qui

---

[76] Ibid. 139, lines 5065–8.
[77] *Book of Margery Kempe*, i, ch. xxii, pp. 50–1, lines 32–3; i, ch. lxxxvi, pp. 213–14.
[78] Carol Hilles argues more strongly than Delany for the existence of a Yorkist agenda in Bokenham's text: 'Gender and politics in Osbern Bokenham's Legendary', in W. Scase, R. Copeland and D. Lawton (eds), *New medieval literatures*, iv, Oxford 2001, 189–212, esp. pp. 196–7.
[79] *Hooly wummen*, 158, lines 5780–93.
[80] She has a lesser twin on the rood-screen at Sotherton church, Suffolk.
[81] NCC, reg. Spyltymber, fo. 7 (Clerke), 1507. Edmund Clerke left to 'the emending of the good Rode and his aungells in Bramfield church 10s'. See also Middleton-Stewart, *Inward purity*, 133, 231–2.

tollis peccata mundi' and 'misere nobis'. Beneath the cross bar, a further two angels proclaim 'gratias agimus tibi propter magnam gloriam tuam'. The cross is also central to the design of the magnificently vibrant carving of the wooden vault of the rood-screen, where it is repeated throughout the paint-retaining tracery on the nave side. The Magdalen on this screen thus remains at the foot of the cross in perpetuity, in the company of the tellers of her story in the Gospels, Mark, Matthew, Luke and John. The parish church must have been, in effect, a *tableau* of the passion, in which the authoritative and enigmatic figure of Mary Magdalen was central. A similar cultic devotion to the holy rood is glimpsed at the parish church of St Giles-on-the-hill, Norwich, which, Blomefield records, possessed a venerated and 'famous rood called the Brown rood', though whether to denote its colour or the name of its donor is unknown: in the south aisle, near the door, it attracted bequests and proximal burial.[82]

Bokenham's Magdalen, an icon of female erudition and evangelism, was the exponent of the Word made flesh, marked in her legend by her miraculous raising from the dead of the princess of Marseilles.[83] Identifying the Magdalen as a preacher was a daring departure by Bokenham and ran counter to the prohibition of mother Church.[84] More than this, Bokenham's *vita* does not focus upon the penitent prostitute, but rather records the 'adventures of the thirteenth apostle'.[85] Mary's apostolic 'adventures' foreground a story of fertility and the almost supernatural powers of the female body.[86] This apparent subversion of gender roles was partly redressed by the Magdalen referring her convert, Prince Maxymyn, to St Peter in Rome for further instruction in the faith.[87] A nod in this direction is also apparent in the books of Julian of Norwich and Margery Kempe, both very keen not to be officially condemned as preaching, teaching women, though patently their spiritual autobiographies demonstrate elements of both priestly activities. Nor did either wish to be denounced as a Lollard.[88] Both knew the potentially fatal outcome of such allegations.[89]

---

[82] Blomefield, *History of Norfolk*, iv. 239.

[83] *Hooly wummen*, 166, lines 6095–101.

[84] Delaney, *Impolitic bodies*, 90.

[85] Hilles, 'Gender and politics', 196–7.

[86] The association of fertility with piety in the *vita* highlights Isabelle Bourgchier's own situation. Her fecundity and that of her prolific family is reinforced by a genealogy of her own line and that of York at the conclusion of the work.

[87] *Hooly wummen*, 164, lines 6018–28.

[88] Julian of Norwich, *Showings*, pt II, ch. xxxiv, p. 431, lines 15–20; *Book of Margery Kempe*, i, ch. lii, p. 126, lines 18–20.

[89] *Book of Margery Kempe*, i, chs liv–lv, pp. 131–6. William Sawtree, sometime priest of Lynn, was burned at Smithfield in March 1401: ibid. introduction at p. xlix. See also L. Staley, *Margery Kempe's dissenting fictions*, Philadelphia 1994, 147.

Personal commemoration and perceptions of the after-life

A near-contemporary and namesake of Lady Bourgchier, Isabella, countess of Warwick, who died in 1439, fostered a singular devotion to Mary Magdalen. She chose her as the patron of her chapel in Tewkesbury Abbey, and, more spectacularly, elected to emulate her in the memorial effigy on her tomb, as her will records: 'And my Image to be made all naked, and no thyng on my hede but myn here cast bakwardys ... and at my hede Mary Mawdelen leyng my handes a-cross.'[90] The countess directed that her celestial advocate be portrayed for posterity in the act of crossing her arms in the sign of the passion, a dramatic demonstration of eternal penitence and supplication. Like Margery Kempe, the countess displayed a humility so extreme as to invert it into spiritual pride of some magnitude. But was the countess demonstrating something other than personal piety in this planned memorial of her naked body? Inescapably, female flesh is being made a focus in a startling and highly ambiguous way, only possible through the cult of the equally ambiguous and iconic Magdalen. The countess chose to employ the sexual economy of her legend to account and record, at the least, her own commitment to penitential piety. By so doing, she effectively engaged the Magdalen to act as an intercessor and a guarantor of her own claim to salvation. It is probable, too, that she intended to convey a much more layered message to do with lineage, status and the centrality of the aristocratic female line.[91]

In a more subtle way, another fifteenth-century noblewoman, the formidable Alice Chaucer (d.1475), also commissioned the advocacy and image of the Magdalen. Alice, by her third marriage countess and ultimately duchess of Suffolk, is commemorated by an extraordinary and innovative *transi* tomb at Ewelme church, on her estates in Oxfordshire.[92] This consists of an effigy of her wasted naked corpse in its shroud, the breasts exposed, their flesh deeply striated, suggesting either age or scars from self-mortification, beneath another of her arrayed in the splendour of her ducal coronet and Order of the

---

[90] *The fifty earliest English wills in the court of probate, London*, ed. F. J. Furnivall, London 1882, 116–17. The countess also left her tablet with an image of the Virgin to the church of Walsingham, together with her gown of 'alyz cloth of gold' with wide sleeves, and a silver tabernacle 'like to that of Our Lady of Caversham'. See also Blomefield, *History of Norfolk*, iv. 279.

[91] Hilles, 'Gender and politics', 201. Hilles stresses Bokenham's evocation of Yorkist female fecundity as being exceptional enough to overcome the customary rules of primogeniture.

[92] Alice and her third husband William, earl of Suffolk, had a fraught relationship with the city of Norwich. In 1442 the earl's arbitration between the city and the priory found for the priory. The citizens were ordered to destroy their new mills: Tanner, *Church in Norwich*, 147–8. All three of Alice's husbands died violently, a sign of the volatility of the times.

Garter.[93] Such a display of penitential piety, with its implicit renunciation of the glittering prizes of worldly wealth and status is not without precedent, but is it convincing?[94] It is particularly interesting, however, because the saints that she chose to have painted above the lower, emaciated figure are not easily visible, even to a recumbent viewer.[95] The corpse-image and paintings are obscured by the narrow open-work arches surrounding them, and their proximity to the ground, which emphasise the solitude of death, and its 'levelling' of all status. So hidden are these saints that they have remained intact and untouched. Images of the Annunciation, the Virgin and Gabriel, an icon of incarnational and contemplative piety, face the half-open eyes of the cadaver image of Alice, her head and neck arched towards them, her mouth open in the rictus of death.[96] The painted figures of St Mary Magdalen and St John the Baptist are at her feet, as in life they were each, in their turn, once at Christ's.[97] Mary, companion and supporter at his passion, now accompanies the duchess in death, coupled with the assurance of the first sacrament, baptism, thus promising redemption and eternal life.[98] At some level Alice is identifying herself with the crucified Christ as well as the holy poor.[99] On the other hand the grandeur of the upper section of the tomb, its fine carving bedecked with heraldry proclaiming Alice's noblest connections, may seem to contradict aspirations to spiritual poverty. The holy name, such a feature of her chantry, is stencilled repeatedly on every wall including the arch which forms the canopy of her parents' tomb, providing a written representation of the vocal adoration of the many angels in the roof, a facsimile of heaven,[100] while the repeated use of heraldic devices around the 'public'

[93]   J. A. A. Goodall, *God's house at Ewelme: life, devotion and architecture in a fifteenth-century almshouse*, Aldershot 2001, 183. This is a unique survival in England of a female cadaver effigy. Goodall has captured the almost inaccessible in his photographs.

[94]   It may be that the duchess of Warwick was similarly commissioning a cadaver figure, signifying penitence and humility, 'coloured' by her devotion to the Magdalen.

[95]   C. M. Meale, 'Reading women's culture in fifteenth-century England: the case of Alice Chaucer', in P. Boitani and A. Torti (eds), *Mediaevalitas: reading the Middle Ages*, Cambridge 1996, 81–101 at p. 100. See also Goodall, *God's house*, 187–9.

[96]   It is notable that the hair of the cadaver effigy is 'cast backwardys', like Isabella of Warwick's instruction for her own image, and loose save for a single ribbon or string around its head. Mary Magdalen's principal attribute, apart from her pot, was of course her unbound or abundant hair.

[97]   John i.26–7.

[98]   Goodall, *God's house*, 174–91.

[99]   A carved figure of the Magdalen (paired with St Katherine) is also featured as an arch stop on the wall above the tomb of Maud and Thomas Chaucer, which, surrounded by the Holy Name, offered an icon of infallible protection to Alice and her intercessors, as well as being her mother's name-saint: ibid. 172, 236–7. The church building itself is central to a complex of Alice's foundations, the choice of which demonstrates her aspiration toward the fulfilment of the spiritual, as well as the corporal works of mercy.

[100]   It is interesting that the first recorded gild dedicated to the Name of Jesus was at Upper Sheringham All Saints, Norfolk, which lies between the shrines of Walsingham and Bromholme: personal communication with Christopher Harper-Bill.

figure on her tomb, and indeed, that of her parents, fulfils a similar function of temporal worship and acclamation. The arms, supported (and thus
endorsed) by angels, feathered or robed, provide a 'crowd of witnesses' to her
earthly lineage and status, a crowd she shortly intended to join in heaven.[101]

Alice's documented inclination, when needed, to assume a costume of
disguise shows her grasp of the power of the image as well as the utility of
anonymity. In 1448, while still countess of Suffolk, Alice was apprehended
by a ditcher, a city employee, in Lakenham Wood, in the Norwich suburbs,
'disguysed like an huswyfe of the cuntre'. She was, significantly, accompanied by three local men, including the rapacious Thomas Tuddenham, who
claimed to be out at night 'to tak the ayr'.[102] Tuddenham and his friend, the
infamous John Heydon, both loathed and feared by the city rulers for their
corruption, violence and over-bearing infringement of the city's liberties,
were not likely companions for a woman bent entirely on her own spiritual
improvement. Although its true purpose cannot be discovered, this incident
in the woods, which ended in a fight between the ditcher and Tuddenham,
was given as the reason for the Suffolks' abiding animosity toward the city
government and their own political alliance with the 'opposition', including
the prior of Holy Trinity.[103] The Pastons, among others, would have judged
that Alice and her family had need of a good deal of intercession in order
to expunge their recurring transgressions. Fourteen years later, in 1462,
Margaret Paston, writing to her husband, John I, remarked on the local
political climate and its antagonism toward the now dowager duchess, and
her son, the new duke: 'They loue not in no wyse the Dwke of Sowthfolk nor
hys modyr … they sey that all the tretourys and extorsyonerys of thys contré
be meyntynyd by them and by sych as they get to them wyth her goodys.'[104]

A retrospective view of Alice Chaucer defies simple definition; she is
patently a motivated and complex woman. A certain element of coercion in
her dealings with her social inferiors would not have been thought particularly strange in one of her standing, nor would it preclude charitable or pious
investment; indeed, it might make it an imperative. Not only was she a
benefactor of the divinity school at Oxford between 1454 and 1461, she was
also a patron of John Lydgate, whom she commissioned to write a work on
the virtues of the mass. One of her last pious acts, in 1473, was the foundation of a gild dedicated to 'The Body of Our Lord Jesus Christ' at the parish
church of Leighton Buzzard, in Bedfordshire (an acquisition from her early

---

101 Goodall, God's house, 193–7.
102 RCN i. 344–5. The ditcher was imprisoned as a result. See also Blomefield, History
of Norfolk, iii. 153–5.
103 Alice and William had a manor at Costessey, in the suburbs. Blomefield records that
'he (Suffolk) kept much at Cossey, to the grief of the city': History of Norfolk, iii. 154.
104 Paston letters, i. 279, letter 168 (1462). Three years later (1465) Margaret was refusing
to plead her complaints to 'mine old lady', but would petition the king if necessary: ibid.
i. 310, letter 188.

marriage to John Phelip).[105] A dedication more redolent of incarnational piety would be hard to find, incorporating as it does a belief in the salvific nature of Christ's wounds and the eucharist. The extensive accommodation offered by the impressive surviving almshouses and the adjacent school, both founded by Alice and attached to Ewelme church, and close by her first and final home, signify substantial investment in the efficacy of intercessory prayer. Perhaps by then Alice was thinking increasingly of the reckoning to come, as the thematic iconography of her tomb may also indicate.

It is evident from the attachment of noblewomen (especially the tenacious such as Alice Chaucer), as well as wives of merchants and artisans to the cult of the Magdalen, that other issues, in addition to penitence and salvation, were involved in devotion to this Mary. The stature of the Magdalen as a royal personage, and, even more, as *apostola apostolorum*, made her a deeply desirable and influential patron saint among the elite, and therefore a fashionable one among the upwardly mobile and ambitious, whether that ambition was spiritual or temporal. The legendary Magdalen had, after all, performed a key role in redirecting the lives of the prince and princess of Marseilles.

It is apparent, too, that Norwich and its citizens were touched by her multiplex iconography, as the furnishing of its parish churches and bequests to them show. In smaller but integral ways Norwich women's commitment to the comfortable works, as seen through the prism of Magdalen-influenced piety, is apparent in their bequests to the spiritual poor and the marginalised: the servants of friends, including solitaries; some, like friends of alderman's widow Katherine Brasyer (d. 1457), working as nursing sisters in Norwich hospitals.[106] Katherine carefully requested that each leper at the city gates be given 3*d.* but, unlike many, also remembered those lepers who had elected to be at the Magdalen hospital in Sprowston, a mile outside. A generation older, another alderman's widow, Agnes Segryme (d. 1474), did likewise, leaving 20*d.* to the 'leprese of Mawdelyn be Norwych'.[107] At another level of expression, the Magdalen's iconic status as contemplative, preacher and teacher and, as Petrarch called her, 'sweet friend of God', had authorised other women, from St Catherine of Siena (d. 1380) to Julian of Norwich and Margery Kemp, to speak with exceptional spiritual authority, to explain, admonish and correct.[108]

---

[105] Goodall, *God's house*, 12.

[106] NCC, Brosyard, fos 58–9 (Katherine Brasier), 1457. Katherine left gifts for all the sisters at St Paul's hospital, but named Alice Cofeld (6*s.* 8*d.*), Joan Baron (20*d.*) and Cecily Rante (12*d.*). Her friend Dame Margaret Purdans, to whom she left 6*s.* 8*d.*, also left a legacy to Dame Alice Sowe (6*s.* 8*d.*), a sister at St Paul's.

[107] NCC, reg. Gelour, fos 81–2 (Segryme), 1474/6.

[108] *The life of solitude by Francis Petrarch*, ed. and trans. J. Zeitlin, Urbana 1924. 'The fifth tractate' (ch. i, 253–4) also refers to the Magdalen as 'the sweet hostess of Christ', a title that describes the epitome of a practitioner of the seven comfortable works.

Eve's exiled daughters were returning to Eden, some, like Katherine Brasyer and Agnes Segryme, in penitent humility and with charity, but others, like Alice Chaucer, determined to exact their temporal and spiritual due. Her contemporary, Margaret Purdans, for many years a single parent, left to the nuns of Thetford 'an English book of St Brigette', then a very widely known book of revelations which emphasised a mother's responsibility for her children's spiritual health and salvation. It could be argued that this female step up the ladder to uphold the ultimate duty of care was a direct result of the piety associated with the aspirational cult of the Magdalen.

4

St Bridget of Sweden

Motherhood and the imperative of salvation

And þan cried the feende, 'Alas! I can nowþir finde þe sinnes [no] haue minde of þe time þat he sinned in'. Þan saide the aungell, '… þe praiers of his modir, and hir teris, and hir grete morninges for Þis sinne, for þai gat him contricion of his sinne, and grace to shriue him of þame: and þerfore þai are oute of þi mind'.[1]

In St Bridget's vision, Christ makes a clear and telling analogy between the birth process that produces the infant and the good soul, 'God's wife', that brings forth good works that please him. The implication is that, like birth, a good spiritual outcome is not without cost or pain, especially as Bridget continues this theme with a metaphor of 'swete froyte (fruit) and bittir'. Bridget's text is full of imagery redolent of birth and the trials of family life and it is easy to see why it became so central to the instruction and inspiration of late medieval women. Having examined local devotion to two legendary saints – St Anne and St Margaret – and a biblical saint – St Mary Magdalen – the popularity of the revelations of, to them, a recently living saint, may point to more pragmatic female concerns. In particular it may highlight women's responsibility for the spiritual education, indeed, salvation of their families, as promoted by St Bridget (albeit transmitted by her male confessors, scribes and translators), and on female involvement in charitable deeds and good works as outlined in her book: in effect, a promotion of the *devotio moderna* as practised by women.

Bridget (Birgitta Birgersotter) was born into the Swedish nobility, to a family of politicians and churchmen. At the age of forty, after a thirty-year marriage and eight children, she was widowed. Believing that she had been called to be a 'spousa Christi', a bride of Christ, she maintained her widowhood as a privileged spiritual status that authorised her subsequent activities.[2]

Norwich had a unique connection with St Bridget because of a talented 'local boy made good', Adam, later Cardinal, Easton (b.c.1330), who was probably schooled at St Leonard's priory, Mousehold, became a monk at Norwich's Benedictine cathedral priory, where he was a contemporary of

---

[1] *Liber celestis*, 478, lines 16–21.
[2] For the historical background of Bridget's Swedish family and times see Claire L. Sahlin, *Birgitta of Sweden and the voice of prophecy*, Woodbridge 2001, 13–33.

Thomas Brinton (in the 1390s bishop of Rochester), and, like him, as a promising student, sent to Oxford to study. Easton became a renowned preacher and defender of orthodoxy. During a disrupted, dramatic and highly traumatic career in Rome, probably between 1385 and 1389, he wrote his *Defensorium Sanctae Birgittae* to gainsay dissenting voices criticising Bridget's speedy canonisation in 1391, though the attacks against her authenticity had begun even in her lifetime.[3] He died, restored to his office of cardinal, bequeathing 288 books to his monastery in Norwich. This tremendous boost to the priory library was loaded into six barrels and duly arrived in 1407.[4] Whether this gift contained Brigettine material is not known, but in view of Easton's preoccupations in his last active years it would be remarkable if his library was denuded of any trace of the saint's revelations.

The Benedictine Adam Easton and the Carmelite Alan of Lynn, it could be argued, embody in their divergent lives and works many possibilities for the dissemination of Bridget's teaching in Norfolk, but perhaps the Carmelite mediation of her work is now easier to distinguish.[5] Even today a fifteenth-century screen panel representing Bridget survives at Horsham St Faith, an ancient priory church on the northern periphery of Norwich, which, uniquely for a Norfolk screen panel, depicts St Bridget receiving a vision of the godhead, seated with a book, perhaps her book.[6] The popularity with the English of the prayers called the 'Oes of St Bridget' is indubitable, the more so after William Caxton had translated and printed them in the vernacular (1490s) and thus made available to a new and less elite market books of hours suitably illuminated with detailed block-prints of the eponymous saint.[7] But the spoken transmission of an English version of Bridget's work had been accomplished considerably earlier, as Margery Kempe's text shows.[8]

In the medieval perception of the heavenly hierarchy and what might be termed highly desirable spiritual sponsorship the Blessed Virgin Mary was considered the *nonpareil*, the highest and ultimate level of mediation with the godhead, especially in matters pertaining to family difficulty or dysfunc-

---

[3] There is no evidence that they ever met, although he did meet her daughter, St Catherine of Vadstena (d.1381): J. Hogg, 'Adam Easton's *Defensorium Santae Birgittae*', in M. Glasscoe (ed.), *The medieval mystical tradition: England, Ireland and Wales*, Cambridge 1999, 213–40 at p. 231.

[4] Tanner, *Church in Norwich*, 35.

[5] N. K. Yoshikawa, *Margery Kempe's meditations: the context of medieval devotional literature, liturgy and iconography*, Cardiff 2007, 64–5, 118–19. Margery consulted William Southfield, Carmelite and visionary of Norwich, before visiting Julian.

[6] Williamson's rood-screen survey, undertaken fifty years ago, mistakenly calls her queen of Sweden: 'Saints on Norfolk rood-screens', 310. This priory was an early eleventh-century foundation, a dependant of Conques, in Normandy.

[7] E. Duffy, *Marking the hours: English people and their prayers, 1240–1570*, New Haven–London 2006, 135–6. See also Jennifer Summit, *Lost property: the woman writer and English literary history, 1380–1589*, Chicago 2000, 115–22.

[8] *Book of Margery Kempe*, i, chs xxviii, xxxix.

tion. She played a primary role in the revelations and meditations of both St Bridget and Margery Kempe, if with very different emphases, but authorising and affirming each of them. It is clear in Margery's text that she identified strongly with St Bridget's maternal anxiety concerning her own son's physical and spiritual wellbeing; in particular Margery feared his vulnerability to sexual activity unsanctioned by marriage.[9] She had long been familiar with Bridget's revelations and book through the mediation of the priest who read to her for seven years. In Margery's struggle to lead a holy life Bridget's book provided a clear exemplar and demonstrated a then unrivalled model of what a woman could achieve personally, or even internationally, first by a direct relationship with God, and second by the validation and authority obtained by recording such unmediated spiritual experiences. Bridget's vocation to prophecy and its intended goal of political and spiritual renaissance was, in her devotee Margery, confined to a more immediate and pragmatic prospect of accomplishing the repentance and salvation of those, whether family, fellow-pilgrims or bishops, who crossed her peripatetic path as she repeatedly dug herself into the moral high ground. That said, she also aspired in her meditations to 'save the world', by her intercession with and through Christ.[10] Ultimately, as a woman of high spiritual aspiration, not to say ambition, Margery had the great satisfaction of knowing that she had, at least, succeeded in her maternal religious duty toward her own errant son, being the agent and catalyst of his conversion and state of grace in time for his subsequent death.[11]

St Bridget had markedly failed to reach this goal with her own consistently unregenerate son, Karl. In the quotation from her *Liber celestis* is glimpsed some of the tension and anxiety experienced by Bridget over Karl's perceived spiritual shortcomings, about which she anxiously meditated throughout his life and after his death. In one of over seven hundred revelations an angel reveals to 'the fiend' (and to Bridget) that her prayers, tears and grief have brought Karl to contrition, thus wiping his slate (and the devil's memory) clean of his sin and saving him from hell. In a subsequent revelation of the Virgin, Bridget is consoled to know that Mary acted as Karl's spiritual 'midwife' in death, granting him her aid physically in his last throes and her spiritual protection thereafter so that the 'feendes hade no pouer Þan to touché his saule'.[12] This envisioning of Karl's death as a rebirth into salvation, with the Virgin acting as midwife to his safe 'delivery' thereto, fulfils Bridget's life-long intercession, albeit posthumously for her dissolute child, and achieves what his mother's years of earthly exhortations

---

9   Ibid. ii, ch. i.
10 Ibid. ii, chs i, ii.
11 Margery says that her son's skin lesions made him look leprous, hinting at her concern for his moral welfare. Despite his sickness she refused to visit him until he had repented, confessed and had been absolved.
12 *Liber celestis*, 477, lines 13–19.

could not. Paradoxically, such interpretation of this vision confirmed his mother's responsibility for his redemption rather than obviated it. Doubtless there were to be many mothers, apart from Mrs Kempe, in and around late medieval Norwich who could empathise to some extent with this situation, Margaret Paston (d.c. 1484) among them.

In 1471 the Paston letters indicate the deteriorating relationship between Margaret Paston and her sons, John III and his younger brother, Edmund, blamed by both men on the malign and over-mighty influence on their mother of James Gloys, a priest in her employ.[13] Significantly, and not for the first time, matters had come to a head for Margaret Paston over issues of reckless sexual misconduct combined with what she doubtless saw as loss of family reputation and of public virtue in the management of estate workers, for whom the family bore the responsibility of good lordship. On this occasion Margaret had summarily dismissed the alleged instigator, Gregory, Edmund's manservant, despite the latter's evident chagrin and letters of vehement protest to his mother. Margaret had heard that Gregory had admitted a prostitute to her manor of Mautby to service himself and (at the least, one imagines) two working ploughmen, who, by chance, saw what Gregory was about in the stables and asked to join in. This was a year of recurring pestilence in Norfolk with consequent labour shortages, but, notwithstanding that good servants were becoming scarce, Margaret Paston's priority was the moral welfare and probity of her household, especially of the young Edmund. Retaining Gregory in her family's service was no more an option for her than had been the retention of her valued steward, Richard Calle, following his alleged clandestine marriage to her young daughter, Margery, two years before.[14] St Bridget and Margery Kempe would have loudly applauded her stand, though the direct influence of the Brigettine text would be hard to prove:

> 'And þerefore, right as þe woman berys þe child, so a gude saule, þat is Godes wife, brynges furth gude werkes þat are plesynge to Gode.'[15]

Despite her life-long shrewd management of household and estates, Margaret Paston, now a widow of some years standing, demonstrated in her will a Brigettine commitment to charitable deeds and good books.[16] She gave 3s. 4d. to each of three solitaries, including two women, and she left 20s. to each order of friars in Norwich and Great Yarmouth. She particularly asked

---

[13] This incident is explored in the wider context in Helen Castor, *Blood and roses: the Paston family in the fifteenth century*, London 2004, 241–2. See also *Paston letters*, 395.

[14] In Margery Paston's case, she bore the brunt of the family's ire, and was temporarily lodged in the household of former mayor, Roger Best, pending the bishop's judgement, 'for', as her mother said, 'she shall not be suffered there to play the brothel': *Paston letters*, 203.

[15] *Liber celestis*, 311, lines 14–16.

[16] NCC, Reg. Caston (Margaret Paston), 1481/4.

for a 'dirige' and a mass for her soul to be sung at the hospital of St Giles, for which she left 20s., but was less generous to its inhabitants, the sisters and their charges, who each received 2d. However, she did fulfil her responsibilities in charitable giving in parishes where the family held lands or interests, leaving chasubles and albs to six churches, thus enriching the provision of the sacraments, gifts to three other churches and monetary gifts to poor households in seven parishes. These were mainly for her own tenants, and ranged from 4d. to 12d., the last for her natal family parish of Mautby, where she was buried with some ceremony. Margaret asked that twelve 'pore meen' from among her tenants, 'or other if they suffice not', be attired in white at her expense, to attend her bier with torches, these lights to be retained and lit for her commemoration on her year day, until used up. While bequeathing no personal books, at least not in her will, she requested that a 'compleet legende' (service book) and an antiphoner be purveyed by her executors, to remain in Mautby church for the use of its parishioners.[17] She thus commissioned several spiritual works of mercy in the provision of the tools to teach and perform the liturgy and to pray, in addition to her corporal works.

More than fifty years earlier, Margery Kempe's access to Bridget's text attests how very far by the first two decades of the fifteenth century a written and vernacular form of Bridget's revelations had permeated the cultural fabric of East Anglian women seeking a spiritual context for their lives. It is apparent, too, that the skill of reading or the possession of the text itself was not essential for this inculturation to take place. How extensively the saint's book had penetrated the reading of men, other than professed religious, is harder to say, titles of books given in wills being often vague or colloquial when mentioned at all. The elite status of the single English Brigettine monastic foundation, at Syon, Isleworth, in Middlesex, founded in 1415 by Henry V, may indicate more of the pious aspirations of the English well-born and literate governing classes than those of Margery's standing, though, as she tells us at the end of her book, she went there on pilgrimage for the plenary indulgence offered at Lammas tide.[18]

The foundation naturally kept various redactions of Bridget's text, but versions of it were in wide circulation forty years after her death, and this increased rapidly with the advent of printed texts.[19] Indeed, Margery's

---

[17] There were books in the Paston household, as testified by the inventory of John II: Rosenthal, *Telling tales*, 195, n. 130.
[18] *Book of Margery Kempe*, ii, ch. x, pp. 245–6. It may be that Margery could read at this stage of her life: R. Krug, *Reading families: women's literate practice in late medieval England*, Ithaca, NY 2002, 153–206.
[19] Cecily, duchess of York (d.1495), a widow for thirty-five years, had books read to her household, and left some to her granddaughters: to Brigitte, a daughter of Edward IV and Elizabeth Woodvylle, she left her *Legenda aurea*, a *Life* of St Catherine of Siena and her book of Mechtild of Hackeborn (originally, perhaps, her son Richard's copy). To Brigitte's cousin, Anne de la Pole, who was prioress of Syon Abbey, she gave a volume containing writings of Bonaventure and Hilton and, appropriately, a volume of St Bridget's revela-

Carmelite confessor and supporter, Alan of Lynn, was known to have collated indexes of Bridget's revelations and prophecies, so she may have become especially receptive to Bridget's *vita* as mediated by him.[20] And if she was, other women may be assumed to have been similarly open to such cultural exposure. Margaret Purdans was a contemporary of Margaret Paston and possessed 'a book called in English St Brigette', which she bequeathed to the nuns of Thetford, perhaps because her daughter, Alice Yaxley, had pre-deceased her in May 1474. [21] Dame Margaret (her will calls her 'domina' and her husband was not a knight) left another book, *Le doctrine of the herte*, to Alice's sister-in-law, Margaret Yaxley, who was a nun at Bruisyard Abbey, a foundation of Poor Clares in Suffolk.[22] In view of her ownership of books, and evidence of exchange, it might be assumed that Dame Margaret, unlike the young Margery Kempe, could at least read vernacular English.[23]

The case for widowhood: 'a gude soule that is Godes wife'

In a period when many women of the status and pious inclination of Margaret Purdans were choosing the vocation of a chaste vowess in widowhood, rather than the customary remarriage favoured and negotiated by their male relatives and other interested parties, Bridget's book gave validation to their decision. This was the path that the saint had chosen in widowhood, although she acknowledged the validity of other ways. The public role of vowess, as opposed to the life of other pious lay women, was rooted in its requirement for sexual abstinence and the single life, after the model promoted for widows by, for example, St Jerome. The vow was made official by a ceremony of licensing by a bishop, and the bestowal of a designated robe and a ring. But in St Bridget's view 'chastity' came in different guises at different costs: 'For som woman kepys chastite (bot thai loue it noyt), for thai haue no gret stirrynge', and advised yet others to 'coueyt noyt to hye uertu that is abouen thy myght' because that was 'pryde and presumpesion'.[24] Clearly, chastity for the wrong reasons carried no special spiritual merit, and Bridget, it seems, believed in achievable goals. For the saint, as for Julian of Norwich, ultimately, it was 'the will to Christ' that counted, rather than

---

tions. This and other book-reading women are discussed in F. Riddy, '"Women talking about the things of God": a late medieval sub-culture', in C. M. Meale (ed.), *Women and literature in Britain, 1150–1500*, Cambridge 1996, 104–27.

[20] D. Watt, *Secretaries of God: women prophets in late medieval and early modern England*, Woodbridge 2001, 33.

[21] NCC, reg. Caston, fos 163–5 (Margaret Purdans), 1481.

[22] Gilchrist and Oliva, *Religious women*, 23, 33.

[23] Riddy argues that the literary culture of nuns and pious gentlewomen at this period were indistinguishable: 'Women talking', 110.

[24] *Liber celestis*, 277, lines 20–1, 9–10.

marital status: 'Þarefore þi doghtir, wheþir scho schall be wife or maiden still, sho pleses me yf hir will and desir be to me', Christ tells her.[25]

Clearly, too, to take a more pragmatic view of some vocations, the financial and legal autonomy achieved by becoming a vowess in widowhood held many attractions for the comfortably-off woman who did not see any benefit in handing over her hard-won worldly goods, business interests and personal independence to the control of yet another husband. Moreover, the testamentary provision made by some men was dependent upon the widow remaining single, and became null and void if she remarried. Such a condition could be interpreted as retaining control from beyond the grave, or, alternatively, as safeguarding a widow's long-term material interests as a single woman, whether or not as a vowess. A vowed chastity, which excluded vows to poverty and obedience, piously embraced or pragmatically elected (and the wish for autonomy does not necessarily exclude a personal piety), at least gave a widow choices.[26] Margery Kempe's undoubted spiritual aspiration to this chaste state when still married, while not without exceptional precedents, carried a more complex and problematic interpretation of the mixed life of contemplative prayer and charitable works than perhaps was applicable to her similarly vowed but widowed peers.

Margaret Purdans is an interesting woman in this context as something is known of her material and spiritual circumstances. Her husband, Richard, who would appear to have been many years her senior, for he predeceased her by almost fifty years, was in the front rank of the ruling elite in Norwich by 1403, possibly before she was born.[27] When she was a young wife his political life was fraught with tensions and intrigue caused predominantly by the ex-mayor, the combative Thomas Wetherby, and his faction, who tried to manipulate the election of his successor to exclude Purdans, the popular choice. None the less Richard ultimately became mayor, making Margaret a woman with precedence in the city while still relatively young. She and Richard had a long affiliation to St Giles's church: she left it six bequests, despite having property in the parish of St Peter Mancroft. Both chose burial there and their memorial brass can now be seen in the nave central aisle, facing east, in company with their contemporaries, Robert (d.1432) and Cristiana Baxter (*see* plate 17).[28] Moreover, in 1428 the man who became Dame Margaret's mentor, Richard Fernys, priest and hermit, inhabited a hermitage in the churchyard.

---

[25] Ibid. 316, lines 22–4. Bridget's daughter, Catherine, did marry but apparently remained a vowed virgin.

[26] See M. C. Erler, 'Three fifteenth-century vowesses', in Barron and Sutton, *Medieval London widows*, 165–83.

[27] Blomefield shows that in 1403 Richard Purdans was appointed one of the final four bailiffs of the city: *History of Norfolk*, iii. 123.

[28] Robert Baxter left £40 to the hermit Richard Fernys to go on pilgrimage for him both to Rome and Jerusalem. He was instructed to circle Rome fifteen times: NCC, reg. Surflete, fo. 86 (Baxter), 1429.

It would appear that Dame Margaret was a widow and a vowess for most of her adult life, and her extensive and long-pondered will provides insights into the life of women in her position, and in to her piety and that of her network of like-minded friends, as well as into her book collection. It reflects many years of reciprocated friendship and prayerful supports, including the mutual exchange of books as also between lay and professed or reclusive woman. How these relationships, as well as the circulating literature, may have been catalysts for the evolving role of the anchoress, for example, or how well-travelled was Margaret's English book of St Bridget in her lifetime is a matter for conjecture. Nor can there be any certainty about the length of her ownership, but manuscripts had been in circulation for over sixty years when Dame Margaret died.

Like St Bridget, Margaret Purdans numbered several distinguished priests and academics among her friends and supporters, apart from Fernys. In her will these friendships were marked by special gifts in addition to bequests of money. Thomas Carman, vicar of Yaxley, was given an English psalter, while John Steyke, bibliophile rector of St Laurence in Norwich (1480–4), received a reliquary engraved with the passion.[29] The Barly brothers, William (a lawyer) and John (rector of St Michael Coslany, Norwich), both Fellows of Gonville Hall, Cambridge, were remembered by a gift of 6s. 8d. apiece, though this was later crossed out. Perhaps more significantly, Margaret left to their probable sister, Alice Barly, 'a book called Hilton'.[30] Six professed women are named in her will as well as at least five anchoresses, including those of Lynn, whose number, names and status are unknown.[31] One of her legatees was Joan, the recluse of Bishopsgate in the city of London; plainly, Margaret Purdans's concerns and contacts were not merely parochial, though she did leave 12d. to each household in her home parish of St Giles. The female religious, lay and professed, are left sums ranging from 3s. 4d. to 20s., this last for Julian Lampet, the Carrow anchorite, and the same to each of her two servants, a rare equity.[32] Margaret also gave gifts to eight nunneries, including the sisters and brothers of Syon (10s.), the double Brigettine house, and also to the prestigious Charterhouse at Sheen (10s.). These could all be categorised as aspirational relationships, with the expected reciprocity

[29] As Steyke was in this post at the very end of her life, one can only wonder whether Margaret knew him in another context prior to this rectorship. This would not be a casual gift: Erler, *Women, reading*, 80.

[30] This was likely to be Walter Hilton's *Mixed life* or his *Scale of perfection*, or extracts from both texts in one compendium.

[31] It is not known how many anchoresses were concurrent in Lynn Episcopi at this time. Isabel, who was enclosed at All Saints, South Lynn, in the fourteenth century and her later successor, Katherine Samson (d. c. 1417), are known for their gifts to their home church over a century before Dame Margaret's death: *Inventory of church goods, 1368*, ii. 208.

[32] This was deleted in the will, probably because Lampet had pre-deceased Margaret by two or three years.

of powerful intercessory prayer, but Margaret's will similarly demonstrates a detailed knowledge and care of her own servants and even those of other people, as well as bequests to her peers.

The practice of the corporal works of mercy too was clearly taken seriously by Dame Margaret and her friends. The poor, as proclaimed in Matthew xxv, were believed to be the elect co-judges with Christ of those who had defaulted in the Christian duty of charity. Their prayers became sought-after, along with those of others of the marginalised, such as lepers and prisoners, who, by their sufferings, were believed to have already 'paid the price'. Margaret was aware that some of her servants had no home or income beyond her death, and was generous enough to arrange that they would not be immediately destitute. Her servant Alice Catelyn was given a modest 20d., but also a life-long share in a messuage owned by her employer in the parish of St Peter Mancroft, a very desirable 'top end' address. Her recently retired servants Margaret Hurry and Katherine Grene were each bequeathed 3s. 4d., Margaret Hurry being given an additional gift of a painted cloth with an image of Dorothy, presumably the popular virgin saint. Margery Smyth was also left a cloth with St Giles painted on it, perhaps a shared parish patron. To each of her surviving servants she left blankets and linen and a basin, providing the wherewithal to sleep and wash in their next lodging or form the basis of a marital home, and to two former servants of one Rose Crowlow, who were lodged in the parish of St Andrew, she gave 8d. each.

Similar preoccupations are evidenced in the will of Dame Margaret's friend and benefactor of her younger days, Katherine Brasyer (d. 1457), another aldermanic Norwich widow, but of St Stephen's parish, who also left gifts, if of more modest amounts, to a veritable army of fourteen named servants, including other people's dependants.[33] She left Margaret Purdans 6s. 8d. and made gifts to many other named female friends who were professed religious, anchoresses and nursing sisters. She seems to have had a special relationship with St Paul's hospital, naming three sisters but leaving varying bequests to them all, and remembering especially the hospital's bailiff, Robert Toly (3s. 4d.), his wife Mary (6s. 8d.) and their daughter, Katherine (20d.), who was possibly her goddaughter. She also gave 6s. 8d. to Sister Alice Cofeld at St Paul's, a substantial gift, the same amount as she left to Mary Toly and Dame Margaret. It is interesting to note that, apart from bequests to St Stephen's church, this is her highest personal gift, aside from the bequests to two hermits which exceed the rest. Like Margaret's, Katherine's will covers a spectrum of academic clerics and other priests (fourteen) as well as three hermits.[34]

Margaret Purdans distributed her goods with as much close attention to her poorer dependants as she gave to her personal friends and family to

---

[33] NCC, Brosyard, fos 58–9. Unlike Margaret Purdans, however, no gifts of books or paxes are mentioned.

[34] Richard Fernys, John Felton and Thomas, both the latter in Fernys's will too.

whom she passed her fine religious artefacts such as her four paxes, two of which were decorated with coral and crystal, her rosary beads and her six books, none of which treasured possessions, incidentally, did she leave to her own son, William.[35] She gave to Elizabeth Yaxley, her granddaughter by Alice, a pair of coral paxes, while the crystal and coral pair went to William's wife, Mary, along with her best gown and furred mantle. Paxes were used at the climax of the mass, being passed from hand to hand and reverently kissed by members of the congregation. They were usually engraved with images associated with the passion or its symbols, often alongside the donor's inscribed name, and became objects of significance and potency, imbued with communal prayer. Margaret left all her four paxes to women, the other two to friends: Christiane Veyl, a favourite of Richard Fernys and a beneficiary of his will, and Joan Sylvester. She points out that her 'first psalter', which she left to Richard Yaxley, her widowed son-in-law, was originally owned by Richard Poringland, another Cambridge doctor of divinity and Fellow of Peterhouse, formerly vicar of St Stephen's, and therefore a successor to the venerated Richard Caister. Poringland, who was also an executor of Fernys's will, had many years previously, like Dame Margaret, been kindly remembered in the will of Katherine Brasyer, their mutual friend, his legacy (13s. 4d.) only exceeded by Katherine's gift to the hermit Richard Fernys (£4). Clearly, as these years of reciprocity of prayer and artefacts show, these four people – Poringland, Fernys, Margaret Purdans and Katherine Brasyer – all knew and had a continuing high regard for each other till death and, through Margaret's bequests and redistribution, the chain of prayer and commemoration continued beyond into the succeeding generation.

The insight that her will provides into Dame Margaret's book collection is very unusual. Evidence of wills and inventories in Norwich has shown that lay book ownership reached its peak in the period 1440–89, but it is numerically disappointing.[36] However, the omission of books from wills does not necessarily signify non-ownership. It may rather indicate that books were already passed on, in circulation or regarded as group or family possessions. It is obvious that Margaret's interest in books was an important aspect of her spiritual life. Two of her books were in English, one given to the nuns of Carrow, title unknown, and Bridget's book, a gift to the nuns at Thetford. Books in return for intercessory prayer, as well as the reciprocity of friend-

---

[35] Following a bequest to William of £40 to be paid in instalments over several years, a section of the will has been crossed out. He was also left some silver, linen and best bedding.

[36] Tanner, *Church in Norwich*, appendix 6 at pp. 193–7. In a prosperous city that was an international depot for trade it is inconceivable that so few books as appear in the documents were owned by the mercantile and governing elite. In the lay wills of 1440–89 (525), only twenty-nine mention books.

ship, may be key here.[37] Margaret's *Le doctrine of the herte*, a text designed for women living under a rule, and focused on examination of conscience and confession, was left to Sr Margaret Yaxley of Bruisyard, to be passed at her death to the ownership of her sister nuns, which might confirm the reciprocal aspect of the gift. Dame Margaret's two psalters, one given to the priest, Thomas Carman, the other to Richard Yaxley, 'my beloved son', perhaps carry this chain of remembrance and prayer outside the conventual walls into a more male-dominated world, but it was the world with which she had successfully engaged all her adult life, through her family, clerical mentors and influential friends.

Dame Margaret's will shows us a generous and pious woman of some wealth and substance which, realistically, could not have been maintained by a long life simply given over to withdrawal and contemplative prayer. The pragmatism of medieval women who combined their piety with engagement with 'the world', both in commerce and in acts of charity, is a recurring trope. It is seen in the life of St Bridget; the life of her noble devotee, Cecily Neville, duchess of York (d. 1495), who had the saint's book read to her dining household and had very problematic sons;[38] in the letters and will of Margaret Paston, who certainly had the sons if not the book; in the wills of Katherine Brasyer and her friend, Margaret Purdans, and others; and, above all, in the book of Bridget's disciple and imitator, Margery Kempe. All became what might be termed 'career widows' with defined temporal goals in pursuit of highly spiritual ends, for themselves and their friends. The 'good soul that brought forth good works', was, Bridget implied, a moral choice: 'if Gode hase ordaynde all saules to saluacion of entent of hys makes, zet may a man, of fredome of hys will, chese weþir he will be saufe or dampned'.[39] For medieval Christian men and women the means of salvation, as Christ taught, was through the commissioning and practice of the corporal works of mercy and, when possible, by the reciprocity of the spiritual works of mercy. It was a challenge eagerly embraced by many women in fifteenth-century Norwich.

---

[37] Ehrler, *Women, reading*, 27–8.
[38] Sahlin, *Birgitta of Sweden*, 4 and n. 8.
[39] *Liber celestis*, 311, lines 11–13.

5

Norwich Women and the Seven Corporal Works of Mercy

Succour and suffrage

'I concell and I preye euerichon of you to conceyue and knowe that Oure
Lorde God at the Day of Dome shall shewe ryght with-oute mercye, full rygo-
rysly, full sturnely, and aske of vs howe that we haue spende the vij verkes of
mercy, as the gospell wittenes ... These vij verkes thou arte bonden to fulfill
by verke and dede ziff thi powere be, or els by thi good will ziff thi powere
faill, in payne of euer lastynge dampnacion ziff thou repente not. *For of these
werkes of mercy Criste shall speke inspeciall of at the Day of Dome. I praye eueriche
of you to haue this in mynde.*'[1]

This preacher thus exhorted his congregation to follow the charitable ideal
expounded by Christ and recorded in Matthew xxv, putting great emphasis
on the utility of good works as a sure means of salvation. He made plain the
horrors of an inescapable last judgement:

Then shall the kynge saye unto them that shalbe on the lyffte hande: departe
from me ye coursed into everlastynge fire, which is prepared for the devyll and
hys angels. For I was an hungred, and ye gave me no meate. I thursted, and ye
gave me no drynke. I was herbroulesse, and ye lodged me nott. I was naked,
and ye clothed me nott. I was sycke and in preson, and ye visited me not.
Then shall they also answere hym sayinge: master when saw we the enhun-
gred, or a thurst, or herbroulesse, or naked, or sicke, or in preson, and have
not ministred unto the? Then shall he answere them, and saye: Verely I say
unto you, *in as moche as ye dyd it nott to won of the leest of these, ye did it nott to
me. And these shall go into everlastinge payne: And the rightous into lyfe eternall.* [2]

From Old Testament times spiritual merit was attached to good works on
behalf of the poor, as the psalmist proclaims: 'He hath dispersed abroad; he
hath given to the poor: his righteousness remaineth forever.'[3] By the late
Middle Ages the imperative of works for the needy, as if for the suffering
body of Christ on earth, was entrenched deep within the consciousness of all
believers, whatever the degree of practical compliance. To gain some insight

---

[1] *Middle English sermons*, 18–19. These date from the late fourteenth to the early
fifteenth century (my italics).
[2] Matt. xxv.34–46.
[3] Psalm cxii.9.

into this mindset, it is vital to be aware of the centrality of the sacrifice of the mass in medieval worship and devotion, indeed, in everyday language and culture. This should be understood and contextualised in order to understand the almost universal belief in, and adherence to, the seven corporal works of mercy. They were, to devout men and women, the accomplishment of a spiritual and redemptive ideal, as well as a pragmatic and reciprocal programme of social welfare:

> I am thatt livynge breed which is cam doune from heven. Yf any man eat of this breed, he shall live for ever. And the breed that I will geve, is my flesshe, which I will geve for the lyfe of the worlde … Whosoever eateth my flesshe, and drynketh my bloudde, the same hath eternal lyfe: And I will rayse hym up at the last daye.[4]

In these words is encapsulated the concept of the body and blood of Christ as *caritas*, of self-giving as a redemptive act. In such a context, charity, as a central element of the passion, has eucharistic connotations. This sacrifice was expressed in art forms readily visible to any congregation. For example, the central roof boss in the Norwich parish church of St Peter Hungate (virtually rebuilt by Margaret and John Paston in the mid-fifteenth century) shows the last judgement with Christ enthroned on a rainbow, with hands raised and body bared to exhibit his wounds. Below his right foot a naked soul rises to heaven, and below his left, the souls of the damned are dragged by a demon into the mouth of a dragon, signifying hell.

The development of devotion to the host as the body of Christ is seen particularly among pious women.[5] The revelatory writings of St Bridget of Sweden, who, with her daughter St Catherine of Vadstena, was permitted weekly communion, influenced Margery Kempe, not least in her own determination to obtain a similar dispensation.[6] Whether or not such devotion later motivated Margaret Paston in 1471 to obtain the same concession must remain a matter for conjecture.[7] For whatever reason, both Margery and Margaret obtained this right. For some women who sought this privilege there may have been aspects of imitating their social superiors, as well as their spiritual exemplars.

Whatever the hermeneutics deployed in assessing Margery's book, it seems not to detract from, but to support, the implication that a great deal of female activity was taking place without clerical or male approval. Even if Margery had no discrete existence as a woman raised in the mercantile elite of late fourteenth-century Bishop's Lynn, she would remain an essentially

---

4 John vi.51, 54.
5 M. Rubin, *Corpus Christi: the eucharist in late medieval culture*, Cambridge 1991, 120–?.
6 Bridget was canonised by Pope Benedict IX in 1391; her daughter was never formally canonised: *Book of Margery Kempe*, i, ch. lviii, p. 143.
7 *Paston letters*, i. 34, 585. Rosenthal has found that Margaret's use of holy days to date letters far exceeds the average use of other members of the family: *Telling tales*, 95–147.

truthful (if subjective) expression of a spectrum of female spiritual aspirations that often called down the opprobrium of men.

For the medieval Christian, the seven corporal works of mercy were an extension of the incarnation. They were both a development and an ever-extending expression of the celebration of the sacrifice of the mass and the communion of saints, dead and alive. An extensive series of wall-paintings at Potter Heigham parish church, Norfolk, shows a dominant recurring female figure representing 'Charity' administering the comfortable works. Though almost lost in places, it confirms how central to worship and the mass were concepts of charity and self-giving. The living, worshipping Church was the body of Christ on earth: the Church Militant commissioned by him to continue his work. The fate of the immortal soul depended on the practical accomplishment of these ideals. This was the context of the highly popular cult of Elizabeth of Hungary, which was so firmly established in Norwich by the mid-fifteenth century. The saint's *vita*, in the then popular *Golden legend* of Jacobus de Voragine, provided a perfect exemplar for pious married women devoted to the provision of comfortable works (*see* plate 18).[8] When she was a twenty-year-old widow, Elizabeth took a subversive decision and renounced her status and wealth, not to mention her young children, and became a Franciscan tertiary in pursuit of 'wylful pouerte wyth chast clennesse'.[9] She founded a hospital for lepers and other sick paupers where she herself worked and undertook menial nursing tasks. A monastic foundation would have been more socially acceptable to her male relatives, as would remarriage, which she also refused.

According to Voragine, Elizabeth beat an old bedridden woman in her hospital for refusing confession and the eucharist.[10] The point of this, to us shocking, story was not the saint's offended religious sensibilities, but the fact that the old woman was refusing absolution, healing and redemption, the medicine of the 'Great Physician'.[11] And that not only for herself but for others who expected her to pray for them. Worse was that this woman, who was receiving intensive spiritual and physical care and charity, should decline participation in the great reciprocal act required of all 'even christians' in the mass: to be the body of Christ.[12] It was unthinkable. To Elizabeth's contemporaries (and, no doubt, the authors and editors of her *vita*), if the sick poor did not participate in the *opus dei*, their being in hospital

---

[8] *Golden legend*, i. 302–18. To Voragine (d. 1298), writing in the thirteenth century, St Elizabeth would have been recent history.

[9] For her perceived rebellious and subversive behaviour see *Hooly wummen*, 275–80.

[10] *Golden legend*, ii. 311.

[11] This concept combined the theology of St Augustine of Hippo with the twelfth-century western reception of Aristotelian works emphasising the harmony and balance of body and spirit to achieve good health: Rawcliffe, *Medicine and society*, 26 n. 17, 32. Augustine categorised disease as an evil arising from the body as a consequence of original sin.

[12] 1 Cor. xii.25–7.

became not only pointless but a potential source of a spiritual miasma of sin, detrimental to the health of all its occupants.[13] Canon 22 of the Fourth Lateran Council (1215) made obligatory confession and absolution, followed by reception of the host, before the cure of the soul could be mirrored in the healing of the body. How could anyone intercede for another when she had patently abandoned interest in her own salvation?

The politically subversive Elizabeth did not permit spiritual subversion among her patients. The recipient of a corporal work of mercy was expected to reciprocate with a spiritual work: prayer for the benefit of all, but especially the donor.[14] The accumulation of intercessory prayer as a 'treasury of merit' was believed to result in a speedier journey through purgatory. John Clopton, wealthy benefactor of Long Melford church, Suffolk, stated in his elaborate will of 1494 that 'I knowe well that prayers is a singular remedie for the deliverance of soules in purgatory', an understanding shared by many of his contemporaries who had also risen to positions of wealth and influence.[15] However, in view of the devotion to the body of Christ in all its manifestations characteristic of late medieval society, and especially, it may be argued, of women, it should not be assumed that the only, or even primary, motivation for performing works of mercy was mere self-interest.[16] However, reciprocity was quintessential both to their practical execution and to the perception of their spiritual merit.

The recurring *leit-motifen* in St Elizabeth's *vita* are the giving away of food to the poor (without male consent) and her own self-abnegation.[17] She could be said to be extending, even breaking, the bounds of the traditional female role, which might account, in part, for the popularity of her hagiography with many women. Her attraction to holy poverty and humility, to the point of abandoning all else, was characteristic of a growing spiritual focus on the poor in body and spirit which placed an increasing emphasis on the eucharist and veneration of the wounded Jesus:[18] St Francis of Assisi, Elizabeth's contemporary, was a particularly brilliant trailblazer for such devotion. Osbern Bokenham's *Life* of Elizabeth significantly shows her pursuing most of the seven comfortable works within and without her hospital foundation.[19] Hospitals were inevitably a focus for the practice of all seven of the works,

---

[13] P. Horden, 'A non-natural environment: medicine without doctors and the medieval European hospital', in B. S. Bowers (ed.), *The medieval hospital and medical practice*, Aldershot 2007, 133–45 at pp. 139, 143.

[14] The spiritual works of mercy were to counsel, correct, console, relieve, forbear, pray and instruct: *Oxford dictionary of the Christian Church*, 1302.

[15] PCC, reg. Home, fo. 17 (Clopton), 1494. See also Duffy, *Stripping of the altars*, 346–54.

[16] Rubin, *Corpus Christi*, 302–16.

[17] *Golden legend*, ii. 308.

[18] Bynum, *Holy feast*, 48–69.

[19] *Hooly wummen*, 271–3.

and bequests to them and their sisters should be viewed in this light.[20] Simi-larly, the overlap between hospital provision for the poor infirm and the increase in almshouse foundation to the same end testifies to a desire that had permeated the ranks of the merchant elite for the selective support of deserving intercessors.[21]

The wide appeal of the *devotio moderna* in the late Middle Ages was possibly rooted in its adaptability to local cults and religious practices, as a result of cross-fertilisation throughout northern Europe.[22] In Bishop's Lynn, for example, the influence of its Flemish forms was apparent in familiarity with the *vita* of Marie d'Oignies (d. 1213). [23] Her story, as a married beguine from Brabant, whose life of holy poverty was recorded by her chosen disciple, Jacques de Vitry, Parisian academic and later cardinal of Louvain, became well-known to Margery Kempe, even in the days when she could not yet read.[24] Through reading Marie's *vita*, a previously hostile friar-preacher of Lynn experienced a *volte-face* regarding his opinion of Margery's uncontrol-lable sobbing. Indeed, he even began to experience similar emotions himself whilst reading the Gospel.[25] The *devotio moderna* was embraced by pious lay women, who were particularly attracted by its combination of contemplative piety with the possibility of community action in practically implemented good works. It also enabled a degree of autonomy of movement and choice, valued by many women who had little enough of either.[26]

By the end of the fourteenth and the beginning of the fifteenth century the influence of Christian humanism and a purifying classicism, which included a preference for patristic doctrines, were also factors influencing the practice of this kind of piety.[27] The latter is manifest in Norfolk in the recur-ring choice of subjects in contemporary rood-screen panels: for example, St Jerome and other Fathers of the Church. Jerome's ideas about Christ, in particular, are reflected in late medieval images that survive in the region. The glass *pietà* in a window high up in the north-west wall at Long Melford church, for example, shows an image of Christ's body which reflects Jerome's

---

[20] The medieval hospital in Lübeck, a town frequented by many East Anglian merchants, contains an early fifteenth-century cycle of paintings of St Elizabeth.

[21] M. McIntosh, *Controlling misbehaviour in England, 1370–1600*, Cambridge 1998, 117.

[22] R. Swanson, *Church and society in late medieval England*, Oxford 1993, 263–5.

[23] *Book of Margery Kempe*, i, ch. lxii, p. 153, lines 1–3.

[24] *Jacques de Vitry: the Life of Marie d'Oignies*, ed. M. H. King and M. Marsolais, Toronto 1993. See also Petroff, *Visionary literature*, 299–307, and *Book of Margery Kempe*, i, ch. lxii, pp. 152–3 (and ch. lxxxii, p. 198, for a parallel experience).

[25] *Book of Margery Kempe*, i, ch. lxii, p. 153, lines 16–22. So much so that 'he wett hys vestiment & ornamentys of the awter'.

[26] See Swanson, *Church and society*, 262–4. Stephanie Adams, citing the work of B. Hanawalt, argues this motive for women's investment in creating 'female' space in their parish churches: 'Religion, society and godly women', 78.

[27] Swanson, *Church and society*, 347.

attachment to extreme asceticism, as do the painted panels of the crucifixion forming retables now housed in Norwich cathedral.

Pious contemplation of the wounded sacred body, represented in such artefacts as the holy rood, *pietàs* and the 'Man of Sorrows', together with good, even sacrificial, works for that body on earth, as represented by the poor and sick poor, lie at the centre of the late medieval perception of the comfortable works. The nature of the works meant that they were inter-preted as services to both the human and the divine body at the same time, whether in care of the sick, provision of food or preparation of corpses for burial, all of which were undertaken on an individual *ad hoc* basis, as well as in Norwich hospitals. Such tasks were emphatically, if not exclusively, the domain of, and largely executed by, women.

The works of mercy promoted by the iconography of joint parish commis-sions found a ready response among many Norwich women, both in deploy-ment of their resources at the time and later, in their funerary bequests, which were sometimes extensive and comprehensive, and, most important, reciprocated. The wills, for example of such women as Katherine Brasyer and Margaret Purdans, thus afford crucial glimpses into women's pragmatism and conjoint spiritual aspirations.

Extensive analysis of late medieval Norwich testators has established that nearly a third, men and women alike, were donors of funds to hospital sisters.[28] This may seem remarkable given the citizens' general reluctance to 'invest' in charitable works that did not involve reciprocal masses; a compa-rable analysis of London testators identified fewer than a fifth making similar bequests.[29] What does this convey of the regard in which hospital sisters in Norwich were held? And how was their role interpreted in the greater context of the comfortable works? Although it is apparent that more men than women were executors of wills, there is less hard evidence that identifies the gender balance of the people who actually implemented these bequests. Women, especially of the humbler to middling sort, rolled up their sleeves to distribute bread and drink, visit and nurse the sick and shelter the traveller. Woman's function and natural affinity was toward the flesh and the servicing of it.[30] Washing and tending bodies, whether those of infants, the sick or the dead, was traditionally their business. The popular legends surrounding the Virgin Mary and the Magdalen, as well as the cult of St Elizabeth of Hungary, accorded a deep significance to such occupations, a significance that by the high Middle Ages imbued them with sacramental resonance.

The growing emphasis upon the works of mercy went hand-in-hand with perceptions of the 'incarnate body' at work within the community, as well

---

28 Tanner, *Church in Norwich*, 132–7.
29 Thomson, 'Piety and charity in late medieval London', 187.
30 C. Rawcliffe, 'Hospital nurses and their work', in R. Britnell (ed.), *Daily life in the late Middle Ages*, Stroud 1998, 43–64. For a more spiritual interpretation of this affinity see Bynum, *Holy feast*, 248–9, 251–9.

as contributing to the honour of the corporate body, whether gild, parish or wider Church. The pragmatic aspects of reciprocity, especially when it benefited the poor, sick poor, aged or industrially injured, were highly valued. Indeed, the practice of charitable works, personal or corporate, constituted the only poor relief available to most.[31] So necessary was this support that the benefactor could be confident of the grateful recipient's intercessory prayer, and would continue to invest in it financially and spiritually. As Agnes Paston (d.1479), no wet liberal she, wrote to her son John I, in 1465, 'this world is but a thorugh-fare and ful of woo, and whan we departe ther-fro, rigth nougght bere with vs but our good dedys and ylle'.[32] In the next line of her letter Agnes makes clear the connection in her own mind between 'good dedys' and redemption: 'And ther knoweth no man how soon God wol clepe (call) hym, and ther-for it is good for euery creature to be redy.'

Even if not to an ideal extent, it is clear that many affluent Norwich women attempted a pragmatic fulfilment of what was understood as a spiritual obligation. Those who were enjoying the benefits of commercial success, some at a very prestigious level, were left in no doubt by the iconography displayed in their parish churches, or by the sermons and poems celebrating their favourite saints, where their charitable responsibilities lay. How much their good works were stimulated by feelings of guilt, or motivated by fear of retribution, even damnation, rather than unalloyed compassion, must remain the subject of a pointless debate. What is certain is that many of them were disposed to dispense alms, some from their own tables.

Feeding the hungry: women's initiatives

The first comfortable work has the most obvious eucharistic connections: 'Jesus toke breede, gave thankes, and gave it to them and sayd: Take, eate, Thys is my body.'[33] The concept of the body of Christ as a loaf is made explicit in a Middle English sermon which also emphasised the priestly role in its distribution among the laity:

> By this feeste that Crist made I vnderstond the grett feest that oure Lorde maketh to euery Cristen man with v loves and ij fisshes. Crist with oo loffe this day, that is ys owen precious body in the forme of brede, fedith many

---

[31] Swanson, *Church and society*, 299–300; S. Shahar, *Growing old in the Middle Ages: 'winter clothes us in shadow and pain'*, Tel-Aviv 1995, 163–70.

[32] *Paston letters*, i. 43–4, letter 30. Agnes was, according to her will, a sister (tertiary) of the Norwich Whitefriars (Carmelites) to whom she left £20 (i. 34, letter 13). Her tough pragmatism did not seem to her to conflict with her religious obligations (for example i, 415, letter 46).

[33] Mark xiv.22.

hundreth thousaundes of men … For-sothe thei be the argvmentes and the skill that may be of the Sacramente, and that longeth not to the.[34]

While this sacerdotal monopoly obtained in the celebration of the mass and the distribution of the eucharist, the same comfortable work permitted lay people, and particularly women, a kind of parallel activity, heavy with redemptive symbolism. The association made in this sermon between the mass and the miracle of the loaves and fishes highlights the significance of charitable doles of food given as an act of piety.

Feeding, of course, except for higher-status medieval women, who employed stewards, male kitchen staff and cooks, in its broader sense of management, planning, purchase, preparation and service, was a woman's designated role in the household. Higher status women would oversee these activities, but others, especially of the artisanal classes, did everything them-selves.[35] Norwich widow Katherine de Norwich (d. 1341/3) kept careful household accounts, which survive for the year September 1336–September 1337. Such detailed documentary evidence rarely survives for women, and Katherine's accounts provide a fascinating glimpse of her life in Norwich. In a literal and measured sense they record Katherine's 'treasury of merit' and her keen awareness of it, as well as revealing her wealth, status and sense of obligation to the destitute. The accounts demonstrate that she was a committed exponent of the first work on a daily basis, giving doles of food: apart from feeding a large household, with many regular additional dinner guests, rising to sixty-two on Christmas day and fifty-three on the feast of the Epiphany, Katherine daily supplied thirteen paupers with bread and herrings in some form, either fresh ('novo'), or smoked ('allec rubium de stauro'), though whether she did so at her own table is unknown. The number signi-fied Christ and his Apostles, a very literal interpretation of 'doing unto the least of these' as if to Christ himself. While dried and smoked fish was a staple for many, probably most, Norwich households, its Gospel connota-tions are clear.[36]

[34] *Middle English sermons*, 128.

[35] F. Swabey, *Medieval gentlewoman: life in a widow's household in the later Middle Ages*, Stroud 1999, 22–3. Some women worked unofficially as cooks, as the York cooks' own gild ordinances of 1424 acknowledge: M. Carlin, 'Fast food and urban living standards in medieval England', in M. Carlin and J. Rosenthal (eds), *Food and eating in medieval Europe*, London 1998, 27–51 at p. 40.

[36] *Household accounts from medieval England*, i, ed. C. M. Woolgar, Oxford 1992, 203–27. Katherine, married first to Piers Braunche (d. 1296), had dower interests in several Norfolk and Suffolk manors, which she held jointly with Walter. It is interesting that Katherine and Walter purchased the house in Newport, Norwich, previously owned by another significant local benefactor, Lettice Payn (d. 1312), widow, who founded the St Anne chapel in St Stephen's church, and another chantry in St Peter Mancroft: Blome-field, *History of Norfolk*, iv. 155.

To mark the eighth anniversary of the death in 1329 of her husband, Walter, on the feast of SS Fabian and Sebastian (20 January), Katherine provided an extravagant memorial feast which consumed a substantial portion of her annual budget – the prodigious sum of £10 18s. 8d., almost one sixth of her household expenses that year. The fare provided included a heron, thirteen plovers, five ducks, twenty-seven hens, four cygnets, four woodcocks, as well as a whole pig, an entire sheep and a very large quantity of beef. At the same time, the regular dole was supplemented by a large quantity of wastel-bread, a kind of cake, to the high value of 4s., and many more than the usual thirteen paupers were fed.[37] In this way the very poor became participants, even if not at her table. Katherine's charitable deed is noted as the very first entry for the day, unlike the other daily accounts. She was clearly determined that no one should forget to intercede for her distinguished husband, or for herself, the provider and president of this banquet. The intercessory prayers of the poor, as highlighted here, were believed to be especially efficacious.

In particular, the dole of wastel-bread indicates that prayers and remembrance were sought from a sizeable number of paupers even eight years after Walter's death. Doubtless Katherine also thought in terms of her own spiritual 'insurance'. To this end, she also made generous gifts to the religious orders of Norwich for their intercession: 'Item in dono pro anima domini priori et conventui sancte trinitatis lxs [60s.] Item fratribus minoribus xs [10s.], item fratribus carmelitis predicatoribus et Sancti Augustini xxs [20s.]'. Although she favoured three houses of friars, the Franciscans, the Carmelites and the Austin friars, it is clear that her greatest generosity was reserved for the cathedral priory and its monks. Whether she was honouring her husband's preferences rather than following her own must, however, remain uncertain.[38]

The survival of Katherine de Norwich's accounts is exceptional. The giving of food by women at home is generally less easy to document than its idealised depiction in memorial glass and other medieval imagery suggests: sadly, the panels showing St Elizabeth feeding the poor in the windows of St Peter Mancroft are not matched by a supporting body of local evidence, apart from odd glimpses in wills. Another East Anglian widow, however, Lady Alice de Bryene (d.1435) of Acton, near Sudbury, Suffolk, who, almost a century later, practised the seven comfortable works, has also left a surviving set of accounts. These show that, on Maundy Thursday of 1412 and 1413, she ordered thirty extra white loaves to be sent to her table before

---

[37] Norwich market boasted a 'wastel market': J. Kirkpatrick, *The streets and lanes of Norwich*, ed. W. Hudson, Norwich 1889. Katherine provided a total of 200 loaves, which, according to her accounts, were bought-in rather than produced within her own kitchens: *Household accounts*, i. 204–5.

[38] *Household acccounts*, i. 204.

distribution to the poor.[39] Such public mediation by a woman of quantities of refined white bread on the eve of the most powerful eucharistic festival of the ecclesiastical year suggests a strongly ritualised statement about the body of Christ, the community and Alice's place in it. Less publicly, through her bailiffs, she also gave more modest doles of grain and dried peas to paupers on her estates at Foxearth and Bures. Lady Bryene's accounts name the individuals who each received half a bushel of grain, evidently because of infirmity rather than simple poverty.[40] In this way her account book, like that of Katherine de Norwich, became a kind of bede-roll.

The giving of life and nurture, both female attributes, were part of the common perception of the eucharist. Furthermore, the wounded body of Jesus, which was such a preoccupation with pious medieval women, religious and lay alike, was seen as generative, healing and nutritive at the same time as being redemptive. The writing of a Carthusian prioress of the Lyonnaise, Marguerite d'Oingt (d.1310), graphically explored the connections between these attributes using the metaphor of childbirth: 'How bitterly you were in labour for me all through your life … Oh, Sweet Lord Jesus Christ, who ever saw any mother suffer such a birth! … your nerves and all your veins were broken … it was no wonder … when you gave birth to the world all in one day.'[41] Marguerite's conceptualisation of her own relationship, and indeed, that of the rest of humanity, to Christ, in the language of motherhood has a strong echo in the later (possibly post-1393) writing of Julian of Norwich. She similarly wrote in her meditations on earlier visions that Christ was: 'oure very moder in grace by takyng of oure kynde made'.[42] She also reflects that 'oure very moder Jhesu … alone beryth vs to joye and to endlesse levyng (living), blessyd mot he be'.[43]

With birth comes breast-feeding, and Christ's wounds were frequently described by both male and female mystics as nurturing and saving the sinner, as a mother suckles her child. Julian developed this idea using the same explicitly maternal imagery employed by Marguerite before her: 'The Moder may geue her chylde to sucke hyr milke, but oure precyous moder Jhesu, he may fede vs wyth hym selfe, and doth full curtesly and full tendyrly with he blessyd sacrament, that is precyous fode of very lyfe.'[44] Depictions of Christ offering his wounded side as a kind of counterpoint to Mary offering her breast were not uncommon. It was believed that breast-milk was the mother's menstrual blood in another form, so that she fed her child

[39] Swabey, *Medieval gentlewoman*, 152. For the founding of Alice's chantry see also Middleton-Stewart, *Inward purity*, 142.
[40] Swabey, *Medieval gentlewoman*, 151. They were Adam Blindman, Agnes Shepherd, John Wafer, Thomas Grye, Bartholomew Hykyn and William Pratt.
[41] *The writings of Margaret of Oingt*, ed. R. Blumenfeld-Kosinski, Woodbridge 1997, 31.
[42] Julian of Norwich, *Showings*, pt II, ch. lix, p. 592, lines 37–8.
[43] Ibid. pt II, ch. lx, p. 595, lines 19–20. See also Bynum, *Jesus as mother*, 129–46.
[44] Julian of Norwich, *Showings*, pt II, ch. lx, pp. 596–7, lines 29–32.

on herself, specifically, on her most distinguishing female attribute.[45] Birth and nurture were, therefore, sacrificial acts like the passion, the theology of which was expressed in iconographic representations, such as carvings of 'the pelican in her piety', found in medieval churches throughout England: in Norfolk, examples may be found at St Stephen's, Norwich, and All Saints, Crostwight, among many others.[46] The sacrificial nature of giving birth was only too apparent in the high risk of maternal death, fears about which were often projected onto the figure of St Margaret of Antioch. An anchorite at Lynn, a spiritual director of Margery Kempe, on hearing of Christ's instruction to her to give up eating meat and focus rather on the sacrament ('thow schalt etyn my flesch & my blod') exclaimed to her: 'Dowtyr, the sowkyn euyn on Crystys brest', echoing Julian's imagery with some precision.[47]

In such a context it should not be a surprise to discover Norwich women with the means to offer charitable gifts of food responding, by means of their bequests, with wholehearted engagement to these ideas. Particularly in the wills of Norwich widows of independent means is this life-long commitment to charitable feeding repeatedly demonstrated. Thus, Margery Dogett, widow of Norwich, in her will proved in 1516, left 'brede to poore folk for my sowle to the value of xiiis iiiid, and to every poor howse in Seynt Petirs and Seynt Vast' parysshes ... an halpenny'.[48] This bequest could have purchased in excess of 3,128 loaves, over and above an additional legacy to the poor households of these parishes. Margery planned to feed bread in generous measure to the poor in her neighbourhood, many probably known to her, and thereby also ensure spiritual nourishment for her soul, by charity and by intercession, at a time when she perceived that she would be most in need of it: at her death.[49] This gift of potentially life-saving bread to the indigent was arguably extending the powerful metaphor of the bread of the eucharist, the Body of Christ. It was, moreover, distributed through the agency and charity of a Norwich lay woman, a widow with the freedom and resources to determine with some exactitude the people she wished to help. A contemporary of Margery, Maud Radbode *alias* Bewflower of the parish of St George Colgate, had also made provision when she died in 1490 to supply bread and ale to the poor, thus ensuring a good turnout. For the ease of her intercessors,

[45] D. Jacquart and C. Thomasset, *Sexuality and medicine in the Middle Ages*, trans. M. Adamson, Princeton 1988, 100.
[46] The pelican was believed to feed its young on blood taken from its own breast. Its act of regurgitation to feed chicks makes it appear to be pecking its breast. The image, taken from the *Physiologus* and the legends of the bestiary, is an allusion to Christ's sacrifice and saving wounds and the proffering of his sacramental blood in the eucharist: Rubin, *Corpus Christi*, 310–12.
[47] *Book of Margery Kempe*, i, ch. v, pp. 16–18.
[48] ANC, reg. Cook, fos 46–7 (Dogett), 1516.
[49] Familiarity was an important factor. See the will of Elizabeth Browne (born Paston), May 1487, which specified that her bequests to the poor should go 'moste specially souche as haue knowen me and I thaym': PCC, reg. Milles, fo. 12.

her corpse was to rest at St George's for a mass on the way to burial at the Austin friars.[50]

The further provisions of Widow Dogett's will demonstrate a sharp percep-tion of the theological imperatives of other of the seven corporal works of mercy. She made gifts to the bedridden in the parishes of St Michael at Plea, St Andrew, St Mary the Less and St Peter Hungate; to lepers and others in the five hospitals at the city gates; and to hospital sisters. She remembered the prisoners in both Norwich gaols, and every poor person in the parish of her burial, St Michael at Plea. It is notable, however, that little mention is made of masses for her soul. Indeed, apart from 13s. 4d. to be paid to priests and clerks on the day of her burial for funeral offices, and a request that a 'certyne be founde for my sowle' at her year's mind, she asked for none. Nor does she mention her deceased husband. Clearly she was depending on the efficacy of her own acts of charity and the prayers of intercession that they inspired, together with eleven separate bequests for lights before the altars and images of two city parish churches and the cathedral, to see her through.[51] *Caritas*, as a demonstration of a belief in a continuing and redemptive incarnation, may be the motivating concept here.

It may be posited that such charity had far more to do with custom and convention than piety, or even to the desire to make a good showing among one's acquaintance. How may such distinctions be drawn at this remove? Would such a line of enquiry be anachronistic? Choice and focus may provide at least some clues. Katherine de Norwich, Alice de Bryene and Margery Dogett, widows in different times, with very different financial resources, chose the distribution of bread as a main plank of their practice of the comfortable works. Margery Dogett's funeral obsequies were, appar-ently, basic and unostentatious, so the desire for dramatic gestures may be discounted. She was possibly of a similar cast of mind as Lady Katherine Felbrigge (d. 1459) of Norwich, whose will was quite explicit: 'I do not, indeed, I expressly forbid, my executors to lay on large banquets or other useless provisions, rather they are to provide for my burial rites in a discreet

---

[50] NCC, reg. Wolman fo. 151 (Radbode/Bewflower), 1490.
[51] Margery demonstrated a personal devotion to the Virgin, St Anne and St Nicholas. She also left to St Julian's church 'my coverlight nexte the beste'. St Julian's had by now accommodated over a century of anchoresses: Julian of Norwich; another anchoress (possibly another Julian) until 1429; Juliana of Conesford , c.1439–43; Agnes or Anneys c.?1445/9–75; Elizabeth Scott c.1481–1511; and Agnes Edryge c.1524. They had estab-lished a reputation for intercessory prayer and good counsel in the industrial heart of the city as the wills cited by Tanner prove. Gilchrist and Oliva, *Religious women*, table 4, p. 98, offer a list of anchoresses but the dates of some wills cited as evidence are erroneous and unreliable. For example, Thomas Wetherby died 1444/5, and his will was proved in 1445, whereas it is there presented as evidence for two apparently different Agneses, in 1472 and 1524. Julian Lampet is also mistakenly identified by them (and Clay) as a successor to Julian of Norwich. Lampet is known to have been enclosed at Carrow from the 1430s until 1481, and not at St Julian's: Tanner, *Church in Norwich*, appendix 7 at p. 200.

and fitting manner as will better please God and help my soul.'[52] Practical charitable provision was the key-note. Katherine was buried next to her distinguished husband at Blackfriars, and left a munificent bequest of £20 to the building of the friars-preachers' steeple, the bells of which would have been audible throughout the city, tolling the hours of the *opus dei* and marking the passing of the dead.[53] She was, perhaps, aware of the parable of the great supper:

> When thou makest a dinner, or a supper: call not thy frendes, nor thy brethren, nether thy kinsmen, nor yet riche neghbours: lest they bidde the agayne, and make the recompence. Butt when thou makest a feast, call the povre, the maymed, the lame, and the blinde, and thou shalt be happy: For they cannot recompence the. Butt thou shalt be recompensed at the resurreccion of the iuste men.[54]

Certainly, Katherine was assisting in the burial of the dead through her contribution towards the steeple for bells and thus also accomplishing the seventh and last comfortable work.

Drink to the thirsty

> 'Whosoever shall drynke of the water that I shall geve hym, shall never be moare a thyrst: But the water that I shall geve hym, shalbe in hym a well of water spryngynge up into everlastynge lyfe.'[55]

The second work of mercy also had sacramental resonances because of its association with the waters of baptism, the first sacrament to be received, and with the cleansing and absolution of the confessional. Water too had parallels with the blood of Christ. It was a powerful metaphor of spiritual survival as exemplified in Christ's conversation with the Samarian woman at the well.[56] Moreover, the value of clean water to a medieval urban community would be hard to overestimate, reinforcing its symbolic potency as a metaphor of salvation.[57] In Norwich many trades associated with the processing of cloth and hides and the working of metals relied on its availability, which meant fierce competition for access to the Wensum. The inevitable problem

---

[52] NCC, reg. Brosyard, fo. 185 (Felbrigge), 1460 (translation).
[53] Adams argues that in Bristol there was a tendency to a gendered focus in such provision, female bequests tending to interior works in the parish church, and male to the exterior fabric: 'Religion, society, and godly women', 79. This was clearly not the case in Norwich, or Norfolk generally, where many women contributed to steeples and bells, for example: Hill, 'Some incarnational aspects of late medieval female piety', 28.
[54] Luke xiv.12–14.
[55] John iv.14.
[56] John iv.10–14.
[57] Matt. iii.11; Mark i. 8; John i. 33.

of heavy pollution of city water supplies and the scarcity of wholesome water to drink reinforced the importance of this work of mercy. Water quite simply was a matter of life and death; whoever controlled its supply ruled. It could hardly be drunk unless made into the small beer or ale which constituted a staple of medieval life. Regular washing of the body with 'clean' water was largely confined to infants, the otherwise incontinent, the affluent and the dead. Civic attempts to safeguard the water supply in urban areas of dense population from high levels of pollution and blockage, as well as unauthorised industrial use, continued, despite the increasingly unfavourable odds created by commercial success.[58]

It may have been that the people gaining most material advantage from 'dirty' commercial activity, likely to interfere with the enjoyment of public spaces, were the ones who would feel most inclined to leave bequests to 'fying' the river, or cleaning blocked city ditches. Norwich, like some other medieval cities, owed its commercial success to the proximity of internationally accessible waterways. However, such bequests are considerably less numerous in Norwich than in London, although there was a slight increase in this kind of testamentary concern among the aldermanic elite of Norwich around 1500.[59]

Excavations of the Norwich Greyfriars' site have confirmed the friars' interest in securing ready access to water, and then developing a piped water system as their house became more complex and extensive. Possibly for symbolic reasons, but certainly for mundane practicality, they actively maintained their rights of access to the Dallingflete (which flowed into the Wensum) granted by Roger Verly, between 1335 and 1344 five times bailiff of Norwich.[60] This important grant was confirmed in 1405 by Elizabeth Elmham, who added the right to clean out the dyke and fish there for a period of two hundred years.[61] In 1466 this lease was further extended for another two hundred years by William Skipwith, whose widow, Margaret, was also a generous patron of the foundation. When she died, twenty-two years after William, she elected to be buried in the friars' church and left

---

[58] E. L. Sabine, 'Latrines and cesspools of medieval London', *Speculum* ix (1934), 303–21 at pp. 310–11; C. Rawcliffe, 'Sickness and health', in Rawcliffe and Wilson, *Medieval Norwich*, 301–26; D. Keene, 'Issues of water in medieval London to c. 1300', *Urban History* xxviii (2000–1), 161–79.

[59] PCC, reg. Moone, fo. 2 (Jowell), 1500/1. John Jowell left £20 'to the use of the commonalty of the city of Norwich, to be expended on the walls and the river'. Jowell, a bedweaver by trade, and obviously an extremely successful and prosperous one, was the fourth of the five husbands of Elizabeth Drake of Norwich (d. 1508).

[60] J. Kirkpatrick, *History of the religious orders and communities, and of the hospitals and castle of Norwich, written about the year 1725*, ed. D. Turner, Yarmouth 1845, 115–18. The symbolic aspects of water provision should not be underestimated. In London it was seen as an important work of mercy for the poor, in a context of emphasis on physical cleansing and purity as opposed to the elimination of moral pollution: Keene, 'Issues of water', 174–9.

[61] Emery and Rutledge, *Norwich Greyfriars*, ch. v, 1.17; 3.10.

them a handsome gift of five marks (£3 6s. 8d.).[62] It was no coincidence that it was the Franciscan order in Norwich that carefully developed a complex and sophisticated water-system. Franciscans had promoted the popular focus on Christ within the context of his earthly family, which found such a profound response among many pious women. Significantly moreover, the Norwich Greyfriars had a chapel of St Anne.[63]

The centrality of water to baptism meant that it took on a particular significance for women involved in midwifery. The high incidence of neonatal death meant that infants were baptised as soon after birth as possible. Where there was doubt about the child's survival during birth the midwife was instructed and authorised to baptise the child, or any part of it that she could reach.[64] In such a context, midwifery could thus cross the boundary between a charitable work and the administration of a sacrament, a priestly function.[65] That the midwife, usually a married (therefore not celibate) woman, who could never be an ordained clerk, should do this was, strictly, unorthodox.[66] John Mirk, canon-regular, writing c. 1400, circumnavigates this issue by instructing that in extreme situations the midwife should 'calle a mon', but only, as he specifies, to help her, should her nerve fail, to 'open' the women to extract the child.[67] A priest intent on such an emergency baptism would have found himself at risk of contamination from the blood of parturition and the stuff of concupiscence. Mirk does not instruct the midwife to call a priest in such circumstances. Given the rate of infant mortality, especially among the Norwich poor living in cramped and filthy conditions, any woman offering aid during birth must have had to administer baptism regularly.[68] One can only conclude that where emergency baptism was necessary priests were, on balance, content for orthodox practice to remain a grey area and leave it to the midwife.[69]

---

[62] NCC, reg. Wolman, fo. 18 (Skipwith), 1488. Margaret Skipwith clearly knew the friars well: she asked that Friar Nicholas Lucas should pray for her in the chapel of St Mary for the first two years of a planned five-year programme.
[63] It has been remarked that St Anne was often perceived as a patron of water with healing, nurturing or life-giving properties: Sautman, 'St Anne in folk tradition', 82–3.
[64] Mirk's instructions, 74.
[65] Leyser, Medieval women, 126–9. See also P. Biller, 'Childbirth in the Middle Ages', History Today (Aug. 1986), 42.
[66] M. Aston, Lollards and reformers: images and literacy in late medieval religion, London 1984, 52. Aston points out that the primacy of this sacrament, and the fact that women were able to administer it, led to speculation among the unorthodox about other aspects of women's administration of priestly functions.
[67] Mirk's instructions, 73, line 105.
[68] Bown and Stirland, 'Criminals and paupers', ch. ii. The skeletons studied indicate the poverty and environmental insults likely to impinge on a life expectancy that equates with that suffered in many developing countries today. Malnourishment of small children (and their pregnant mothers) resulted in stunted growth, rickets and, sometimes, extremes of deformity, and provided no resistance to opportunistic infection or injury.
[69] Considering the daily importance of their role, midwives are not well documented

Visiting the sick

> The good preste … fel in gret sekenes, & sche was steryd in hir sowle to
> kepyn hym in Goddys stede. &, whan sche faylde swech as was nedful for
> hym, sche went abowtyn to good men & good women & gate swech thyng
> as was necessary vn-to hym.[70]

Margery Kempe supported her friend, 'the good preste', by visiting and
by supplying him with essentials, until her own resources failed. She then
alerted people of good will, who donated what 'was necessary vn-to hym'.
That is, she set up a system of community care. Such an individual response
was the first practical resort: the priest, it should be remembered, would
probably have had no immediate family to supply his material needs during
an acute illness.[71] Margery makes plain that this support was inspired by the
Holy Spirit, that she was 'steryd in hir sowle to kepyn hym in Goddys stede',
that is to look after him as though he were Christ himself. Her predisposition
to see elements of Christ's passion in the everyday is dramatically emphasised
in Margery's text by her 'cryings', as she termed them, at the sight of a beaten
child or a whipped animal.[72] The passion was as central to care for the sick
as to the other six works. A more pragmatic, but similarly heart-felt concern
is apparent in the 1516 will of Margaret Norman, widow of the parish of St
John, Ber Street, Norwich: 'I will that the surgen shalbe payed ye xs that is
owynge to hym, kepynge his p(ro)myse that he shall make Peter Syer hool
of his disease.'[73]

Visiting the sick had its primary exemplar in the life of Christ. The many
miracles recorded in the Gospels would have been comprehended as meta-
phors of spiritual revelation, as well as literal accounts of bodily healing.
Christ's visits to Peter's sick mother-in-law and Jairus' dying daughter made
clear the obligation of the Church Militant to visit the sick.[74] Moreover,
after restoring Jairus' daughter to life, 'Christus medicus' commanded that
she be given something to eat. For the medieval Christian this detail placed
the healing visit in a eucharistic and incarnational framework. At a more
practical level, the parable accorded well with contemporary medical theory,
notably regarding the *regimen sanitatis* with its regulation of diet, the first

in Norwich nor any other English cities, though see Rawcliffe, 'Women, childbirth, and
religion', 110.
[70] *Book of Margery Kempe*, i, ch. lx, p. 147.
[71] Institutional care of the aged and infirm priest was to become a major issue for the
Church as increasing numbers of corrodies in hospitals and other monastic foundations,
established specifically for this purpose, were sold to the laity to raise funds: Swanson,
Church and society, 236–7.
[72] *Book of Margery Kempe*, i, ch. xxviii, p. 69.
[73] H. Harrod, 'Extracts from early Norfolk wills', *NA* i (1847), 111–28 at p. 124.
[74] Luke iv.39–9; Mark v.38–43.

of the non-naturals.[75] The revitalised child was being encouraged to rejoin the community, eating being a social activity, a communion. The healing of Peter's mother-in-law also ended with a reference to a shared meal, in that, once restored, the old woman instantly rose up from her bed and 'ministered unto them'. This affirmed the reciprocity among members of the body, as well as underscoring the fact that, like caring for the sick, feeding, especially of the convalescent, was women's domain.

There was certainly a general assumption that a woman's place, whatever her station, was in the sickroom, and this extended to the obligation felt by women at all social levels to assist others in childbirth. The Paston letters reveal such an obligation on the part of gentry women (and their husbands) to attend others, especially the influential, in childbirth,[76] while the wives of Norwich's more affluent men were also doubtless aware of the Christian imperative to help respectable poor women in labour.[77]

In the more general context of care for the sick, the evidence of wills shows Margery Dogett, for example, leaving bequests for the bedridden in her own and three adjacent parishes, some of whom she undoubtedly knew personally, and possibly visited: 'Item to every person beynge bedred withinne the parysshes of Seynt Myghell of Mustowe, Seynt Andrewes, Seynt Mary Litill and Seynt Petir of Hundegate, to eche of them iid.'[78] To be bedridden, young or old, meant to be incapable of earning a wage and, therefore, reduced to dependence and often penury. Margery also left 3s. 4d. to each of the four orders of friars in Norwich traditionally associated with ministry to the poor, and the substantial sum of 13s. 4d. to be spent 'in wynter to poor folkes in woode'. Wood was a charitable *post-mortem* gift favoured by the affluent residents of Norwich, which strongly suggests that the bedridden and disabled were thus receiving practical assistance in preparing their food and fires. Alice Crome, for example, in her will of 1516, specifyed that 'in tyme of

---

[75] Bynum, *Holy feast*, 48; Siraisi, *Medieval and early Renaissance medicine*, 120–3.

[76] 'I vnderstand that my lady wold be ryght glad to have yow a-bought hyr at hyr labore jn so myche that she hath axyd the questyon of dyuers gentyllwomen whedyr they thought that ye wold awayte on hyr at that season or nought. And they aswered that they durst sey that ye wold wyth ryght good wyll awayte on hyr at that tyme … Wherfor, for Godys sake have your horse and all your gere redy wyth yow wherso euer ye be': John Paston III to his mother, Margaret, March 1476, concerning the lying-in of the duchess of Norfolk: *Paston Letters*, i. 601–2, letter 371. Margaret would then have been in her fifties. Any pregnant land-holding woman confined to her rural estates naturally sought to engage a midwife of established reputation, whatever the obstacles. Thus when Margaret Paston herself, pregnant for the first time in the winter of 1441, wrote to her London-based husband John that 'Elisabet Peverel hath leye seke xv or xvj wekys of the seyetyka (sciatica), but sche sent my modyr word be Kate that sche xuld come hedyr wanne God sent tyme, thoov sche xuld be crod in a barwe (barrow)': ibid. i, letter 125, pp. 216–17.

[77] Bequests were made to lazar houses and other institutions open to destitute women and their babies and to orphans. See, for example, the will of Annor, wife of John Gilbert: NCC, reg. Jekkys, fos 49–50 (Gilbert), 1466.

[78] ANC, reg. Cook, fos 46–7 (Dogett), 1516.

wynter whan most nede shalbe sen that ther shalbe cwt (hundredweight: 112lbs) of wode to be distribute to the pore people by the space of time of iij yerys after my decese'.[79] Alice belonged to the parish of St George 'of Muspole', along the road from Margery Dogett, and she, too, obviously intended her gifts to help her neighbours upon whose prayers she could rely.

Such female almsgiving, surely performed for the salvation of the women's deceased friends, as well for as their own spiritual health, was probably widespread, but it is only visible in this particular context through the bequests of widows: active widows, particularly the pious, needed the validation of philanthropy in order to preserve their reputations in a close community. However, the performance of day-to-day deeds of charity in a domestic environment was achievable by most women at some level, whatever their status. It found expression, for example, in the thirteenth century in devotion to St Sitha (or Zita) of Lucca, a life-long servant, depicted on a screen panel at Barton Turf as a very young servant-girl, clutching the household keys and her rosary which became her symbols (*see* plate 19).[80] Her popularity may also be a reflection of the many young women moving from rural to city employment after the plague, to fill the resultant gaps in domestic service. Arguably, those people whose material acquisitions (accumulated, sometimes inevitably, as a consequence of someone else's death or other loss) conflicted with their spiritual aspirations felt most heavily the pressure to discharge this spiritual duty.

Certainly the imperative on the affluent to look to those in want was constantly reinforced in preaching, as was the promise of redemption to follow. Thus, the Dominican preacher John Bromyard on the future role of the poor:

> And with boldness will they be able to put their plaint before God and seek justice, speaking with Christ as judge … 'We have hungered and died of famine, and those yonder did detain our goods that were owing to us … (and) We were made infirm. Those yonder did it, who beat us and afflicted us with blows.…Their satiety was our famine; their merriment was our wretchedness. Their feasts, delectations, pomps, vanities, excesses, and superfluities were our fastings, penalties, wants, calamities and spoliation'.[81]

---

[79] NCC, reg. Gylys, fos 94–5 (Crome), 1516.
[80] The cult of St Sitha or Zita of Lucca (1218–78), patron of servant girls, rose to prominence in England in the fifteenth century: Duffy, *Stripping of the altars*, 164. Sitha had worked in the household of a wealthy weaver, where her patient and exemplary behaviour did not endear her to fellow-servants. She was a model of female submission and conformity triumphant. She was once to be found painted on a chest at Denton church, Norfolk, and on the screens at Barton Turf, North Elmham and Norwich St James: Williamson, 'Saints on Norfolk rood-screens', 313. Her cult was also established in the cathedral priory church by 1363, where her image attracted a substantial £2 6s. 4½d. that year: Shinners, 'Veneration of saints', 138.
[81] Owst, *Literature and pulpit*, 300–1.

Such strong language of exhortation, even prophecy, could only sharpen the desire for the prayers and intercession of the indigent. Sermons, indeed, and their content may give some clue to the general understanding of concepts of charity, redemption and their interdependence. John Mirk's sermon for the feast of St Martin tells of the saint as a young knight, who, 'among other knyghtys ... kyt his mantell yn too partes, and yaf halfe to a pore man that was naket. Wherfor yn the nyght aftyr he saw Cryst clothyd yn the same clothe'.[82] This literal interpretation of Christ's redemptive body as *caritas*, clothed in the gifts of humanity, is a recurring theme. The life of St Elizabeth of Hungary, perhaps more than any other, promoted the close connection between Christ's body and charity to the poor. Bokenham's *vita* designates the saint 'Modyr of pore men', who to 'the seuene werkys of mercy / Wyth greth dylygence...dede intende'. The poet highlights her personal engagement, noting that 'Wyth hyr owyn handys (she) wul spyn & dresse / To makyn of cloth ... she myht doon almesse / To pore men wych askyd for crystys honour.' [83] As spinning was a back-up activity for nearly all Norwich women, regardless of trade or occupation, this was an interpretation of a daily function that could be grasped and placed in a spiritual framework.

Clothing the naked

Clothing the poor both concentrated and emphasised the general focus on the physical body of Christ – in the sense that Christ as the incarnate God was perceived as putting on human flesh, like a garment – and his passion, in preparation for which St Matthew's Gospel simply says: 'And they stripped him'.[84] The stripping of Christ itself became a focus of penitential meditation, appearing from the sixteenth century onwards as the tenth station of the cross. St Paul informed the Galatian church that '[you] have put Christ on you'.[85] The nakedness and vulnerability of a god who had taken on Mary's flesh were made explicit in the old tradition of the Virgin swaddling the infant Christ in her veil, an image promoted by the pseudo-Bonaventure in his *Meditationes vitae Christi*. The connection of the incarnation with the passion is made clear when the Virgin covers her son's crucified nakedness because 'she is saddened and shamed beyond measure when she sees him entirely nude ... and girds him with the veil from her head'.[86] In his 'Homily on Lent' (c. 1400), John Mirk observed that when 'Cristes clothys wern drawn of hym ... his modyr, wonde hyr kerchef about hym to hyll his

---

[82] *Mirk's festial*, 66, 272.

[83] *Hooly wummen*, 270–1.

[84] Matt. xxvii.28.

[85] Galatians iii.27.

[86] *Meditationes vitae Christi of the Pseudo-Bonaventure*, ed. and trans. J. de Vinck, Paterson 1960, 333.

136

membbrys.'[87] The Virgin's veil, like the houselling cloths and towels used in the mass for catching up the eucharistic body, had, like her, become its vessel.

The parable of the prodigal son uses the gift of fine clothing to demonstrate forgiveness, redemption and renewal of a relationship with the Father: 'Bringe forth that best garment, and put it on hym ... for this my sonne was deed, and is alive agayne. He was loste and ys nowe founde.'[88] The taking of the habit for the professed religious, as with the mantle and the ring of the vowess, was symbolic of the same transformation, of dying to the old life and robing for the new. Gilds and fraternities in Norwich too placed great importance on the distinction of their livery robes, which might display such emblems as the cross of St George and be worn by almsmen and women as well as gild members.[89]

The charitable offering of clothing is demonstrated in an undated steward's account where Lady Alice de Bryene provided thirty-six lengths of wool-russet, a heavy-duty everyday cloth, for thirty-six paupers, together with thirty-six bowls. She may have been sponsoring the local Palm Sunday observances while simultaneously commemorating the thirty-sixth anniversary of the death of her husband, Sir Guy:[90] the association of significant anniversaries with major religious festivals can best be understood in the context of continued remembrance and the stimulation of further intercession, both for the deceased and, in particular, for the surviving benefactor. Lady Alice's gift could also be interpreted as a supremely theatrical statement of her wealth and social standing during this festival and its procession if, that is, the paupers actually processed on Palm Sunday, as they customarily did during funerals.[91] But the fact that Alice, at the same time, also caused the erection of a cross in the churchyard may throw another light on her gift. She was plainly aware of the significance of the passion iconography as a demonstration of the means to salvation for herself and for all her 'dependants' who would pass the cross, either on foot or on a bier. Alice cannot have been unmindful, either, that her name would be forever associated with it and the popular recollection that on such a day she had clothed thirty-six paupers.

From the fifteenth century onwards bequests for funeral clothing for groups of five became more frequent, in honour of the five wounds of Christ with all the redemptive connotations. The Mass of the Five Wounds

---

[87] Mirk's festial, pt I, 247.

[88] Luke xv.22, 24.

[89] B. McRee, 'Religious gilds and civic order: the case of Norwich in the late Middle Ages', Speculum lxvii (1992), 77.

[90] Swabey, Medieval gentlewoman, 158, citing TNA, SC 6/1297/22. Sir Guy's thirty-sixth anniversary would have been in 1422.

[91] For example, Alderman Robert Jannys of Norwich, in his will of 1530, bequeathed 'at my buryall day to xl poore men and women xl gownes lyned and made': PCC, reg. Thrower, fo.1 (Jannys), 1531/3.

(ascribed incorrectly in many *Horae* to Pope Gregory the Great), also gained high favour.[92] This cult was connected to the veneration of the Image of Pity, or Man of Sorrows, depicting a living and wounded Christ, and many crude representations were circulating in the late Middle Ages, some worn as amulets to stop the flow of blood.[93] Funerary gifts of clothing dressed the poor in the 'livery' of the rich donor at the time of his or her greatest need. Like the robes frequently worn by hospital patients, they served the dual purpose of advertising the generosity of a patron while simultaneously eliciting intercessory prayer.[94] This practice permitted a metaphorical representation of the passion, whether in number (the five wounds, the twelve Apostles, the forty days in the wilderness or multiples of these) or in the use of the poor themselves to personify the naked Body of Christ now clothed by a compassionate donor. Such a physical representation of his wounded body is apparent in the will of Margaret Purdans. She requested that her executors should find five male and five female paupers (for the five wounds) to attend her daily requiem masses for thirty days and pray for her, for which service they were to be paid 2*d*. apiece.[95] In this case, however, no mention is made of any provision of clothing for the paupers. The giving of clothing for paupers, impoverished nuns, hospital sisters and other needy individuals, can, however, be documented in the case of Elizabeth, widow of John Yaxley, a prestigious serjeant-at-law, who in her widowhood lived at Carrow Abbey. In her will of 1530 she bequeathed gifts of £20 each to the London Charterhouse and to Syon Abbey, the Brigettine foundation. Her close relationship with Carrow is also evident in her bequests. For example she left a pension to an older nun, Dame Mawte (Maud), for the term of her life, as well as a selection of household utensils and linen, and 'xs of lawfull money'.[96] It is probable that they were related, by affection and friendship, if not by blood. More revealing, perhaps, was her long-term commitment to the care and support of a man who was mentally incapacitated to the point of dependence on the charity of others. Her will suggests that she had kept him in her lifetime, and now arranged matters so that her son could continue to do so after her death:

[92] Duffy, *Stripping of the altars*, 238. Edward Ive, in his will of 1513, asked for five masses of 'the five wounds' on the day of his burial, the same mass to be repeated five times every year for four years in addition to a *dirige* and *requiem* mass: ANC, reg. Gloys, fo. 110 (Ive), 1509/19.

[93] Rubin, *Corpus Christi*, 305.

[94] Rawcliffe, *Medicine for the soul*, 177.

[95] NCC, reg. Caston, fos 163–5 (Purdans), 1483. The cult of 'the five wounds' was a sister-cult to that of 'the name of Jesus'. Pfaff reports a surviving Norwich missal of 1397 which contained the mass of 'the five wounds', but not 'the Jesus mass': *New liturgical feasts*, 67, 84–91.

[96] This was rent from land held at Burgate, which brought in 3*s*. 4*d*. After Mawte's death, the prioress was to dispose of the land and use the money 'for hyr soule and myne': NCC, reg. Platfoote, fos 105–6.

To Antony Yaxley to the intente that he shall sufficently kepe Wyllam Hamonde ydiot with mete, drynke and clothyng duryng his naturall lyef with other necessaries accordyng to hym Cs [£5]. To Wyllam Hamonde, a matres, bolster, pair of blankets, a coveryng and two pair of course shetes with apparel fit for him.[97]

In a material sense, Elizabeth's support of William Hammond was inclusive of most of the corporal works of mercy. We do not know if he could pray for his benefactress; Elizabeth probably thought her ministrations were sufficient before God to obtain her salvation. Perhaps she was simply a compassionate woman. Her concern for her servants after her death, when they would be without employment or home, is also demonstrated:

Also, I wylle that my supervisour shall see my seruauntes have that I beqethe them or rather more shortely aftre my deathe. Also I wyll that my seruauntes shall go to borde with my lady priores a moneth aftre my decease. And she to haue xijd a weke payde for a pece by myn executours.[98]

Elizabeth Yaxley may well have been expecting a degree of resistance from her son, as she expressed the hope in her will that he would not forget the kindness she had shown him in his own need. She evidently held letters of obligation binding Antony, which she instructed her executors to enforce at law if he contested her wishes. No doubt many an heir saw his mother's charity as a drain on his inheritance.

A significant proportion of Norwich women were employed in domestic spinning, in weaving and as seamstresses in the production of clothes. It could be argued that they were also more closely involved in the distribution of these personal items, and were, by extension, 'clothing the naked'. Inevitably, more is known about the activities of the elite. A prioress of Carrow, probably Joan Spalding, is recorded in 1484/5 as giving in alms the substantial wardrobe of 'divers pairs of shoes, hose, shorts, tunics and other garments provided for Parnel Paternoster, a servant in the kitchen' whom she herself supported. She also paid 1s. 6d. for the repair of clothes and shoes of other poor servants.[99] Her largesse did not, according to the accounts, extend to those outside her employ.

[97] Ibid. fos 104–8 at fo. 105.
[98] Ibid. fo. 107. Many testators made similar provision for servants, some of whom were relatives.
[99] 'Three Carrow account rolls', ed. L. J. Redstone, NA: The Centenary Volume xxix (1946), 72–3. At this time Margery Palmer, nun, was cellaress, and possibly acting as almoner.

Relieving the prisoner

'Then was Peter kepte in preson. But prayer was made without ceasynge of the congregacion unto god for hym.'[100]

The material relief of prisoners was a regular feature of funerary bequests in Norwich, as in all late medieval English cities. The examples of Christ, St Peter and St Paul as innocent prisoners 'for the faith', as well as Christ's injunction to his followers that they should visit and relieve those in prison as if they were himself, made this a mandatory work of mercy. And the threat of imprisonment was no respecter of social standing, as is demonstrated by both John Paston I[101] and Alderman Robert Toppes.[102] Previous good standing offered no protection should trading debts overwhelm or political misjudgements prove disastrous.[103] In such a situation the wives of gentry, merchants or tradesman could find themselves acutely vulnerable or liable to extensive extra responsibilities: this may have strengthened their inclination towards this work of mercy.

Margery Dogett, widow of Norwich, left bequests of 4d. to every anchorite and anchoress in Norwich, and 4d. to each of the five lazar houses at the city gates, the same amount that she gave to the prisons.[104] The connection between these bequests is not a fanciful one: Christ was imprisoned by Pontius Pilate, and his flogged body was described by St Jerome as being *quasi leprosus*. Medieval iconography such as *pietà* clearly exploited this imagery, dwelling upon the suffering experienced by God in human form.[105] No leper, male or female, could have hoped for more powerful propaganda. Recluses, too, who were 'prisoners of God', were encouraged to meditate on this theme, thereby achieving a degree of heightened spirituality. This clearly struck a plangent chord with the worldly elite of late medieval Norwich.[106] Certainly, bequests to prisoners, lepers and anchorites are often grouped together.

It has been calculated that 16 per cent of the Norwich laity and 11 per cent of the clergy made some testamentary provision for prisoners, although

---

[100] Acts vii. 4–5.
[101] *Paston letters*, i. 304–5, letter 184, lines 15–19.
[102] Toppes was in the Fleet prison from 13 February until 25 March, 1441: Wedgwood and Holt, *Parliament*, 863. On 27 July 1443 he was granted a pardon, together with his first wife Alice, and his son, Robert, 'for all offences committed by them before 14 July last and any consequent outlawry and waiver': *CPR, 1441–1446*, 189.
[103] *RCN* ii. 26, no. xxxv.
[104] ANC, reg. Cook, fos 46–7 (Dogett), 1516, 1503/38.
[105] John xix.1–5.
[106] The author of the *Ancrene riwle* told his readers (p. 77) that their vocation necessitated the development of falling sickness (epilepsy) of the soul in order to attain humility. It was a metaphor taken very literally in the dramatic expression of the spiritual by Margery Kempe, as became clear on her pilgrimage to the holy places of Jerusalem: *Book of Margery Kempe*, i, ch. xxviii, p. 68.

this is a lower percentage than in London.[107] Some were probably well aware of the extreme, even life-threatening conditions of the indigent chained and fettered prisoners, unable even to hire a blanket from the gaoler, and made quite specific arrangements.[108] Thus Alice Crome directed in her will of 1516 that 'Half an hundred of wod [56lbs] ... (should be) deuyded a mongte the prisoners in the castell and the guyhald in wynter – the space of tyme of iij yeres.'[109] Her plan for a long-term provision of heating suggests an understanding of the harsh realities of prison life borne of experience. It can be no coincidence that she also left a gift to the gild of St Barbara, patron saint of prisoners, which met, as she clearly notes, at the Carmelite friary, and the same amount (12*d*.) to the gild of St Margaret at the 'ffryer Austyne'. St Margaret's legend, like that of St Barbara, featured imprisonment, in her case in both a solid dungeon and the depths of the metaphorical devil-dragon. It is likely that Alice's *post mortem* gift of fuel for heating, or for cooking, was supplemented by gifts of food from the living. Alice's contemporary, Margery Dogett, left 'to either howse in Castell and Guild Halle in Norwich, ivd'. Bearing in mind that sheets cost one penny a night to hire and a peck of coal cost a half-penny, a bequest of 4*d*. per goal would not make much difference unless through the accretion of widespread donations from both the living and the dead.[110] Extant records of testamentary gifts should probably therefore be regarded as the tip of a sizeable iceberg, by means of which the city's prisons and charitable institutions continued to function.

Lepers: the suffering elect

Those who were sequestered by their disease or infirmity, such as lepers or the crippled, may well have attracted support for similar reasons. 'Imprisonment' by disease was frequently seen to be a punishment for moral shortcomings in the same way as a prison cell seemed a just response to debt or some other civil offence.[111] An alternative view was that sickness, especially chronic and progressive disease, was a sign of spiritual election, whereby earthly suffering

---

[107] Tanner, *Church in Norwich*, 135.
[108] Gangrene caused by abrasion of fetters and chains could occur, and the risk of epidemic disease was notorious: H. Harrod, 'Extracts from the assize and plea rolls of the thirteenth century about Norwich thieves, etc', *NA* vii (1872), 263–88 at p. 267.
[109] NCC, reg. Gylys, fos 94–5 (Crome), 1516.
[110] *Illustrated letters of the Paston family: private life in the fifteenth century*, ed. R. Virgoe, London 1989, 126, referring to the ordinances of Newgate prison, which was rebuilt in 1420 by the gift of Alderman Richard Whittington.
[111] See the archive of the dean and chapter of Norwich Priory Church, NRO, DCN 39/1, where one of the post-dissolution *leprosaria* is described as being for the 'sustentacion, releeff and comfourte of the prysoners of almyghty God, vexed with suche sykenes and diseases that they of necessitee ar constreyned and compelled to eschewe and avoyde oute and from the company of al peopyll'.

ameliorated the future ineluctable pains of purgatory. They had been chosen to be 'prisoners of God', a high spiritual calling. It was, therefore, a burden to be borne by the sufferer with thanksgiving, and one which rendered such a person especially appealing to a potential benefactor. The worthy sick who had made full atonement for their sins naturally attracted widespread support, as their prayers seemed more effective.[112]

Lepers came into such a category, being incurable and dependent, and, in some towns, though not Norwich, unable to beg for alms in public places. Christ's depiction in glass and paint as *quasi-leprosus* and thus sin-bearer, became more common as the cult of his humanity grew in popularity.[113] The *vitae* of such recent saints as St Elizabeth and St Francis of Assisi, both dedicated to nursing lepers, reinforced the validity of charitable giving for their support.[114] 'Plague saints', such as St Sebastian and St Roche, whose wounds were carefully depicted in the iconography of the later Middle Ages, further enlisted compassion for those whom society was otherwise inclined to reject.[115] (Fear of the miasmas of disease maintained a powerful hold on urban populations during times of repeated outbreaks of sickness, both infectious and famine-related.)

It was entirely within the context of the Franciscan tradition that Margery Kempe, like St Francis and many holy women before her, felt the desire to embrace lepers.[116] She, too, associated their sores with Christ's wounds and passion:

[112] Tanner, *Church in Norwich*, 223 n. 3.
[113] The *pietà* window at Long Melford church has been mentioned. The conflation of the lesions of leprosy with the stigmatic wounds suffered by St Francis embodies with some economy the essential thinking behind this kind of incarnational piety. So, too, the identification of the wounded Christ with the marginalised 'living dead'; the connection of humiliation with the final judgement is intrinsic: MacDonald, Ridderbos and Schlusemann, *The broken body*, 162–3; C. W. Bynum, *Fragmentation and redemption: essays on gender and the human body in medieval religion*, New York 1992, 276.
[114] In the painted glass of St Peter Mancroft the image of St Elizabeth feeding lepers, among others, was visibly linked with the donor figure of the Franciscan, Robert Ringman. These panels were dedicated in 1455: King, 'Glazier', 222. For St Francis and possible evidence of him being a leper see J. Schatzlein and P. D. Sulmasy, 'The diagnosis of St Francis: the evidence for leprosy', *Franciscan Studies* xlvii (1987), 181–27.
[115] SS Roche and Sebastian are both depicted on the screen at North Tuddenham where Roche displays his plague sore. They were both also associated with leprosy because of their skin lesions, Sebastian's caused by arrows.
[116] Queen Mathilda (d.1118), wife of Henry I, was an early practitioner of leper-kissing: Rawcliffe, *Hospitals of medieval Norwich*, 44. The beguine, Marie d'Oignies of Brabant (1177–1213) and the Franciscan tertiary St Elizabeth of Hungary (1207–31) were particularly noted for founding institutions for the care of lepers as part of a vocation of contemplation combined with holy poverty and compassionate good works for the poor: 'Marie d'Oignies: the *Life* of Marie d'Oignies by Jaques de Vitry', ed. M. King, in Petroff, *Visionary literature*, 179–83; *Hooly wummen*, 263–4, 271–2. The mystic, Angela de Foligno (1238–1309) talked about the taste of a leper's scab in the context of the eucharist: *Angela of Foligno: memorial*, ed. C. Mazzoni, Woodbridge 1999, 16.

So sche cryid & so sche wept as zyf sche had sen owr Lord Ihesu Crist wyth hys wowndys bledyng, & so sche dede in the syght of hir sowle, for *thorw the beheldyng of the seke man hir mende was al takyn in-to owr Lord Ihesu Crist … Than had sche gret mornyng & sorwyng for sche myth not kyssyn the lazerys whan sche sey hem.*[117]

The penitent Magdalen was, naturally, a protector and patron saint of lepers: she had anointed Christ's feet in the house of Simon the leper; and her withdrawal to the desert mirrored their marginal existence.[118] Although none of the other five leper hospitals situated at the city gates provided intercession on anything like the scale of the leper house dedicated to the Magdalen at Sprowston, it is easy to see why they continued to attract such widespread *post mortem* gifts.[119] The visible suffering of the lepers, combined with some level of personal engagement, enhanced their prospects for intercession.

In fact they were sustained by a level of donations in excess of anything received at Sprowston. The hospital of SS Mary and Clement, a *leprosarium* outside St Augustine's gate, was founded by a lay woman, probably Margaret de Lungespee (d. by 1310), first wife of Henry de Lacy, earl of Lincoln.[120] Over many years other men and women supported this and other *leprosaria* with modest bequests, much as they did the prisoners in the castle and gildhall. Doubtless the elite of Norwich, daily going about their business, saw 'the leper at the gate, full of sores', and were obliged to recollect the fate of Dives in the parable, despatched to hell for his hubristic indifference. In 1476 Agnes Segryme gave money to the five houses at the gates, and also made special mention of the 'Leprese of Mawdelyn be Norwych' to whom she left 20*d.* to be shared.[121] Margaret Purdans particularly remembered the lepers outside the gates of St Giles in her own parish (perhaps personally known to her), each one receiving 4*d.*, twice the amount she gave to lepers living at the other city gates, who were each to receive 2*d.*, the same amount she left to the prisoners.[122]

---

[117] *Book of Margery Kempe*, ch. lxxiv, p. 176, lines 27–34.

[118] *Hooly wummen*, 168, lines 6151–60. Jansen, *Making of the Magdalen*, 174. Rawcliffe quotes a medieval poem about the fate of Cresseid, whose 'wantoun blude' brought her to a lazar house: *Medicine and society*, 15. The links between sexual passion, and prostitution, and leprosy is clear.

[119] Between 1370 and 1532 at least a third of those who left wills remembered the lepers at the gates: Tanner, *Church in Norwich*, 223.

[120] NRO, Misc. 1/5.

[121] NCC, reg. Gelour, fos 81–2 (Segryme), 1474/6.

[122] NCC, reg. Caston, fos 163–5 (Purdans), 1481/3.

Anchorites and fund management

The metaphor of exclusion or separation that so often attached to the leper could also be applied to anchorites, even though they actively sought enclosure.[123] Like lepers, they were perceived as existing on a liminal plane between the living and the dead and, like many lepers who pursued a religious vocation, they chose to be 'dead to the world'.[124] Theirs was a penitential vocation: 'All our happiness must be in the cross of Jesus Christ. This saying has a particular point for recluses, whose joy should consist altogether in God's cross.'[125] Were they perceived as spiritual 'captives' who through their purity, exclusion and prayers were 'ransoming' other members of the Christian community?[126] The thirteenth-century writer of the *Ancrene riwle* warned anchoresses not to eat meals with guests, 'for it is very much against the nature of any Order, most of all against the "order" of an anchoress, who is completely dead as far as concerns the world'.[127] Her principle function was to pray from her first awakening, and worship was the objective of every moment of the day. The treatise itself, as a guide to the penitential sequestered life, naturally emphasises the problems of sin and temptation, rather than offering a deep exploration of contemplative piety, which was to be developed more fully in English by the late fourteenth-century anonymous author of *The cloud of unknowing*. Spiritual advice for religious women was also produced by Richard Rolle (d.1349), the hermit of Hampole. He fully and graphically expanded the instructions initially given by the author of the *Ancrene riwle* that anchoresses should meditate on the passion of Christ.[128] The imagery evoked in late medieval anchoresses' prayers, therefore, remained that of all pious women: Christ's passion and his five wounds.

That the anchoresses and other solitaries of Norwich followed a valued vocation there can be no doubt. Many, including the renowned preacher and former Norwich Benedictine, Bishop Thomas Brinton, thought that recent natural disasters, including plague, were brought upon mankind by the rising tide of human sinfulness.[129] Such thinking underpinned something of the

---

[123] Female perception of liminal and 'desert places' is explored in G. M. Gibson, *Contemplation and action: the other monasticism*, Leicester 1995, 157–208.

[124] Ibid. 183–93, esp. p. 190.

[125] *The ancrene riwle; the Corpus MS*, ed. M. Salu, Exeter 1950, repr. London 1990, 154.

[126] A Norwich memorial brass palimpsest of a monk-anchorite, dated 1460, on the obverse of a civilian brass of about 1535, is illustrated in J. Page-Phillips, *Macklin's monumental brasses*, London 1972, 55. The tonsured anchorite is depicted in prayer, gazing out through an elegantly wrought grille which enclosed a doorway, topped by a crocketed arch of some splendour. It was discovered in the Norwich church of St John de Sepulchre. Its current whereabouts are not stated.

[127] *Ancrene riwle*, 183.

[128] 'Meditations on the passion': *English writings of Richard Rolle*, 90–124.

[129] The causative sin might be women's love of extreme fashion, men's drunkenness and sabbath-breaking, or extortion from the poor: Owst, *Literature and pulpit*, 392–3, 435–6.

expanding demand for intercession; penitence and prayer were at a high spiritual premium. Katherine Goodered, widow, in her will written in 1459 and proved in 1464, left 13s. 4d. to Julian Lampet, a generous amount even for a wealthy woman.[130] Katherine's husband, William, had been a justice of the King's bench and she may, through him, have grown familiar with a wide spectrum of local society.

Her gift was only exceeded by an earlier legacy from Lady Bardolf in 1447, who left Lampet ten marks (£6 13s. 4d.), the greatest legacy that she is known to have received.[131] But in this case Lady Bardolf left clear instructions that the anchoress was to give priority to the support of one dependant, perhaps an elderly woman then living with her, who, when she died, was to be succeeded by another. Such *post mortem* arrangements assured the continuation of Lady Bardolf's comfortable works for an indefinite period and constituted a very flexible alternative to the establishment of a short-term chantry. Not only did they promote the intercession of a series of 'pensioners', but also the prayers of the still youthful anchoress herself. Lampet was required by the will to administer this charity, as well as to supervise the practicalities; in a real sense she was being asked to invest in it, materially and spiritually, in the stead of the deceased Lady Bardolf. In such a case, what perception did such benefactors have of Julian Lampet's 'apartness'? It is clear that this family had a high opinion of the anchoress's administrative capability, as well as of her piety. Seventeen years later, in 1464, as the gift from Katherine Goodered shows, bequests to Lampet were still consistent and regular: Agnes, wife of Godefrid Joye, a Norwich alderman, left her 20d., while Margaret Stubbe, who was rather less affluent, still found 16d. for her support.[132] Were these women's more modest bequests made in imitation of their social and economic superiors? Or did they unite in their assistance of Lampet for less tangible and more spiritual reasons? Either motivation would not necessarily be exclusive of the other.[133] Perhaps the particular attachment of women to the female solitary was experienced as a heightening of charitable focus. Conflating the anchoress's meditative experience of the passion with the pragmatic enabling of 'new life' for those to whom the anchoress ministered on behalf of the benefactor echoed Christ's bestowal

---

130   NCC, reg. Brosyard, fo. 330 (Goodered), 1464.

131   NCC, reg. Wylbey, fo. 133 (Bardolf), 1447. Her husband had made a similar gift in his earlier will of 1438, where he directed that ten marks be shared among the poor of Norwich, according to the 'assignment, will, and discretion' of Julian Lampet. William Phelip, Lord Bardolph, was the nephew and heir of Sir Thomas Erpingham (d. 1428), who had also left the young Lampet 23s. 4d., apparently without instruction for disbursement: *The register of Henry Chichele, archbishop of Canterbury, 1414–1443*, iv, ed. F. F. Jacob, Oxford 1943–7, ii. 600, 381. See also Anne K. Warren, *Anchorites and their patrons in medieval England*, Berkeley 1985, 186–221.

132   NCC, reg. Brosyard, fo. 332 (Joye), 1464; NCC, reg. Botyngs, fo. 164 (Stubbe), 1464.

133   For an extended discussion of anchoresses and other pious women in Norwich see Hill, 'Julian and her sisters', 165–87.

from the cross of his mother into the care of John the Evangelist, which effectively encompassed all seven comfortable works.[134] Certainly, whether investing in the holy poverty expressed by the solitary vocation, or in other contiguous charitable works, many Norwich women clearly felt a desire to be associated to a greater or lesser degree with acts that were perceived as salvific.

In another variant, Agnes Alblastyr, widow of Worstead, where the finest Norfolk worsted cloth was produced for finishing in the city, made three significant gifts to marginalised women in her will proved in 1524: 'To the porre women dwellynct in the almesse house, xijd. Also to Margaret lyppar (leper), xijd. Also to the blynd woman Mother Botoe, xijd.'[135] The will reads as if these women lived at Worstead and were well known to Agnes. There is a sense of exclusion and separation, even liminality about them that might have led Agnes to remember them and value their intercession.[136]

Sheltering the homeless

'Foxes have holes and bryddes of the ayer have nestes: but the sonne of man hath nott wheron to laye hys heed.'[137]

This comfortable work, rooted in the Old Testament tribal and religious imperative of hospitality to the stranger, becomes in the New Testament a directive to treat everyone as the incarnated Jesus, who saw himself as home-less and itinerant, not a desirable condition in late medieval Norwich.[138] The letters of St Paul emphasised the metaphor of the inclusive social body and its mutual dependence under the headship of Christ.[139] Such imagery stressed the interdependence of Christians both in adversity and in the sharing of gifts of the spirit. It was also a metaphor for good order and governance in the body politic, demonstrated in the spectacles which marked the visits to Norwich of itinerant justices, as well as the civic and religious pageants

[134] John xix.26–7.
[135] NCC, reg. Grundisburgh, fos 57–8 (Alblastyr), 1524.
[136] The Alblastyrs were also the major donors of the magnificent rood-screen at Worstead St Mary church, where Agnes and her husband, John, were buried. The screen is inscribed with the date 1512, but John died, as his will attests, in 1520. Agnes, who survived her husband by about four years, probably supervised the execution of his will and the administration of his estate. Clearly, much of the practical sponsorship and plan-ning of sections of the screen, some panels of which are very Flemish in subject and execution, were carried out in their lifetimes. See Mitchell, 'Painting in East Anglia around 1500', 375.
[137] Luke ix.58.
[138] Matt. xxv.44–6.
[139] 1 Cor. xii for example.

which peppered the official calendar.[140] The hierarchy of city officials under the leadership of the mayor mirrored in microcosm this concept of heavenly order, and was duly authenticated by it.[141] For the fifteenth-century parishioner in the pew the possibility of reciprocal aid in time of hardship had its attractions,[142] but those provisions that existed were, none the less, extremely selective in being designed to succour the deserving, rather than the feckless poor.

The rise of the mercantile class and the growing prosperity of those with craft and trade skills in the difficult years following successive outbreaks of plague meant that these influential but vulnerable groups found a common bond in gild and fraternity membership. It was the skilled and established rather than the casually employed labouring poor who could afford the entrance fee and to whom the gilds had most to offer. Although Norwich was home to a Gild of Poor Men, poor women had no such provision. That some women in the skilled and employed socio-economic groups may have enjoyed gild and fraternity membership on relatively equal terms with their husbands is, however, reflected in the wording of the surviving regulations. The Norwich Gild of the Trinity, for example, ruled 'yat alle ye bretheren and sisteren of yis fraternite shul kepen and begynnen her deuocioun on ye euen of ye feste of ye Trinite'.[143] Though these societies were primarily religious organisations based on mutual aid, both temporal and spiritual, they may well also have functioned as a limb of government and civic order.[144] Support was clearly primarily intended for those already housed and working in the city whose business had encountered difficulty through reasons beyond their control. Since tradesmen often worked where they lived, domestic and work space was necessarily combined. Thus in times of hardship and underemployment, the risk of losing the home also meant certain threat to the chances of paid employment. When trade gilds offered help they did so in expectation of foreseeable recovery and repayment. Excessive risk, fecklessness or poor judgement rendered them culpable and disqualified them from relief. The ordinance of the Norwich Gild of Peltiers was quite emphatic: 'But if it be his foly, he schal nout han of ye elmes' (if it is his own fault, he shall not receive alms).[145] Help was not for the vagrant poor or homeless, but intended as short-term aid in a crisis until business could be resumed,

---

[140] P. Maddern, 'Order and disorder', in Rawcliffe and Wilson, *Medieval Norwich*, 189–212.

[141] Ibid. For a discussion of the interdependence of Church and State see Swanson, *Church and society*, 103–22.

[142] B. McRee, 'Charity and gild solidarity in late medieval England', *Journal of British Studies* xxxii (1993), 195–225, esp. pp. 209–11.

[143] 'Fraternitas Sancte Trinitatis in ecclesia Cathedrale', in *English gilds: the original ordinances*, ed. L. T. Smith and L. Brentano (EETS o.s. xl, 1963), 25. Members were each fined one pound of wax for non-attendance at gild meetings.

[144] McRee, 'Religious gilds', 70–3.

[145] *English gilds*, 31.

or as support for the elderly or disabled who had worked hard all their lives. Even the Poor Men's Gild of Norwich proclaimed in its ordinances that 'if any brother or sister of this pouere gilde falle in any pouerte or secknesse, or any other meschef be the sendyng of Crist, *and he may nought helpe him-self with his owen godis*', he or she might have 'iij. pens *til that he be recured*'.[146]

Hard times

Recurring plague, other endemic diseases, cattle murrain and famine-related sickness, sometimes concurrent, meant that sudden death was always a possibility and, with it, the collapse of a business and, for the widow, often the loss of a home. Where the house was owned rather than rented, primogeniture ensured that the eldest son displaced his mother in authority, if not actually removing her physically. The increase in corrodies offered by monastic foundations, such as Norwich cathedral priory, and the nationwide founding of almshouses highlight how demographic changes were creating housing problems, even at the middle level of society.[147] Christian Umby, widow of Dunwich, Suffolk, stated in her will of 1495 that her house standing next to All Saints' church currently accommodated Agnes Pye and Agnes Netherby. The two almswomen were to remain there until they died, when 'other ii por folks to have their dwelling in the same … that they keep reparacion … also to paie in rent Robert Christon or his assignes'.[148] Clearly, these tenants were respectable 'shame-faced poor' rather than itinerants completely without funds. A property was sometimes divided to provide both rented accommodation and an almshouse, thereby realising income for the owner in addition to intercessory prayer. It may be noted, too, that the cost of repairs was, in this case, written into the lease. This interlocking of pragmatism with spiritual aspiration appears to have been a recurring feature of late medieval charity. Even the anchoress Julian Lampet was commissioned to oversee such an arrangement.

In Norwich, almshouse foundation was heavily outnumbered by bequests for parochial relief to existing hospitals and to the leper-houses outside five of the city gates (about a third of Norwich wills proved between 1370 and 1532 gave to the lazar houses, whose almost total dependence on public charity was well-known). Alice Crome (d. 1516), who requested that the residue of her goods be disposed 'that itt may be to the most pleasure of god & wele (health) of my Sowle', established seven almshouses during her life, which stood together, as she described, 'att the west ende of the chyrch

---

146 Ibid. 40 (my italics).
147 Dyer points out the overlap of provision between hospital corrodies and almshouse occupation: *Standards of living*, 243.
148 Middleton-Stewart, *Inward purity*, 84; NCC, reg. Woolman, fos 248–9 (Umby), 1495.

[St George, Muspole] northward'.[149] Alice indicated her intention that the properties 'shall remayne styll as almeshowsys for evermore as they do att the present tyme'. That is, one was 'letyn' commercially for rent, which was to be used for the 'reparacon of all the other'. Alice, though not specific in her will about the occupants, or their standing, had presumably chosen the current ones herself, as had Christian Umby. Though there is a tradition that Alice Crome's foundation was for the shelter of poor widows, there is no corroborative evidence.[150]

It appears that founders of almhouses, who were mainly of the mercantile or artisanal class, were offering shelter to those lower down the social scale who, through infirmity or age, were incapable of work: the 'lame, crooked, blind, bedridden'.[151] But governors of these establishments were highly selective in their admission procedures; the almshouse depended for its existence on the maintenance of rigid social and economic inequalities.[152] The occupants were to be sober, honest and of 'good fame', able to regulate their own actions, that is, not mentally unstable, and not 'tavern haunters'. Nor, as might be expected in a godly foundation, were men and women permitted to enter each other's rooms. The implementation of codes of behaviour, as specified in gild ordinances, was carried to even greater extremes in some almshouses in order to achieve a purity of intercessory prayer among those whose main occupation this was meant to be. That such charity in Norwich was almost always confined to hospital sisters and patients, or else concentrated on parochial relief, rather than invested in almshouses, sets it apart from other English cities. In Norwich almshouses remained an individual initiative of the few.

Hospital corrodies were bought by individuals with endowments of land or cash, for which bed, board and sometimes clothing were provided.[153] Theoretically, at least, corrodies at St Paul's hospital, Norwich, cost just above £6 in the 1490s, which was a considerable sum beyond the reach of most.[154] The close and patent rolls show that, between 1446 and 1485, Norwich cathedral priory granted a number of corrodies to lay men and women, largely under pressure from the crown.[155] However deserving such corrodians were, a shift was taking place away from the original concept of the shelter of the poorest, meaning the truly destitute. The 'deserving' or 'shame-faced poor' were increasingly seen as the late medieval equivalent of an association of distressed gentlefolk, or at least the lower middling sort and

---

149   NCC, reg. Gylys, fos 94–5 (Crome), 1516.
150   E. Phillips, 'Charitable institutions in Norfolk and Suffolk, c. 1350–1600', unpubl. PhD diss. UEA 2002, 121–2, 132–3; Blomefield, History of Norfolk, iv. 472.
151   The ordinances of the Saffron Walden almshouses, c. 1400: Dyer, Standards of living, 243. See also McIntosh, Controlling misbehaviour, 116–19.
152   Dyer, Standards of living, 246.
153   Ibid. 243–4.
154   Rawcliffe, Hospitals of medieval Norwich, 74–6.
155   Tanner, Church in Norwich, 67.

upward. Concern had become focused, along with charity, on the temporarily impoverished who might be expected to return to work, and upon
those who had grown infirm or entered a respectable old age. The destitute
and sick poor, it is tacitly implied, might be burdensome, or worse, danger-
ously disordered, and unlikely ever to function in a society based on a hierarchy of reciprocity. Such *vulnerati* had to depend on the charity dispensed
by individuals or religious foundations, although, even here, the criteria for
acceptability were becoming increasingly selective.[156]

Burial of the dead: 'Passio Christi conforta me'

This was not a commission given by Christ in the Gospels but is recorded
among deeds of alms in the Book of Tobit: 'if I saw any of my nation dead, or
cast about the walls of Nineve, I buried him'.[157] What had been in the Apocrypha the vocation, even obsession, of Tobit, became in the New Testament
telling of the passion a ritual that was embraced by women; more specifically
women who had ministered to Christ in his life and in his dying.[158] It was
these women who returned with spices to prepare his body for the grave. In
the medieval period burial was perceived as a reciprocal duty of care within
the inclusive body of the Church. Such was the intense focus in lay female
piety on the crucified Christ that the preparation of part of that body on
earth for burial was full of symbolism of the incarnation and redemption.
As Julian of Norwich reminded her 'even christians', her vivid revelation
of the passion had shown the crucified dying body discernible only as 'all
blode', all sacrament. It is not stretching this concept too far, therefore,
to claim for this female role something of a sacramental ritual. 'And when
the sabboth daye was past, Mary Magdalen, and Mary Jacobi, and Salome,
bought oyntmentes, that they myght come and anoynt him.'[159] There are
intimations of coronation and kingship in this statement, in which women
assume a priestly role (*see* plate 20).[160]

Margery Kempe's meditative 'visualisation' of giving comfort to the Virgin
after Christ's burial took the form of an offering of food, designed to be
medicinal. 'Sche mad for owr lady a good cawdel', combining the interment with a symbol of healing, regeneration and communion.[161] A caudle,
containing spice, sugar and wine, was often given as a restorative to women

---

[156] For more personal strategies regarding the poor homeless in Florence at this period
see B. Pullan, *Poverty and charity: Europe, Italy, Venice, 1400–1700*, Aldershot 1994, 188.
[157] Tobit i. 16–22: *The Apocrypha, according to the authorised version*, SPCK edn, Oxford–
London n.d.
[158] Luke xxiv.1.
[159] Mark xvi.1.
[160] For traditional elements of this female role see E. van Houts, *Memory and gender in
medieval Europe, 900–1200*, London 1999, 93–5.
[161] *Book of Margery Kempe*, i, ch. lxxxi, p. 195.

recovering from childbirth, emphasising here the role of the Virgin in the 'new birth' of mankind through her son's death. There was a current belief that the Virgin had experienced the birth of Christ without pain (a concept given form in the revelations of St Bridget of Sweden),[162] and that the Virgin underwent the belated pangs of birth whilst watching him dying, which was the sword that would enter her heart, as prophesied by Simeon in the temple.[163] This conflation of birth with death at the scene of the crucifixion established the physical body of Mary as the dynamic link between earth and heaven, and was a feature of Cistercian and, more especially, Franciscan vernacular piety. 'Jesu, fili mihi, Jesu quis mihi det ut ego tecuum et pro te moriat, fili mi, dulcissime Jesu!' ('Jesus, my son, Jesus permit me to die with you and for you, my son, sweetest Jesus').[164] Her experience of the greatest physical pain was repaid by the highest spiritual joy at Man's redemption, which concept illuminates the perception of the Virgin's unparalled standing as intercessor 'at the hour of our death'. It is difficult, at this remove, to assess the impact of such ideas on the lives and legacies of the women of Norwich, but it is possible to document their close links with the friars of Norwich, whose connections with the female community were extensive and whose promotion of affective piety attracted many Norwich women to invest in them spiritually and financially.[165]

The Friars Minor (Franciscans) in Norwich attracted local support from their arrival (c. 1226) until the Dissolution, and surviving wills show that the brothers were valued for a combination of reasons, both practical and pious. In her will of 1475 Alice Brocher, widow of Norwich, requested burial in their church and gave 20s. to the repair of their dormitory. Alice appointed Friar John Sparke as the supervisor of her will, leaving him 3s. 4d. for his labour.[166] Was this a choice based on a relationship of trust and friendship? Was he her spiritual advisor, assuming a role similar to that of the Carmelite, Aleyn of Lynn, who had supported Margery Kempe?[167] Or was Alice's decision based simply on his reputation for competence and integrity? Friar John's father, Thomas Sparke, coverlet weaver, who died in 1480, also appointed his son to this task, though that is less surprising. It perhaps reflects a close-knit network of patronage, as family connections are

---

162 *Mirk's festial*, 24, 'De annunciacione dominica', 109, lines 20–4; *Liber celestis*, introduction, p. xii.

163 Luke ii. See also the vernacular poems of the Franciscan Jacopone da Todi, cited by Warner, *Alone of all her sex*, 211–14.

164 St Bonaventure (1221–74), 1 sent. 48.4, quoted in D. L. Jeffrey, *The early English lyric and Franciscan spirituality*, Lincoln, NE 1975, 61–3.

165 The vernacular writing of the period suggests a different and more earthy view of the friars and their relationship with women: *The political songs of England, from the reign of John to that of Edward II*, ed. T. Wright (Camden vi, 1839), i. 263; ii. 249: 'Freeres, freeres, wo ze be!/ *ministi maloram*/ For many a mannes soule bringe ye/ *ad paenas infernorum*'.

166 NCC, Reg. Gelour, fo. 61 (Brocher), 1474.

167 *Book of Margery Kempe*, i, ch. lxix, pp. 167–9.

clearly to be found between the brothers and their benefactors, just as those at Carrow Abbey bound the nuns to their patrons.[168] Margaret Fissher (d. 1486), widow of Norwich and mother of Friar John Fyssher, asked for burial in the Greyfriars' church, and left them 10s. To her son she remitted the 6s. 6d. he owed her, and, in addition, allocated 20s. for him to pray for her soul for three months. Lastly, she bequeathed him one pair of linen sheets.[169] Linen sheets, while a pragmatic and lasting gift, may just conceivably, to Margaret Fyssher's mind, have provided the wherewithal to perform for her own son, in imitation of the mother of Christ, the seventh work of mercy, in supplying his winding sheets.

Women who were connected to the Greyfriars by confraternity tended to make this clear in their wills. Thus, Joan Cook, widow of North Walsham, a thriving centre of cloth production that serviced Norwich, left one comb of barley to the Friars Minor, 'of which I am a sister' (*consorer*).[170] Margaret Est (d. 1484), widow of Norwich, left them 6d. She had obtained a letter of pardon, or indulgence, from the Greyfriars, 'unto which I am sustyr', and requested a mass in the friary if her estate could afford it.[171] Significantly, such affiliation, which the four orders of friars offered women as well as men, is accorded prominence in their wills, including those of the less affluent. It highlighted a special relationship that gave access to almost unlimited reserves of intercessory prayer. Such contact also offered women, who were more restricted in movement than their husbands and brothers, the possibility of personal spiritual direction beyond the parish church. It must be assumed, too, that such a venue offered copious opportunity for women to meet each other. Sometimes it also promised access to books.[172]

The *Ars moriendi* reflected the priority given to spiritual preparation for death, especially the 'good death', which meant primarily being shriven: that

---

[168] *Carrow abbey: otherwise Carrow priory near Norwich in the county of Norfolk; its foundations, buildings, officers & inmates, with appendices, charters, proceedings, extracts from wills, landed possessions, founders, architectural description of the remains of the buildings and some account of the family of the present owners*, ed. W. Rye, Norwich 1889, appendix 9, pp. viii–xxix. Another popular friar was John Fyssher, son of Margaret (d. 1486), and nephew of William Herbert of Swardeston, who asked him to celebrate mass on his behalf for two years: NCC, reg. Gelour, fo. 180 (Herbert), 1477. Roger Aylemer also asked Friar Fyssher to go on pilgrimage for him to Rome: NCC, reg. Moulton, fo. 49 (Aylemer), 1497; *Norwich Greyfriars*, appendix 2. In contrast, Adams has found few sons and daughters of the mercantile elite of Bristol taking holy orders in this period: 'Religion, society, and godly women', 73.

[169] NCC, reg. Aubry, fo. 61 (Fissher), 1486.

[170] NCC, reg. Gelour, fo. 216 (Cook), 1478.

[171] NCC, reg. Caston, fo. 203 (Est), 1484. For the background to such bequests see Harper-Bill and Rawcliffe, 'Religious houses'.

[172] *Book of Margery Kempe*, i, ch. ix, p. 22, lines 11–22. The widow Margaret Wetherby left a munificent legacy for the building of the Austen friars' library, so long as it was emblazoned with the names of Margaret and Thomas Wetherby as a prompt to remembrance.

is penitent, confessed and absolved.[173] This was priests' work; but illuminated books used for prayer and meditation show that the preparation of the body at home was clearly women's. The deposition from the cross, a favourite subject for many northern European artists of the period, often depicted this task. It was 'The wemen that folowed after whych cam with hym from galile, (who) behelde the sepulcre and howe hys body was layed … and prepared swete odoures, and oyntmentes'.[174] Among these women, Mary Magdalen is given the central role and is described in John's Gospel as standing at the foot of the cross. She was also the first to see the risen Christ.[175] The Magdalen is the central figure, after Christ, in almost every depiction of the deposition. In a context where she was venerated second only to the Virgin Mary, and associated with the preparation of Christ's body for burial, such a visible female role in death takes on a deeper dimension.[176] This is suggested in the opening pages of Julian of Norwich's short text where, with some longing, she identifies with the Magdalen's special affinity to Christ's body: 'I woulde haue ben that tyme with Magdaleyne and with other that were Christus louers, that I might have seen bodilie the passion that our lord suffered for me.'[177] The veneration of, and identification with, Mary Magdalen, and the influence of her *cultus* on the practice of the comfortable works as penitential and redemptive, in parallel with Christ's wounds, is apparent here. So, too, is the subtle interplay of this piety with a more complex understanding of the sacrament of the mass.

The importance of this final act of charity to the body went far beyond the physical decencies. Personal *post-mortem* arrangements must be seen in the context that ceremonies and benefactions alike were experienced as corporate realities by all 'even christians'. Funerary rituals were not merely the preoccupation of the about-to-be-dead; the mass, in which they were enacted, was believed to be inclusive of and interactive between all generations: the living and the dead and God. The corporate and inclusive nature of such rituals is central to an understanding of their meaning, as is the wider context of the mass.[178] No less an authority than St Augustine of Hippo supported the view that merit was available 'For all that at the messe stondith a-bowte, / & for all Crysten people, that be well moo, / That labowr the comen vele in the world a-bowte / Than to pray for thy frend haue thou no dowt.'[179] The preparation of the body for burial, imbued as it was with

---

[173] Ibid. i, ch. xlv, p. 110.
[174] Luke xxiii.55–6.
[175] John xix.25; xx.14.
[176] St Mary Magdalen features on seven, possibly eight, surviving rood-screen panels in Norfolk: Williamson, 'Saints on Norfolk rood-screens', 305.
[177] Julian of Norwich, *Showings*, pt II, ch. ii, p. 285.
[178] Duffy, *Stripping of the altars*, 327–37.
[179] *Songs, carols, and other miscellaneous poems: from the Balliol MS 354, Richard Hill's common-place book*, ed. R. Dyboski (EETS e.s. ci, 1907), nos 72, 70. See also Rubin, *Corpus Christi*, 153.

sacramental potency, began the process of transition from Church Militant to Church Triumphant to which all believers aspired. Testamentary instructions detailing masses, lights, charity, groups of intercessors (the poor, priests, friars, friends, the recluse) were written in the confident expectation that others would do for the deceased as s/he had many times done for others.

The distress of the bereaved in times of epidemic disease when the numerous dead could not be buried with appropriate obsequies can be thus comprehended. The resulting exponential increase in demand for intercession and remembrance reinforced the value of this comfortable work. The swift deliverance from the pains of purgatory required immediate prayers of intercession and masses. What began as a ritual washing of the corpse accompanied by prayers for the dead was integral to the spiritual necessity of a well-attended 'send-off' of continuing intercessory prayer. It was, therefore, a corporal act of mercy that evolved into a spiritual work of ultimate importance. Bequests of commemorative gifts promoting the remembrance of deceased family, friends and patrons for whom one was obliged to pray should be seen in a similar light: corporate and reciprocal acts of charity, the response to which was intercessory prayer.

In an age when thoughts of sudden death and judgement loomed frighteningly large, the funeral was for all but the richest the last opportunity for the giving of alms. The prayers of the poor, to whom Christ was believed to be especially receptive because of his identification with them, were valued and repeatedly commissioned on such occasions. Margarete Odeham, widow of Bury St Edmunds, in her will of 1492 instructed her executors to 'vysite the pore men and other that be dysposed to take almes eche man and woman and chylde to have ob (half-penny) and euy bedredman jd as hastely as it may be don after my deth'.[180] A bell-man was employed to go around the parish between the death of the parishioner and the burial to invoke prayers of intercession for the dead and also as a signal to clergy, friends and poor folk alike to attend the burial, that is to pray.[181] With this in mind, Margarete Odeham also instructed that: 'myn executors do make a good dyner as hastely as thei may coueniently after my dethe to my neybours and other good louers'.[182] So serious a view did Margarete take of immediate *post-mortem* intercession that, in addition to ordering another dinner for the local prisoners, she invested very heavily in the prayers of the professed religious, in a sense the elite 'cavalry' in support of the 'storm troops' of the poor. The four orders of friars in nine East Anglian towns were each to receive 6s. 8d., while each nun in thirteen named convents in the same region was promised 12d. This is intercession planned with the precision of a field-marshal leading a two-pronged attack on the heavenly city.

---

[180] *Wills and inventories from the registers of the commissary of Bury St Edmunds and the archdeaconry of Sudbury*, ed. S. Tymms (Camden o.s. xlix, 1850), 73–80.
[181] Duffy, *Stripping of the altars*, 357.
[182] *Wills and inventories*, 74.

Funerary gifts to parish churches and other foundations, which clearly displayed the name of the benefactor, made permanently visible appeals to 'well-wishers' for intercessory prayer, sometimes for generations. The Peacock chalice, formed by a foot taken from a pre-Reformation pyx (dated 1507) joined to a later cup, carries this legend around the foot: 'Praye for the solle of Stewyn Pekoc and Marget hys wyff, which gave this in the worshippe of the Sacrement.'[183] Bequests for mass vessels and associated artefacts used regularly in close proximity to the sacrament, elevated for all to see at the powerful climax of the mass, the 'sacring', enriched parish liturgy and fulfilled a deeply felt need for lasting commemoration.

An even more munificent gift of plate, including a paten with the vernicle, was made to furnish the mass at St Peter Mancroft church by Robert and Cristiane Holdy in the early years of the sixteenth century. This and other surviving late medieval patens in Norfolk suggest evidence of a growing cult of the vernicle.[184] Of the twenty-eight datable patens surviving from the period 1420 to 1530, twenty-two are engraved with the face of Christ. Of the remainder, five feature the monogram of the 'name of Jesus' and one, the *Agnus Dei*.[185] In this incarnational context, too, Alice (d. 1521), widow of John Buxton, a worsted weaver, in the parish of St Martin Coslany, Norwich, left £5 towards the cost of a red cope to be worn during the mass, an appropriate gift from a woman associated with the textile industry, the colour redolent of the blood of Christ.[186] Joan Thurlock (d. 1505) of Cley-next-the-Sea, Norfolk, bequeathed 'a slevid surplesse for the parson or the parish prest to were in the service of god'.[187] Joan also left an altar cloth to the 'Hey Awter', ensuring with these gifts her remembrance at every mass. In the parish of Raynham St Mary, Norfolk, Margarete Champeneye similarly obtained assurance of prayer through the donation of a silver chalice, 'j calix argenteus', to embellish the altar in 1368.[188] At the parish church of St Agnes, Cawston, in the prosperous weaving heartlands serving the city, Idonée (d. after 1376), wife of Robert Sparham, left a tapestry of black worsted, embroidered with their initials in gold, to be used 'pro mortuis', as a pall covering the bier. This not only served as a splendid personal memorial to Idonée and Robert at every requiem mass, but was intended to accomplish

---

[183] C. Platt, *The parish churches of medieval England*, London 1995, 101.
[184] Hope, 'Inventories', 153–240 at p. 206.
[185] See C. R. Manning, 'Medieval patens in Norfolk', NA xii (1895), 85–99, from which the figures are taken. Four of the five monogram patens are early, the earliest being from Salle (1420) and Wood Dalling (1420), both within the cloth-weaving areas. The earliest patens with the vernicle came from Beeston Regis (1450), Hanworth (1450) and Suffield (1480), all *en route* or in proximity to Bromholme Priory by way of Trimingham and its 'head of St John the Baptist'.
[186] Blomefield, *History of Norfolk*, ii. 836.
[187] Harrod, 'Extracts from early Norfolk wills', 122.
[188] *Inventory of church goods*, 99–100.

the last of the comfortable works in helping to bury the dead of this parish in what was construed as a decent and honourable manner.

The same imperatives of commemoration and proximity to the sacred applied to the choice of burial sites, especially within the church building or at its thresholds. Sites close to the sanctuary and the celebration of the mass, or near the chapel or altar of a favoured saint, or the rood, were thought to be especially potent. They were also very sought after, as burial in such a prominent position constituted a statement of wealth and status. First Margaret, then her husband, Robert Blyklyng (d. 1452), chose to be buried in the conventual church of St Mary the Virgin at Carrow abbey, among the nuns, and left a handsome gift of 20s. to their anchoress, Dame Julian Lampet, perhaps in the hope of what they viewed as gilt-edged intercession.[189] Margaret Blyklyng is unusual among lay female testators of this period in her request for burial at Carrow, the ratio in the surviving records being eighteen men to just four women, ten of the men being in holy orders.[190] It may be that Robert's endorsement of his wife's choice of burial site made this for him the fulfilment of the seventh work, in a more personalised and special way.

Another of these exceptions, Elizabeth Yaxley, who died in March 1533, asked to be buried at Mellis if she were living there at the time of her death, or at Carrow, should she be in residence.[191] Perhaps Carrow Abbey was her Norwich *pied à terre*: it may be that she spent her declining years in their community and had close friends among the sisters.[192] She bequeathed to the nuns' church a tapestry depicting scenes typical of the iconography of incarnational piety. Perhaps such an act allowed Elizabeth, and others like her, to continue performing both the corporal and spiritual works after death. It could be argued that the fine tapestry constituted a more effective inducement to prayer for the Yaxleys than Elizabeth's gifts of money, which, once spent, could easily be forgotten. To the prioress, Isobel Wygon, who witnessed Elizabeth's will in 1530 and was executrix, Elizabeth also left a cloth depicting the three Magi, and to the nuns a generous 'v marces [£3 6s. 8d.] equally dyvyded and to praye for me'. She also promised to 'yche of hyr systres a remembrance as it shall please myn executours'.[193] Elizabeth's gift of 'a remembrance' to each of the nuns suggests that, apart from or knowing them personally, she well understood the power of the object to call to mind its owner. Elizabeth was a granddaughter of Margaret and Richard Purdans, so her affinity and piety is, perhaps, not surprising.

Earlier, Elizabeth, widow of Henry Lovell, Lord Morley, in her will proved in February 1500, had also requested burial in the nuns' church. In this case

---

189   NCC, reg. Aleyn, fo. 230 (Blyklyng), 1452.
190   Figures taken from *Carrow abbey, otherwise Carrow priory*, appendix ix, pp. xiii–xxix. According to their wills at least three of these men were chaplains at Carrow.
191   NCC, reg. Platfoote, fo. 104 (Yaxley), 1533.
192   Ibid. fo. 108.
193   Ibid. fo. 106.

the prioress was to benefit by 6s. 8d., and every nun by 3s. 4d.[194] It would appear that burial at Carrow was for the affluent minority, some of whom were already resident there. That so few women, apparently, chose Carrow as a burial location, even if their daughters were nuns there, had no direct correlation with the numbers leaving *post mortem* gifts to the community. For example, Agnes, widow of Ralph Segryme, a prominent alderman of Norwich, left bequests to the prioress and every sister in her will, proved in 1474.[195] Their daughter, Catherine, was a nun at Carrow (later to become prioress), but Agnes still opted for burial in her parish church, St John Maddermarket, alongside her husband and in front of their screen, on which their initials, and Ralph's merchant's mark, were then inscribed.[196]

Across the city in the wealthy riverside parish of St Michael Coslany, Agnes Parker (d. 1505) asked to be buried in the chapel of St John the Baptist within her parish church. She also left rents to fund a lamp before the rood, thus placing a perpetual 'prayer' before the crucifixion represented above the screen.[197] At her death, in 1521, Alice Buxton chose to be buried next to her husband in the nearby churchyard of St Martin Coslany, 'before the image of Our lady in the Oke'. This image was an object of much local veneration to which her husband, John, had left 6d. in 1513, and to which Alice herself was clearly devoted.[198] Perhaps their choice of locus was dictated by the knowledge that their friends and neighbours would regularly offer prayers there too.[199]

Post-mortem commemoration could, however, prove to be problematic. In November 1471, Margaret Paston wrote to her son John III to complain of his elder brother's negligence and irresponsibility. In particular, Margaret felt that the family had been shamed locally because five and a half years after her husband's death, in May 1466, John II had still not commissioned his gravestone: 'Yt is a schame and a thyng that is myche spokyn of in thys contre, that yowr faders graue ston is not mad. For Goddys loue, let yt be remembyrd and purveyde fore in hast.'[200] She was still writing to Sir John, appealing to him directly about this affront, twelve years later, in May 1478, when she reminded him that she had

> sent yow be Whetele the clothe of golde, chargyng yow that it be not solde to non othere vse than to the performyng of yowyr fadyrs tovmbe as ye send me worde in wrytyng. Yf ye sellyt to any othyr vse, by my trowthe I shall neuer

194 NCC, reg. Cobbalde, fo. 183 (Lovell), 1500.
195 NCC, reg. Gelour, fo. 81 (Segryme), 1474.
196 Cotton, 'Medieval roodscreens', 50.
197 NCC, reg. Ryxe, fos 226–7 (Parker), 1505. See also B. Hanawalt, 'Keepers of the lights: late medieval English parish gilds', *Journal of Medieval and Renaissance Studies* xiii (1984), 21–37.
198 ANC, reg. Johnson, fos 227–8 (Buxton), 1513.
199 Blomefield, *History of Norfolk*, iv. 484.
200 *Paston letters*, i. 358–9, letter 212.

trost yow wyll I leve. Remembyr that yt coste me xx marke the pleggyng owte of yt, and yf I where nat glad to se that made I wolde nat departe from it.[201]

Margaret clearly felt she had not completely accomplished the seventh work for her husband, whose soul, along with her own and that of their children and ancestors, might thus be imperilled. Furthermore, the public 'worship' of the Pastons was badly damaged. The urgency of the task left undone demanded the sacrifice of Margaret's treasured cloth of gold, and her sorrow and chagrin at her son's insensitivity is palpable in this, her last surviving letter.

Women's wishes regarding their own burial are now generally unknown, unless they were widows whose wills have either survived or were recorded by antiquaries. Married women would be far less likely to draw up wills or testaments if their husbands were living, as such documents would have had no legal standing without their consent. This, however, was sometimes given. One such case was Helen Moundeforde, the Norwich glazier,[202] who worked on some of the high-quality glass commissioned in St Peter Mancroft church in the 1450s,[203] and may have helped to create some of the panels portraying scenes from the life of St Elizabeth.[204] Helen asked to be buried in the cemetery of St Mary Coslany, a parish church popular with the successful tradesmen and artisans of both sexes who worked or lived in this parish, and whose prayers she could anticipate with confidence.[205]

In this context the extensive use of lights, that is wax candles, tapers and torches, at funerals and burials was a commonplace practice throughout Christendom, and was held to be a major part of funerary ritual and of worship in general. As a symbol of Christ overcoming evil and hell, light in the form of candles or torches was a powerful and living sign. Burning candles were also believed to have apotropaic power, being a symbol of Christ's incarnation in Man's dark world, while simultaneously constituting a prayer of intercession on their own account.[206] It was feared that demons in the guise of temptations to despair or self-pity would make a concerted last-ditch attempt to obtain the soul of the dying, therefore the deployment of lights around death-beds, biers, hearses and graves was understandably popular with testators, both humble and great.[207] Even poorer members of gilds and parishes could participate in this, the seventh work, by the accumu-

---

201 Ibid. i. 380, letter. 228.
202 NCC, reg. Brosyard, fos 84–5 (Moundeford), 1458.
203 King, 'Glazier', 216.
204 Ibid. 222.
205 Unlike most of her contemporaries the married Helen felt it necessary to draw up a will. Her trade may have been the catalyst here. Being a glazier was not without physical risk, and her husband, like Helen, could expect to be commissioned to work far from home.
206 Duffy, Stripping of the altars, 96, 361–2.
207 Hanawalt, 'Keepers of the lights', 28, 32.

lation of small donations to buy a candle or torch for the bier or the requiem mass. Spiritual merit would be attached to such giving, both for the person so honoured and for the giver.[208]

Margaret Stannow, for example, widow of Aylsham, Norfolk, in her will of 1487, bequeathed 'to the lyte of our lady in the same Chyrch [St Michael's, Aylsham] xijd … [and] jli of waxe to a candell, to be brente be forn the ymage of or lady in the chapell in the East ther … to the sustentacon of the lyght, brenyng be forn the partyble upon the perke xijd' (the light burning in front of the great crucifix and set on the rood beam). She proceeded to request, for further assurance, 'that myn executors, after my deth, fynd & susteyn j lampe, brenyng be fron the sacrament bith nyght and day … be the space of an hole yer'.[209] Margaret chose the deployment of her funerary lights with some thought: the Virgin to intercede; the rood with its depiction of the saving passion and wounds; and the sacrament, the redemptive Body itself.

Wax was a commodity constantly in demand in churches and shrines as part of the liturgy and worship. Aside from the specific role played by candles and lights in the seventh work, votive candles and wax models of afflicted parts of the human body were regularly offered up by suppliants in the hope of intercession for recovery, as is shown in the painted glass of York Minster.[210] The wicks of candles were often cut to a significant length, such as the height of the patient, or the assumed height of Christ, or the length of the nails with which he was crucified.[211] In 1443 Margaret Paston's mother-in-law, Agnes, notably donated to the shrine of Our Lady of Walsingham wax equal to the body-weight of her sick son, John.[212] This, combined with Margaret's promised pilgrimage, was their first resort when news came that he had been taken ill in London, and, in writing to tell him so, she thereby made him a participant in his own recovery.[213] Such a large quantity of wax

[208] The earliest document relating to the gild of St George in Norwich (founded prob-ably c.1385) notes as one of its central functions the support of a light: *Gild of St George*, 9. See also Duffy, *Stripping of the altars*, 142–3. The obligation to provide lights was the same for female as for male members of the gild of St Mary, Norwich, which met in the Franciscan friary: 'Alle the bretheryn and sistyn of the gylde … schullen offeryn a candel and to torches of wax … the to torches scullen ben of xl.*lib.* [40lbs] weyghte': *English gilds*, 14.

[209] Harrod, 'Extracts of wills', 116.

[210] Rawcliffe, *Medicine and society*, 22–3.

[211] Linnell, 'The commonplace book of Robert Reynes', 125.

[212] *Paston letters*, ii. 55.

[213] Margaret also made oblation to St Leonard's Priory, Norwich, home of a highly venerated image of St Leonard, which in the year 1348/9 had raised £38 12s. 9d. of the priory's total income of £46: M. R. V. Heale, 'Veneration and renovation at a small Norfolk priory: St Leonard's, Norwich, in the later Middle Ages', *Historical Research* lxxvi (2003), 431–49 at p. 436. Before the image stood a pyx of ivory, containing the purported cap of the saint, together with a 'girdle of the Blessed Virgin'. Because of her pregnancy, the girdle may also have been of current interest to Margaret (p. 438).

was, presumably, made into votive candles for use at the shrine, becoming part of the reciprocal intercessory activity which, in conjunction with the mass, was its core function. As the wax burned and melted, so it was thought, the illness would likewise diminish. The Paston women, mother and wife, may also have thought that, in the possible event of John's death, provision for his soul was also already underway and the intercession inherent in the seventh work partly accomplished by this gift.

Margery Dogett prioritised her requests for lights, placing them even before charitable bequests in her will of 1515. She left:

> to the sepultur light in the same chirche [St Michael of Mustowe] xiid ... to the light of Seynt Myghell, to the perke light, to the light of Our Lady, the light of Seynt Anne, and to the light of Seynt Nicholas in the same chirche, to iche of them ... vid ... to the lampe afor the highe autyer, to the common light that brenneth over Myghellmess evyn and Myghelmes day, and to the light of Seynt Cristofir in the same chirche, to iche of them iiiid.[214]

Margery's honouring of, and supplication to, the Incarnate Christ and his female antecedents, together with the assayer of souls, St Michael, gives a glimpse of her preoccupations as she prepared for death. Her more mundane gifts to her female friends may have been made in anticipation of their prayers or even of their readiness to prepare her corpse for its 'long home'. Alice Hendrye, Margery Appulton, 'Willdes wiff', Anne Lyston, who got her 'werser cloke', 'Bretens wiff' ('beste kyrtill'), 'Medilgat' doughter' ('kertill'): some or all of her friends may have been entrusted with this task. The reciprocity accorded to these activities should not be underestimated: women's support of each other in this ritual echoed that at childbirth, lying-in and laying-out being part of the same spectrum of mutual care.

It is clear that Norfolk women were closely involved in, and attached to, the practice of the seven corporal works of mercy throughout the fifteenth century and beyond. They invested not only their money and time in them, as did many of their husbands, but also their physical and spiritual energies. Placed in the powerful and all-pervasive context of the eucharist and belief in an incarnate God, during a period when the prospect of sudden, unshriven death was a constant and increasing source of anxiety, the continuity of the redemptive work of his body on earth assumed momentous importance. The identification of Christ as *caritas* reinforced this perception. Margery Kempe reported Julian of Norwich telling her that 'The holy gost meuyth neuer a thing a-geyn charite & yf he dede he were contraryows to hys owyn self for he is al charite.'[215]

---

[214] ANC, reg. Cook, fos 46–7 (Dogett), 1503–38.
[215] *Book of Margery Kempe*, i, ch. xviii, p. 42.

Hospitals and nursing: the concise 'comfortable works' package

Nursing, a largely female occupation of service to the body, was generally performed by women at home, but also by sisters, lay and professed, attached to hospitals. These were usually religious or *quasi*-religious foundations, originally for the care of the poor and destitute sick, lepers, aged or disabled clergy and poor travellers such as pilgrims. The primary focus of this care was the health of the soul, without which, it was believed, the body could not thrive or recover, being part of a conjoint whole. The regular celebration of the eucharist was the central dynamic of hospital life, both as an agent of restoration and comfort for the patients and their carers and as a vehicle of intercession for hospital benefactors.[216]

Nurses were involved in the ministration of food and drink to the frail, and the washing and dressing of infected and foetid wounds and sores: the management of a multitude of suppurating skin lesions and diseases, some, rightly or wrongly, identified as leprous. As an act of pious charity this was full of risk for the nurse, but full of spiritual merit for both nurse and benefactor, and implicitly demanded intercessory prayer from the patient.[217] The act of Jesus in washing the feet of his disciples, described in the Gospel of St John, reinforced the reciprocal nature of the merciful works, giving such humble acts the highest endorsement: 'Yf I then youre lorde and master have wesshed youre fete, ye alsoo ought to wesshe one anothers fete.'[218] Again, the association is with the flesh and service to it, specifically perceived as women's territory: St Elizabeth was sometimes depicted washing her patients.[219] The preparation of the dead for burial was also, for nurses in hospital foundations, a regular and core task, which enabled them to accomplish the seventh comfortable work both as individuals and on behalf of others.[220] When they were depicted, they were often shown about this duty as well as nursing the living. Nurses' prayers were sought-after, as legacies frequently testify. Their *post mortem* administrations had obvious gospel antecedents and played a notable part in the rituals of death and burial. Since the nurses performed this work for the poor of Christ, their actions were judged especially meritorious. In the *N-town play*, 'The announcement to the three Marys' begins, significantly, with the voice of the reformed Mary Magdalen, who links

---

[216] Rawcliffe, 'Nurses', 58, and *Medicine for the soul*, chs i, iv; Rubin, *Corpus Christi*, 84–5.

[217] Margery Dogett's discrete grouping together in her will of all the sisters of Normans, each anchorite in the city and each of the 'howses of syke men' implies an expectation of intercession: ANC, reg. Cook, fos 46–7 (Dogett), 1503–38.

[218] John xiii.14. See also *Jacob's well: an English treatise on the cleansing of man's conscience*, ed. A. Brandeis (EETS o.s. cxv, 1900), 247, esp. lines 20–9. A French bishop, while washing the feet of a leper, is requested by him to cleanse with his tongue the 'snevyl' from his sore nostril, and is rewarded with a jewel in his mouth.

[219] An example is in the altarpiece of the collegiate church of Laüfen, near Basle: Rawcliffe, 'Nurses', 60.

[220] Ibid. 44–5.

Christ ('that tholyd wounde') with redemption and healing (she addresses him as 'my leche' or physician). The women reciprocate, as they themselves go to 'leche Cryst: Swete systeryn, I yow besech, / Heryght now my specyal speche: / Go we with salvys for to leche / Cryst, that tholyd wounde. / He hath us wonnyn owt of wreche./ The ryght wey God wyl us teche / For to seke my Lorde, my leche; / His blood hath me vnbownde'.[221]

Some of the women tentatively identified as living in communities resembling beguinages in Norwich may possibly have been involved in such nursing activities, but outside the more formal sisterhood of Norwich's two major hospitals. Even more than the striking number of anchoresses these households seem to have been an urban phenomenon unique to Norwich.[222] It may be significant that the Carmelites, with whom many East Anglian anchoresses were associated, had been very influential in the development, and finally the enclosure, of the beguines in the Low Countries.[223] Moreover, continental beguines, originating in the diocese of Liège, had been devoted to the body of Christ, both in the veneration of the eucharist and in the selfless nursing of the body on earth as represented by the poor and the marginalised.[224] Bequests were made to communities described in wills as 'sisters living together',[225] 'poor women'[226] or 'sisters dedicated to charity',[227] in the parishes of St Swithin (house of John Pellet) and its neighbour St Laurence (tenement of John Asger)[228] and perhaps in the churchyard of St Peter Hungate, feet away from the anchorhold of Blackfriars.[229] These tightly-knit parishes were within easy walking distance of the hospitals of St Giles and St Paul (Norman's), and close to the four leper houses of St Giles, St Benedict, St Leonard and SS Mary and Clement at the city gates. Significantly, the sisters mentioned in Norwich wills lived close to the sites of former almshouses, and near properties accumulated by the brethren of the hospital of St Giles which were let for rent.[230]

---

[221] N-town play, i. 36, p. 359, lines 1–8.

[222] Gilchrist and Oliva identify seventy-three anchoresses on forty-two sites in the diocese in contrast to thirty-two sites for males: Religious women, 75.

[223] This began after the papal bull of Gregory IX in 1233: Devlin, 'Feminine lay piety', 184.

[224] Rubin, Corpus Christi, 166.

[225] 'Sorores pariter comorantes': NCC, reg. Hyrnyng, fo. 153 (Wylby); 'sorores simul comorantes': reg. Surflete, fo. 86 (Baxter).

[226] 'Mulieres paupercule', NCC, reg. Brosyard, fo. 160 (Child).

[227] 'Castitati dedit', NCC, reg. Aleyn, fo. 58 (Veautre); Tanner, Church in Norwich, 65.

[228] RCN ii. 67, no. lxxxvi.

[229] This particular anchorhold had a long tradition of occupation, until its last known anchoress, Katherine Mann, in 1555. The location itself became the site of much radical preaching. Katherine was a correspondent of Thomas Bilney, who was burned as a relapsed heretic, and herself came under suspicion of heresy: Tanner, Church in Norwich, 164, 199.

[230] Rawcliffe, Medicine for the soul, 95, quoting NRO, NCR, 24A, Great Hospital, Norwich, accounts, 1415–60, recording rentals and their locations.

The possibility that lay nursing sisters were members of such communities does not exclude their involvement in other charitable activities. Perhaps these households constituted temporary *maisons dieu* specifically for women, like others for poor people found in many English towns:[231] chamberlains of the city of York, for example, made a regular payment of 20s. a year to a community of poor women of the *maison dieu* situated on the Ouse Bridge,[232] and there is other evidence in Yorkshire of a bias towards the shelter of their own sex among women who founded or supported *maisons dieu*.[233] In Norwich, the parish churchyard of St Swithin, near where the tenement of John Pellet was situated, became the site of an almshouse for respectable widows in the sixteenth century.[234] It may be that this reflected an earlier tradition of female occupation. Although it has been argued that lower-status nuns, for example, did not return to their families at the Dissolution, like their higher-status sisters, but often congregated together,[235] this would not account for the earlier groups of women who were obviously part of the spiritual map of Norwich. Whoever they were, and however they supported themselves (and they are only once described as paupers, which title itself may simply imply a spiritual status of holy poverty), the significant feature is that these 'sisters' attracted bequests; they were, therefore, deemed worthy of charity and their prayers were valued. The possibility that they were involved in some kind of hospital work may further explain both their popularity with testators and their nomenclature.

The hospital of St Paul *ultra aquam*, a Benedictine foundation run by monks of the cathedral priory, had a chequered history. This may well reflect demographic changes in Norwich, as well as a shift in the expression of female piety and women's adherence to a form of the *devotio moderna*. The early hospital statutes had ruled that an unspecified number of lay brothers and sisters were to live under a *quasi*-monastic rule, obedient to the authority

---

[231] K. Kerby-Fulton argues that households in Norwich identified by Tanner as *quasi-beguinages* were sister-houses of the *devotio moderna* movement and based on the continental model: *Books under suspicion: censorship and tolerance of revelatory writings in late medieval England*, Notre Dame 2006, 249.

[232] J. Ward, 'Townswomen and their households', in Britnell, *Daily life*, 41, citing *York city chamberlains' account rolls*, 107, 124, 250, 16. Richard Britnell's article in the same volume: 'York under the Yorkists', notes (p. 175) that this bridge was also the location of a chapel of St William, six shops, a council chamber, the civic prisons and a public latrine, another example of combining the liminal with the pragmatic that is, perhaps, open to many interpretations.

[233] P. Cullum, '"For pore people harberles": what was the function of the *maison dieu?*', in D. J. Clayton, R. G. Davies and P. McNiven (eds), *Trade, devotion and governance: papers in late medieval history*, Stroud 1994, 36–54, esp. p. 47.

[234] Rawcliffe, *Medicine for the soul*, 192–3.

[235] M. Oliva, *The convent and the community in late medieval England: female monasteries in the diocese of Norwich, 1350–1540*, Woodbridge 1998, 61. However, as Harper-Bill and Rawcliffe point out in 'Religious houses', this claim is not supported by the evidence cited: Rawcliffe and Wilson, *Medieval Norwich*, 73–120.

of the master. By the mid-1370s the lay brothers of St Paul's seem to have vanished, leaving a community of sisters of two kinds, 'half' and 'whole', both kinds fed and clothed by the foundation, but only the latter, apparently, living in.[236] They attracted small but regular bequests from a third of the testators of Norwich between 1370 and 1532, gifts of money being sometimes supplemented by household goods. The half-sisters, unlike their 'whole' *sororum societas*, were not bound forever to the foundation, and the records of St Paul's show that at least two left, one permanently.[237]

The regular bequests of clothing, goods and small amounts of money to sisters, both half and whole, at St Paul's hospital may be interpreted as an attempt to accomplish the practice of the comfortable works in a concise and economical fashion. Hospital foundations by their existence and function daily fulfilled most of the seven, often vicariously through the agency of the nurse. A recurring feature of *post-mortem* arrangements, such charity can also be seen as a further reflection of the incarnational and redemptive piety to which so much hope was attached. Thus, Alice Crome, widow of Norwich, in her will of 1516 bequeathed: 'To evy sister and halff sister of the Normans, ijd'.[238] Alice, unlike many, did not adjust the amount according to the sisters' status, but valued the prayers of both categories.

Another Alice, widow of Thomas Richeman, worsted-weaver, of the parish of St Martin at Oak, Coslany, in her will of 1521, left to 'hol systers and half systers beyond and dwellyng in the hos of Normans, ijd', also making quite explicit her reluctance to distinguish between the resident sisters and those living 'beyond' the precinct. She added a gift of a 'blanket and shett of my household stuf for the pore house ther to be used to the ease of the pore bedryd'.[239] The 'pore house' was for a category of paupers defined by their inability through sickness, infirmity or extreme decrepitude to be self-supporting by labour of any kind.[240] St Paul's Hospital was comparatively unusual in that it had once received pregnant women in need, which may account for the origin of its school. Care of the orphaned babies may have become part of the hospital's response to the destitute poor.[241] Thomas Salter (1478–1558), priest, remembered with affection Dame Katherine Peckham, whose teaching had been the basis of his primary education in Norwich, and in thanksgiving for which he left the 'pore sisters' a gift.[242]

---

[236] Rawcliffe, *Hospitals of medieval Norwich*, 69–70.

[237] Ibid. 74.

[238] NCC, reg. Gylys, fos 94–5 (Crome), 1516. Alice also founded a modest almshouse in the parish of St George, Colgate.

[239] NCC, reg. Allblaster, fos 215–17 (Richeman), 1523.

[240] Cullum, 'Pore people harberles', 41.

[241] There is a full account of St Paul's in Rawcliffe, *Hospitals of medieval Norwich*, 61–89; for its nurses and other staff see pp. 69–77.

[242] Thomas Salter, priest, 1478–1558, left a bequest of regular fresh bread to the sisters of St Paul's in fond remembrance of Dame Katherine, who had taught him to read there seventy-two years before: 'almes I have fownded and willed it to be given *specially to the*

In order for a woman to become a 'whole', i.e. resident, hospital sister, whether she was driven by a vocation or the basic need to find a job with inclusive accommodation, money was required. 'Poor' sisters were often supported by bequests of money, clothes or household articles. Bishop Walter Suffield had stipulated in 1249 that four sisters, of fifty years of age or a little less, should care for the poor sick of his hospital of St Giles. When not so engaged they were required to be active in pious and charitable works. He also stated that services at the chapel should be suspended if any other women entered the precinct. In spirit, if not in letter, his rule began to be breached within sixty years by the selling of corrodies. In 1309 the widowed Mary de Attleburgh sought a form of sheltered accommodation by offering her estates at Seething to the hospital for a corrody as a hospital sister. It seems as if expediency was directing this shift away from the founder's intentions; some women, who were clearly pensioners, were being received into the sisterhood of St Giles.[243] This must, however, remain in part a grey area. The ubiquitous influence of the *cultus* of St Elizabeth of Hungary and the promotion of the importance of the practice of the corporal works of mercy may have inspired some pious widows when electing this course of action. Certainly, the maintenance of thirty beds and care of their occupants guaranteed a life that was no sinecure for the uncommitted. And, naturally, some were not.

Alice Bothumsyll and Dame Elizabeth Ordyng, who entered the sisterhood of St Giles around the same time, in 1517, had to provide the requisite cost of entry in instalments. Alice's kinsman, Stephen, paid the master £3 6s. 8d. over a period of four or five years, while Dame Elizabeth, who had difficulty fulfilling her obligation, was aided by the master, John Hecker, who completed her payment himself.[244] It is interesting that nine years later Alice Bothumsyll left the hospital with a wagon-load of property to live in Watton, demonstrating a certain flexibility with regard to her 'profession'. It may be that Alice had developed an infirmity of body or mind which made her continued presence problematic. Her retention of her personal possessions would indicate, at the least, a life not lived in communal austerity.

The nursing sisters at St Paul's were frequently beneficiaries of small legacies, which helped those with little or no funding. Katherine Brasyer, wealthy Norwich widow and friend of Margaret Purdans, remembered the half and whole sisters of 'Norman's', who each received 4d., except for three

---

said pore sisters bycause I have a greate truste that they will praie for me' (my italics): PCC, reg. Welles, fo. 13; TNA, PRO, 11/42a, p. 101.

[243] Rawcliffe, *Medicine for the soul*, appendix 1 (statutes for the foundation of the Great Hospital, Norwich), article 5 at pp. 241–8; article 10 (revised) at p. 243; article 32 (29) at p. 245; NRO, Phi 311, cited at pp. 171, 297 n. 88.

[244] Hecker commissioned the beautiful pew-end in the nave of St Helen's church depicting St Margaret bursting forth from the dragon. The sisters of St Paul's were also expected to pay 10 marks (£6 13s. 4d.) on entry: Rawcliffe, *Hospitals in medieval Norwich*, 74, referring to the 1492 visitation of Bishop Goldwell.

named sisters: Alice Cofeld (6s. 8d.), Joan Baron (20d.) and Cecily Rante (12d.), who were obviously known to her and whose prayers she clearly sought.[245]

It is arguable that women, in particular, esteemed the sacred symbolism of the role that the physical administration of such works gave them, in addition to their accumulation of spiritual merit. The physical aspects of the works of mercy and the humility required in their administration placed them squarely in the female domain. Indeed, it has been suggested that the lack of widespread almshouse provision in Norwich was offset by a coherent and effective system of parish and hospital relief.[246] It was in this milieu that women significantly featured. Such charity provided many opportunities for them to combine the active with the contemplative life, and assigned to them a significant public and communal role. Mary and Martha of Bethany provided the models for this dual focus of service. Further endorsement came from a society characterised by spiritual reciprocity, in the context of the mass.[247] The sacramental resonance of such activities had a deep and lasting appeal for pious women. In this important respect, it was a role that they were soon to lose.

While it may be argued that charitable works continued to be undertaken by pious women in the reformed Church, and outside it, the context of the mass and the veneration of the sacrament in the company of visible images of the community of saints had gone. Women's role as agents of charity, which they had valued for generations because of the parallels with the sacred, was to become totally bereft of its former terms of engagement. The performance of charity by women outside the household and the mobility that had legitimately come with it ceased to be understood as a redemptive activity, or to be identified with the physical self-giving of Christ. Charity was henceforth to begin, and stay, at home.

[245] NCC, Reg Brosyard, fos 58–9 (Brasyer), 1457.
[246] Phillips, 'Charitable institutions', 290–3.
[247] This was advocated by Nicholas Love, prior of Mount Grace (1410–17) in his *Mirror of the blessed life of Jesus Christ* (ed. M. G. Sargent, Exeter 2005). See also *Book of Margery Kempe*, p. xxxii.

Conclusion

It is indisputable that Norwich's long-established status as an important entrepot for international trade supplied the material foundations, as well as the channel, for what was to become a fertile *milieu* of innovative piety and religious thought of singular interest to women. In particular, the influence of the Low Countries and Germany is demonstrated in surviving painted glass, commemorative brasses, painted panels of rood-screens and, not least, in the content of the revelatory spiritual autobiographies written by two Norfolk women, both living in busy urban centres of industry and trade.[1] The range of charitable bequests recorded in women's wills continued to demonstrate their aspiration to combine the pragmatic with spiritual benefit. This was true even at the cutting edge of religious practice, for example, where a well-known anchoress might be asked to administer funds and accommodation. Gifts to hospital sisters, to friends living in monastic establishments, or to family servants were all intended in their individual way to enhance the *opus dei.*

Women from the city and its hinterlands had an extensive and often multi-layered understanding of the implications of incarnational religion: God made flesh. The feast of the Annunciation and its powerful symbolism made clear how God's offering of himself to mankind was to be responded to by Christians in their own sacrificial charitable works which were to mirror both Mary's response to Gabriel's message and Christ's mode of life and death on earth. In this respect the Annunciation linked firmly with the passion of Jesus, which was perceived as the greatest act of *caritas* possible. It promised redemption for the benefactor who paid for and commissioned good works, the practical implementation of charity, and even for the benefited if they reciprocated by intercessor prayer.

Attachment to the cult of the holy kin in western Christendom enabled women to obtain validation as seekers of an interior spirituality through the exemplars of St Anne and her three married daughters, as well as *auctoritas* in running sometimes very complicated households within a wide network of extended family, including in-laws, godchildren, employees and long-term friends. Examples are numerous, among them Margaret Paston, her kinswoman the five-times-married Elizabeth Drake of Norwich and Agnes Thorpe of St Michael Conslany, twice-married with a husband, Robert, and three sets of in-laws and step-children. The very considerable success of the cult of St Anne in Norwich, as well as in the greater diocese, is a significant

---

[1] King, 'Glazier', 220; Mitchell, 'Painting in East Anglia around 1500', 373–80.

marker of the utility and empowerment that women in particular discovered in her legend and iconography. Like many of her devotees, she began her legend as a wife with a fertility problem, but became through three marriages a fruitful progenitrix of an extensive and influential dynasty, and, like more than a few women in Norwich, ended her life and story as a chaste widow and grandmother, similar to those endorsed by St Jerome.

With marriage came childbirth and, in the medieval period, serious risk of neo-natal death for mother and child. Having argued for female attachment to the cult of the virgin St Margaret for these obvious and understandable reasons, it is clear that her protection and patronage were not merely a matter of pragmatic delivery, but rather of deliverance in its fullest sense. Again, personal empowerment and the protection of mother and infant through dependence on the unmediated intervention of Margaret's direct offices with God come high on her agenda in a way not offered by any other virgin martyr. If there were no other documentary or testamentary evidence, her sixty gild dedications and forty-eight surviving parish churches would surely proclaim her central importance in Norfolk and Norwich.

The Magdalen, the penitent fallen woman risen to spectacular spiritual heights by, like Margaret of Antioch, becoming 'spiritually male', in her case through her association with the living and dead body of Christ, shows another aspect of incarnational piety, demonstrated in the Gospels and taken up in Norwich. Her *persona* and legend, a conflation of several women, became an icon of special interest both to the professed religious and to the aspirational lay. Her teaching and preaching activities were, sadly, doomed to be ever over-shadowed by her image as an exorcised, tearful, reformed harlot of great beauty. The purging of her demons, said the propaganda, allowed space for the works of mercy, both corporal and spiritual, to fill the vacuum. The connectedness of physical and spiritual health, upheld by the Aristotelian and Galenic medicine of the time, made her the patron of *leprosaria* and other shelters. Her importance to the mystical tradition of this region, within and beyond the books of Julian of Norwich and Margery Kempe, is a matter for conjecture. The suspicion remains that many Norfolk churches, apparently dedicated to the Virgin Mary, began their existence under the patronage of quite another Mary, who was to prove far too subversive to the reforming mind. Anne, Margaret, Mary Magdalen gained much of their potency as women whose fleshliness had been justified, triumphant or rehabilitated: a redemption associated with the fleshly vulnerability of Christ's wounded body, which reinforced the attraction.

Last among the cults of female saints here is that of St Bridget of Sweden. The influence of her life and writings in fifteenth-century East Anglia, albeit male-mediated, awaits a full assessment. It is clear, however, that her revelations were popular among urban wives and their professed sisters and daughters vowed to the conventual life. This was so whether they could read or not. It may be that the mendicant orders, as well as other interested clerics, played an active role in the dissemination of the contents of Bridget's book, if not the text itself, as demonstrated by Mrs Kempe. Margaret Purdans was one pious Norwich widow who possessed a vernacular version and it is known that she enjoyed a wide and active circle of spiritually-inclined friends. The manifest increase, in the late Middle Ages, in the cults of saints who were married and mothers signals many things, but it was saints such as Anne, Elizabeth of Hungary and Bridget whose cults promoted marriage as an estate in which piety and even sanctity might flourish. By the same token, the promotion of the seven corporal works of mercy as a means of imitating Christ and obtaining redemption married well with this enhanced status.

The richness of surviving material culture in the many medieval churches of Norwich and Norfolk, and the range of literature written by and for people with local connections, points to the wealth, activity and entrepreneurial spirit of the region. Add to this treasure trove the archive of wills and other city records, and it would be a very closed mind that, once aware, was not receptive to the preoccupations and initiatives of fifteenth-century Norwich women.

It would be unrealistic, however, to assume that every woman in Norwich and its environs was eager to cultivate a life of spiritual poverty, or sought to perform good works as a vocational endeavour. None the less, the surviving material culture alone suggests that an understanding of such ideas prevailed for generations at different levels of perception across the many social divides. Evolving and challenging theological concepts were, moreover, taken up and interpreted in a number of ways, often combining the practical with the spiritual. It is notable, for example, that women's wills often demonstrate an ongoing concern for their servants and other dependants. Agnes Segryme, in her will written in 1474, left to her servant Isabell 20s., along with good household linen and pewter goods, the wherewithal to begin her own house-hold.[2] This mindfulness of the individual situations of one's dependants is occasionally carried over into remembrance of and concern for the servants of others; thus, for example, Margaret Purdans strikingly left 20s. to each of the servants of the anchoress Julian Lampet, to whom she also intended to give an equal gift.[3] This amount of money could have bought substan-tial intercession (specifically, the prayers of three women at the centre of religious life in Norwich) over a long period. Herein is demonstrated the pragmatic interface of pious bequest and works of charity, and the reluctance to divide the material from the spiritual, which is a dominant and recurring characteristic of late female medieval religion. It is seen to be 'writ large' in the female domain precisely because the material and fleshly were perceived

---

[2] NCC, reg. Gelour, fo. 82 (Agnes Segryme), 1474. Agnes is clear that Isabell should 'abyde' with her body until her interment, performing domestically the seventh comfort-able work.

[3] NCC, reg. Caston, fos 163–5 (Margaret Purdans). In the event, Lampet predeceased her.

as central to women's nature as well as pertaining to their area of responsibility. The tensions in the legend of St Margaret reflect this.

The empowerment, even elevated status, bestowed on those performing
the seven corporal works of mercy is exemplified in devotion to the cult of St
Elizabeth of Hungary, whose depiction survives in glass at St Peter Mancroft
in the heart of the city, and on the screen formerly at the suburban church
of St James Pockthorpe, as well as on those at the churches of Barnham
Broom and Upton, in the Norwich hinterlands. Such female aspiration
is further endorsed in the cult of St Anne, whose legend confirmed that
married women with children could indeed aspire to sanctity. The attraction
of combining charitable activity with contemplative, even revelatory, piety
is found, in its different aspects, in devotion to the Magdalen, who occupied
a unique place in Norwich religious life. Her cult, in a sense, embodies the
'cutting edge' of piety as practised by some women in Norwich, who were
themselves supported by innovative, if liminal, sometimes charismatic figures
of marked and acknowledged spiritual stature. It was in many respects distant
from the piety of aristocrats such as Margaret Beaufort, Cecily Neville or
even Alice Chaucer, in that it involved personal engagement with the sick,
the derelict and the dead, in addition to exposure to inspirational literature
and the daily offices. Sufficient evidence remains to claim a vigorous and
evolving incarnational piety at the end of the fifteenth century and beyond
for Norwich women who in a busy industrial and commercial context lived
out their religious aspirations and demonstrated an affective and reciprocal
piety. The frequency with which the sons and daughters of the commercially
successful merchants of Norwich embraced a life in professed religion, many
locally, may also indicate the seriousness with which their mothers often
undertook their spiritual obligations as promoted and endorsed by St Bridget
of Sweden in her influential writings.[4] In this Norwich differs markedly from
the mercantile community of Bristol, for example.

Inevitably, a concluding word must be allowed to Margery Kempe, who,
at the end of her book, in her old age, recorded her prayers of intercession.
Among her petitions, she prays: 'I cry the mercy, Lord, for alle my frendys &
for alle myn enemijs, for alle that arn seke, specialy, for alle lazerys, for alle
bedred men & women, for alle that arn in preson … H aue mercy vp-on
them, & be as gracyows to her sowlys as I wolde that thu wer to myn.'[5] Such
spiritual interconnectedness and reciprocity were the aims of all members of
the Church Militant aspiring to salvation. The practice of the comfortable
works was the means. Many Norwich women attempted to achieve this goal
with the means at their disposal, whether in the unrecorded gift of bread

4   This was clearly understood by Margery Kempe: see p. 109 above.
5   *Book of Margery Kempe*, ii, ch.x, p. 251, lines 15–21.

for a sick neighbour or the bequest of 6*d.* towards the construction of their parish church steeple.[6]

Julian of Norwich, however, has the final say. She regarded charitable activity as evidence of the immanence of the Holy Spirit working in harmony in her 'even christians' to the fulfilment of God's will, human redemption: 'For theyse wurke in vs contynually, alle t(o) geder, and thoo be gret thinges; of whych gretnesse he wylle we haue knowyng here, as it were in an ABC. That is to sey that we haue a lyttlle knowyng, where of we shulde haue fulhed in hevyn; and that is for to spede vs.'[7] Earlier in the Long Text Julian had identified the crux of the matter: the wounded Christ was 'our owne kynde'. *Caritas* was his outworking.

---

[6] Joan Gedney left 6*d.* to the steeple of St Peter Mancroft in 1508: NCC, reg. Spyltymber, fo. 90 (Joan Gedney), 1508. In the same year Amelyn Caster, of Norwich St Laurence, left 6*s.* 8*d.* to the 'fynyshyng of ye stepyll of her own church': NCC, reg. Johnson, fo. 205 (Amelyn Caster), 1508. The tolling of bells as a call to prayer, or to mark a death, constituted a much valued form of intercession. Surviving wills show that women of varying economic status throughout Norfolk were investing in steeples and bells.

[7] Julian of Norwich, *Showings*, pt II, ch. lxxx, p. 708, lines 9–12. Julian here outlines a credal statement of the necessary things: human compassion; the teaching of holy Church; and the action of the holy spirit.

APPENDICES

APPENDIX 1

Material evidence for the cult of St Anne in Norwich and Norfolk

NORWICH

Altars known to have been dedicated to St Anne

St Gregory	Blomefield, *History of Norfolk*, iv. 273. Shared dedication.
St Mary Coslany	Blomefield, *History of Norfolk*, iv. 489. Elizabeth Knowte (d. 1493) requested burial by St Anne's altar: NCC, reg. Aubrey, fos 142–3.
St Michael at Plea	Blomefield, *History of Norfolk*, iv. 325
St Peter Mancroft	Blomefield, *History of Norfolk*, iv. 207; King, *Medieval stained glass*, v. 145, citing will of Thomas de Ryselee (1391)

Chapels known to have been dedicated to St Anne

Carrow priory	*Carrow abbey*, p. xlviii
Cathedral church	Chapel with image *c.*1329; Dodwell, 'William Baucheron', 112; Shinners, 'Veneration of saints', 40, 138; Blomefield, *History of Norfolk*, iv. 38
Greyfriars	Blomefield, *History of Norfolk*, iv. 109–10. Lady Margaret Carbonel (d.1431) buried in this chapel
St Andrew	East end, south aisle: Blomefield, *History of Norfolk*, iv. 302–3
St Anne Conesford	Chapel of ease for St Clement, demolished by 1370 and united with St Clement's: R. C. Taylor, *Index monasticus: the abbeys and other monasteries, alien priories, colleges, collegiate churches and hospitals, with their dependencies, formerly established in the diocese of Norwich and the ancient kingdom of East Anglia, systematically arranged and briefly described, according to the respective orders and denominations in each country*, London 1821, 70

St Clement Conesford Blomefield, *History of Norfolk*, iv. 78. Katherine Marchale (d.1458) gave a silver tablet and chain.

St Margaret Westwick East end, south aisle, gild meeting place: Blomefield, *History of Norfolk*, iv. 258

St Peter Mancroft East end, south aisle, gild meeting place: Blomefield, *History of Norfolk*, iv. 207

St Stephen North aisle, founded by Lettice Pain c.1313, with rents of £6 6s. 8d.: Blomefield, *History of Norfolk*, iv. 163–4.

Church windows recorded as containing images of St Anne

St Peter Mancroft, Norwich East window*: King, *Medieval stained glass*, iv

St Stephen, Norwich East window, German*: David King: personal communication

Gilds known to have been dedicated to the patronage of St Anne

St Martin at Bailey NCC, reg. Heydon, fo. 24 (Ladde)

St Martin at Palace NCC, reg. Ryxe, fo. 194 (Daywell), 449; Blomefield, *History of Norfolk*, iv. 369

St Peter Mancroft NCC, reg. Aubry, fo. 32 (Kempe); Reg. Haywarde fo. 149 (Petifer)

Images and lights known to have been dedicated to St Anne

St Edmund Blomefield, *History of Norfolk*, iv. 405

St Gregory Image in the chapel of St Thomas, south aisle: Blomefield, *History of Norfolk*, iv. 273

St Helen St Giles's hospital possessed an image in the chancel in the fifteenth century: Rawcliffe, *Medicine for the soul*, 125.

St John at Sepulchre An image in tabernacle in nave: Blomefield, *History of Norfolk*, iv. 141

St Martin at Palace Blomefield, *History of Norfolk*, iv. 369

St Mary Coslany In Lady chapel on south side: Blomefield, *History of Norfolk*, iv. 490

St Michael at Plea Blomefield, *History of Norfolk*, iv. 325

St Peter Hungate Blomefield, *History of Norfolk*, iv. 325

St Peter Mancroft Blomefield, *History of Norfolk*, iv. 207

SS Simon and Jude Image in 1531: Blomefield, *History of Norfolk*, iv. 356

St Stephen	Blomefield, *History of Norfolk*, iv. 152–3, 163. Alice Carr left her small coral beads for daily adornment of the image, to be replaced by her best beads on feast days.
Whitefriars	Taylor, *Index monasticus*, 42; Blomefield, *History of Norfolk*, iv. 417. Christian Savage (d. 1440), requested burial before St Anne's image, in the chapel of the Holy Cross: NCC, Reg. Doke, fo.167; Blomefield, *History of Norfolk*, iv. 41. Beneath this chapel was sited one anchorhold of the friary.

NORFOLK

Church windows recorded as containing images of St Anne

Fersfield	East window, south aisle: Blomefield, *History of Norfolk*, i. 105
Ketteringham	roundel *
Mileham	south east chancel
Mulbarton	fragments
Outwell	north chancel
Oxborough	east window, north aisle

Gilds and chapels known to have been dedicated to St Anne

Acle Priory	Taylor, *Index monasticus*, 71
Blakeney Whitefriars	Blomefield, *History of Norfolk*, ix. 455, 1518
Congham	Taylor, *Index monasticus*, 72
Cromer	Blomefield, *History of Norfolk*, viii. 107
East Dereham	Blomefield, *History of Norfolk*, xvii. 96
East Harling	Blomefield, *History of Norfolk*, i. 330. Chapel founded by Anne Harling.
Fersfield	Blomefield, *History of Norfolk*, i.105.
Great Fransham	Blomefield, *History of Norfolk*, ix. 499
Happisburgh	Blomefield, *History of Norfolk*, ix. 301
Hickling	Blomefield, *History of Norfolk*, ix. 307
Horsey	Taylor, *Index monasticus*, 72
Hunworth	Chapel, 1506, with alabaster depicting St Anne and the Virgin: Harrod, 'Extracts from early Norfolk wills', 111–28 at p. 123
Litcham	E. Puddy, *Litcham*, Dereham n.d., 49
Little Walsingham St Peter	Blomefield, *History of Norfolk*, ix. 271
Lynn, location unknown	Nativity of the Blessed Virgin Mary
Lynn Greyfriars	*Making of Kings Lynn*, 325

Lynn St Margaret	Conception (by St Anne) of the Blessed Virgin Mary: TNA C 47/42/240
Lynn St Nicholas	*Making of Kings Lynn*, 29, citing will evidence.
North Barningham	Blomefield, *History of Norfolk*, viii. 96
North Wootton	Blomefield, *History of Norfolk*, ix. 203; L'Estrange cites six bells inscribed with prayers to St Anne: *Church-bells of Norfolk*, 13
Poringland	Blomefield, *History of Norfolk*, v. 442
Shipdham	*Carrow abbey*, 134
Snettisham	Blomefield, *History of Norfolk*, x. 379
South Creake	Blomefield, *History of Norfolk*, vi. 84
Stratton St Michael	Taylor, *Index monasticus*, 74
Swanton Morley	Blomefield, History of Norfolk, x. 57
Thetford St Peter	Gild and chapel, east end, north aisle: Blomefield, *History of Norfolk*, ii, 62. Sibill Tillis (d. 1503) gave 13s. 4d. towards a new tabernacle of St Anne for the saint's chapel: NCC, reg. Popy, fo. 286.
Tottington St Andrew	Nativity of the Blessed Virgin Mary: Blomefield, *History of Norfolk*, ii. 355
Walsoken All Saints	Gild of the nativity of the Blessed Virgin Mary: Blomefield, *History of Norfolk*, ix. 128.
Weybridge Priory	Nichols, *The early art of Norfolk*, 164.
Wiggenhall St Mary	Gild of the nativity of the Blessed Virgin Mary: TNA, C 47/45/36
Wymondham St Mary	WPC, statutes of gild and accounts 1470–1544, gild of the nativity of the Blessed Virgin Mary

Painted glass, wall-painting, screen panel or carving depicting St Anne, or lights, recorded and gone or extant*

East Barsham	Alabaster fragments built into a barn wall, including a figure of St Anne teaching the Virgin to read: Martin, 'Some fragments', 257–8.
Fakenham	South side: Blomefield, *History of Norfolk*, vii. 96
Fersfield	Image and lights: Blomefield, *History of Norfolk*, i. 105.
Great Fransham	An altar c. 1358: *Inventory of church goods temp. Edward III*, ii. 105
Great Plumstead	Commissioning of St Anne's image in alabaster:

	NCC, Reg. Spyltymber fos 42–6, will of Henry Wilton
Harpley St Laurence	Screen: Anne and Joachim teaching the Virgin to read: Williamson, 'Saints on Norfolk rood-screens', 329*
Houghton St Giles	Lady screen: Williamson, 'Saints on Norfolk-rood screens', 330*
Little Walsingham	Image: Blomefield, *History of Norfolk*, ix. 271; NCC, reg. Palgrave, fo. 43 (John Harte) 1526, requested burial before image
Lynn	*Making of Kings Lynn*, 21, 29, cites St Anne's Fort, at port mouth, chapel in St Nicholas's church.
Marsham	Lights: Blomefield, *History of Norfolk*, vi. 287
North Barningham	Image: Blomefield, *History of Norfolk*, viii. 96
North Wootton	Image, 1534 bequest for tabernacle of St Anne: Blomefield, *History of Norfolk*, ix. 203
Outwell	Lights: c. 1514: Williams, 'Some Norfolk churches', 333–44, 339
Oxborough	Image on the north side: Blomefield, *History of Norfolk*, vi. 183
Ranworth St Helen	Image and lights: Duffy, *Stripping of the altars*, 182 n. 73
Stratton Strawless	Lights c. 1490: Harrod, 'Early Norfolk wills', 117
Yarmouth	Image c. 1484/5: A. W. Morant, 'Notices of the church of St Nicholas, Great Yarmouth', *NA* vii (1872), 232

None extant except those marked *

Many of these citations are extracted and collated from Nichols, *The early art of Norfolk*.

Material evidence for the cult of St Margaret of Antioch in Norwich and Norfolk

NORWICH

Gilds known to have been dedicated to the patronage of St Margaret

Austin Friars	Tanner, *Church in Norwich*, 208
St Margaret Fyebridge	Tanner, *Church in Norwich*, 209

Images known to have been dedicated to St Margaret

Cathedral church	Wall-painting on anti-reliquary chapel arch.* Image: Shinners, 'Veneration of saints', 143
St George Tombland	Blomefield, *History of Norfolk*, iv. 474–5
St Gregory, Charing Cross	Image; wall-painting with St George*: Blomefield, *History of Norfolk*, iv. 274
St Helen Bishopgate	Carved pew end of Margaret erupting from dragon situated in the nave* Ceiling boss in Goldwell chantry in same nave*
St James Pockthorpe	Sculpture on font stem*
St Margaret Newbridge	At least two images of the saint, the principal one transferred on its conversion to St George Tombland
St Margaret Westwick	Sculptured north porch spandrels*
St Michael at Plea	Large painted panel (now in a cathedral vestry*)
St Peter Mancroft	Alabaster panel featuring Margaret and mainly local female saints, nine in all* Painted glass scenes from life of Margaret in a fifteenth century series* Basin with blue enamel Vestments
St Peter Parmentergate	Painted glass: Blomefield, *History of Norfolk*, iv. 96
St Stephen	Image of St Margaret: Blomefield, *History of Norfolk*, iv. 154

NORFOLK

Gilds, churches and chapels known to have been dedicated to St Margaret

(All named have documented gilds.)

Antingham St Mary	Blomefield, *History of Norfolk*, viii. 77
Aylsham St Michael	Blomefield, *History of Norfolk*, vi. 277
Barnham Norton St Margaret	Blomefield, *History of Norfolk*, vii. 19
Beachamwell St Mary	TNA, C 47/42/224
Bodham All Saints	Blomefield, *History of Norfolk*, ix. 369
Breckles St Margaret	Blomefield, *History of Norfolk*, ii. 272–3
Briston All Saints	TNA, E 179/150/236
Burgh St Margaret	Blomefield, *History of Norfolk*, xi. 156
Burnham Westgate St Mary	Blomefield, *History of Norfolk*, vii. 38
Cantley St Margaret	Blomefield, *History of Norfolk*, vii. 231
Clenchwarton St Margaret	image: TNA, C 47/42/228
Cley-next-the-Sea St Margaret	Taylor, *Index monasticus*, 71
Drayton St Margaret	Blomefield, *History of Norfolk*, x. 412
East Bradenham St Mary	NCC, reg. Norman, fo. 7r, R. Newman, 1486
East Dereham St Nicholas	Blomefield, *History of Norfolk*, x. 213
Felthorpe St Margaret	Blomefield, *History of Norfolk*, x. 416
Filby All Saints	Blomefield, *History of Norfolk*, xi. 221
Garveston St Margaret	NCC, reg. Ryxe fo. 159r, T. Garnet 1505
Great Snoring St Mary	Blomefield, *History of Norfolk*, ix. 258
Griston St Margaret	Blomefield, *History of Norfolk*, ii. 290
Hardley St Margaret	Blomefield, *History of Norfolk*, x.141
Harpely St Laurence	Blomefield, *History of Norfolk*, viii. 458
Heacham St Mary	Blomefield, *History of Norfolk*, x. 312
Helmingham St Margaret	Blomefield, *History of Norfolk*, viii. 239
Hilborough All Saints	Blomefield, *History of Norfolk*, vi. 115 n. 6
Little Dunham St Margaret	Blomefield, *History of Norfolk*, ix. 481
Lyng St Clement	Blomefield, *History of Norfolk*, viii. 252
Lynn Greyfriars' church	*Making of Kings Lynn*, 325
Lynn St Margaret	TNA, C 47/43/262
North Tuddenham All Saints	Taylor, *Index monasticus*, 74
North Walsham St Nicholas	Blomefield, *History of Norfolk*, xi. 79
Old Buckenham All Saints	TNA, E 179/150/202; E 179/150/235
Ormesby St Margaret	Blomefield, *History of Norfolk*, xi. 239
Ovington St John	Blomefield, *History of Norfolk*, ii. 296
Pudding Norton St Margaret	Blomefield, *History of Norfolk*, vii. 119
Reepham St Mary	Taylor, *Index monasticum*, 74
Runhall All Saints	Blomefield, *History of Norfolk*, ii. 474

Salle SS Peter and Paul	Blomefield, *History of Norfolk*, viii. 276
Saxlingham Nethergate St Mary	Blomefield, *History of Norfolk*, v. 501
Saxlingham St Margaret	Blomefield, *History of Norfolk*, ix. 436
Seething St Margaret	Blomefield, *History of Norfolk*, x. 177
Stanfield St Margaret	Blomefield, *History of Norfolk*, x. 53
Stratton Strawless St Margaret	Blomefield, *History of Norfolk*, vi. 442
Suffield St Margaret	NRO, Gunton Collection, 1424–1523, uncatalogued version of bede roll
Swanington St Margaret	Blomefield, *History of Norfolk*, viii. 265
Tatterford St Margaret	Blomefield, *History of Norfolk*, vii. 192
Thornham All Saints	Blomefield, *History of Norfolk*, viii. 175
Thrigby St Mary	Blomefield, *History of Norfolk*, xi. 254
Thurgarton All Saints	Taylor, *Index monasticum*, 74
Topcroft St Margaret	Blomefield, *History of Norfolk*, x. 189
Tunstead St Mary	Blomefield, *History of Norfolk*, xi. 73
Upton St Margaret	Blomefield, *History of Norfolk*, xi. 134
Wallington cum Thorpland St Margaret	TNA, E 179/150/203
Wereham St Margaret	Blomefield, *History of Norfolk*, vii. 508
Witton St Margaret	Blomefield, *History of Norfolk*, vii. 267
Wolterton St Margaret	Blomefield, *History of Norfolk*, vi. 452
Wymondham St Mary	NRO, ANF Liber I, fo. 135r Stephen Dote 1483; ANF Gillior, fo. 3r William Plomer 1535) image
Yarmouth	Blomefield, *History of Norfolk*, xi. 366

Painted glass, wall-painting, screen panel or carving depicting St Margaret, recorded and gone or extant*

Alderford	Painted glass
Babingley	Screen panel
Brandiston	Painted glass
Bressingham	Painted glass
Catfield	Wall-painting*
Clenchwarton	Image
Cringleford	Painted glass
Docking	Stone carving: font stem*
East Rudham	Painted glass
Felbrigg	Silver paten, 1480–1500 (in use)*
Filby	Screen panel*
Foulden?	No dragon*
Framingham Earl	Painted glass
Gooderstone	Image
Great Massingham	Painted glass

Gressenhall	Screen panel
Haveringland	Screen panel
Heacham	Painted glass*
Hemblington	Stone carving: font stem*
Heydon	Painted glass*
Hingham	Stone carving*
Hockering	Stone carving: font stem*
Ketteringham	Painted glass*
Kimberley	Painted glass*
Lessingham	Screen door
Lynn	Common seal; mayoral seal
Lynn Whitefriars	Seal
Martham	Painted glass: two painted glass panels*
Merton	Painted glass*
Mileham	Painted glass
North Walsham	Screen panel*
Paston	Image
Ranworth	Screen panel*
Repps	Screen panel
Rougham	Stone carving*
Rushforth College	Seal
Salle	Painted glass (not *in situ*)
Sandringham	Painted glass*
Sharrington	Painted glass
Shipdham	Stone carving
Stody	Painted glass fragment*
Stratton St Michael	Painted glass*
Swaffham	Image
Swannington	Stone carving*
Thetford priory	Retable, now at Thornham Parva, Suffolk*
Upton	Image
Walpole St Peter	Image and screen panel*
Walsoken	Stone carving: font stem*
Weasenham St Peter	Painted glass
West Harling	Painted glass*
Wiggenhall St Mary	Stone fragment*; screen panel*
Woodton	Painted glass*
Worthing	Painted glass

For further details see Farnhill, *Guilds and the parish community*, and Nichols, *The early art of Norfolk*, passim.

Material evidence for the cult of St Mary Magdalen in Norwich and Norfolk

NORWICH

There is no surviving documentary evidence for gild patronage by the saint in Norwich.

The first leper hospital in Norwich, which was dedicated to St Mary Magdalen, was sited at Sprowston, about one mile outside the Magdalen Gates to the north of the city. The Sprowston leprosarium owned a lectern hanging emblazoned with the saint's image (*Inventory of church goods temp. Edward III*, i. 33).

Chapels known to have been dedicated to St Mary Magdalen

St Stephen	South aisle, including altar dedication jointly with St John the Evangelist: Blomefield, *History of Norfolk*, iv. 152

Images known to have been dedicated to St Mary Magdalen

St James Pockthorpe	Font stem image, now at St Mary Magdalen, Silver Street*
St Mary Coslany	Bequest for a window next to the image of Mary Magdalen. Unclear whether her image is free-standing or another window: Blomefield, *History of Norfolk*, iv. 490
St Peter Mancroft	Image and lights: Blomefield, *History of Norfolk*, iv. 212

Painted screen panel depicting St Mary Magdalen, extant*

Norwich cathedral	Panel crucifixion*: Lasko and Morgan, *Medieval art*, 37, plate 52

NORFOLK

Gilds known to have been dedicated to the patronage of St Mary Magdalen

East Dereham St Nicholas	Gild, possibly two: Farnhill, *Guilds*, 182; Blomefield, *History of Norfolk*, x. 213
Lynn, location unspecified	Gild, possibly two: Farnhill, *Guilds*, 193.
Pulham St Mary Magdalen	Gild: Farnhill, *Guilds*, 199; Blomefield, *History of Norfolk*, v. 396
Sandringham St Mary Magdalen	Gild: Farnhill, *Guilds*, 200
Wiggenhall St Mary Magdalen	Gild: Farnhill, *Guilds*, 208
Wiggenhall St Peter	Gild: Farnhill, *Guilds*, 209

Images of St Mary Magdalen in painted glass, painted screen panel, wood and stone recorded and gone or extant*

Babingley	Late screen panel
Binham St Mary	Screen panel*
Burnham Deepdale St Mary	Painted glass in chancel*
Cromer SS Peter and Paul	Painted glass
Docking St Mary	Stone carving: damaged font stem*
Field Dalling St Andrew	Painted glass*
Garboldisham St John Baptist with All Saints	Screen panel, defaced*
Hemblington All Saints	Stone carving: font stem*
Hingham St Andrew	Monument*
Irstead St Michael	Stone carving: font stem*
Lessingham All Saints	Screen panel*
Ludham St Catherine	Screen panel*
Lynn Benedictine priory	Image of St Mary Magdalen with St Margaret
Lynn St Mary Magdalen Hospital	Seal
Martham St Mary	Painted glass*
North Elmham St Mary	Screen panel
North Walsham St Nicholas, formerly BVM	Screen panel*
Pulham St Mary	Painted glass*
Repps St Peter	Screen panel
Stody St Mary	Painted glass*
Swaffham SS Peter and Paul	Image: Blomefield, *History of Norfolk*, vi. 217
Thornham All Saints	Screen panel*
Walpole St Peter	?Screen panel:* poor condition

Walsoken All Saints	Stone carving: font stem*
Wiggenhall St Mary	Wood.carving* of the Magdalen; screen panel*
Wiggenhall St Mary Magdalen	Painted glass; image and lights

For source details see Blomefield, *History of Norfolk*; Nichols, *The early art of Norfolk*; and Farnhill, *Guilds*.

Bibliography

Unpublished primary sources

London, The National Archives
Will registers proved in the prerogative court of Canterbury (PCC)
Reg. Blamyr (1501–3)
Reg. Horne (1496–1500)
Reg. Ketchyn (1556)
Reg. Milles (1487–91)
Reg. Moone (1500–1)
Reg. Thrower (1531–3)
Reg. Welles (1558–9)

Norwich, Norfolk Record Office
Archive of the dean and chapter of Norwich Priory Church
DCN 39/1
Gunton collection, 1424–1523. Uncatalogued version of bede roll
Misc 1/5 Founding of leprosarium dedicated to St Mary and St Clement, at St
    Augustine's gate
Reg./4 135 (Castre), 1420

Will registers proved in the Norwich consistory court (NCC)
Reg. Alblaster   (1520–4)
Reg. Aleyn   (1448–55)
Reg. Alpe   (1526–32)
Reg. Attmere   (1527–44)
Reg. Aubry   (1479–93)
Reg. Botyngs (Betyngs)   (1457–71)
Reg. Briggs   (1514–27)
Reg. Brosyard   (1454–64)
Reg. Caston   (1479–88)
Reg. Cobbalde   (1465–8)
Reg. Coppinger   (1514)
Reg. Doke   (1436–44)
Reg. Gelour   (1472–9)
Reg. Godsalve   (1531–42)
Reg. Grundisburgh   (1524–6)
Reg. Gylys   (1516–32)
Reg. Harsyk   (1383–1408)
Reg. Haywarde   (1516–32)
Reg. Heydon   (1370–83)
Reg. Hyrnyng   (1416–26)

Reg. Jekkys   (1464–72)
Reg. Moulton   (1495–8)
Reg. Palgrave   (1518–32)
Reg. Paynot   (1473)
Reg. Platfoote   (1530–5)
Reg. Popy   (1501–4)
Reg. Ryxe   (1504–6)
Reg. Spyltymber   (1507–10)
Reg. Surflete   (1426–36)
Reg. Wolman   (1488–96)
Reg. Wylbey   (1444–8)

Will registers proved in the archdeacon of Norwich's court (ANC)
Reg. Bemond   (1501–5)
Reg. Bulwer   (1501–6)
Reg. Cook   (1503–38)
Reg. Gloys   (1509–19)
Reg. Johnson   (1578–9)

Published primary sources

The ancrene riwle: the Corpus MS, ed. M. Salu, Exeter 1955, repr. London 1990

Angela of Foligno's Memorial, ed. C. Mazzoni, Cambridge 2000

The Apocrypha, according to the authorised version, SPCK edn, Oxford–London n.d.

Aquinas, Thomas, *Nature and grace: selections from the Summa theologica of Thomas Aquinas*, ed. and trans. A. M. Fairweather, London 1954

——— *Summa theologica of Thomas Aquinas*, pt II/1, ed. Fathers of the Dominican Province, London 1915

Archdeaconry of Norwich: inventory of church goods temp. Edward III, ed. A. Watkin (NRS xix/1, 2, 1947–8)

The Bedford hours, ed. J. Backhouse, London 1990

The book of Margery Kempe, ed. S. B. Meech and H. E. Allen (EETS o.s. ccxii, 1940), repr. Oxford 1997

The book of Margery Kempe, ed. B. A. Windeatt, Harmondsworth 1985

The book of Margery Kempe: an abridged translation, ed. L. H. McAvoy, Cambridge 2003

The book of vices and virtues, ed. W. N. Francis (EETS o.s. ccxvii, 1942, repr. 1968)

Calendar of patent rolls (Henry VI), IV: 1441–1446, London 1908, repr. Nendeln, Lichtenstein 1971

Carrow abbey: otherwise Carrow priory near Norwich in the county of Norfolk; its foundations, buildings, officers & inmates, with appendices, charters, proceedings, extracts from wills, landed possessions, founders, architectural description of the remains of the buildings and some account of the family of the present owners, ed. W. Rye, Norwich 1889

The commonplace book of Robert Reynes of Acle, ed. L. Cameron, New York–London 1980

The Digby plays, ed. F. J. Furnivall (EETS e.s. lxx 1896, repr. 1967)

English gilds: the original ordinances, ed. L. T. Smith and L. Brentano (EETS o.s. xl, 1963)

English writings of Richard Rolle, hermit of Hampole, ed. H. E. Allen, Oxford 1931, repr. Gloucester 1988

The fifty earliest English wills in the court of probate, London, ed. F. J. Furnivall, London 1882

Hali meidenhad, ed. F. J. Furnivall and T. O. Cockayne (EETS o.s. xviii, 1865)

Henry of Lancaster: Le Livre de seyntz medicines, ed. E. J. Arnould, Oxford 1940

Historie of the arrivall of Edward IV in England and the finall recouerye of his kingdomes from Henry VI: three chronicles of the reign of Edward IV, ed. J. Bruce, Gloucester 1988

Holy Bible: authorised King James version, London 1953

The hours of Catherine of Cleves, ed. J. Plummer, London 1966

Household accounts from medieval England, i, ed. C. M. Woolgar, Oxford 1992

Illustrated letters of the Paston family: private life in the fifteenth century, ed. R. Virgoe, London 1989

Jacob's well: an English treatise on the cleansing of man's conscience, ed. A. Brandeis (EETS o.s. cxv, 1900)

Jacobus de Voraigne: the golden legend: readings on the saints, ed. W. G. Ryan, Princeton 1993

Jacques de Vitry: the Life of Marie d'Oignies, ed. M. H. King and M. Marsolais, Toronto 1993

John Mirk's instructions for parish priests, ed. G. Kristensson, Lund 1974

Julian of Norwich: A book of showings, ed. E. Colledge and J. Walsh, Toronto 1978

A leechbook, or a collection of medical remedies of the fifteenth century, ed. W. R. Dawson, London 1934

Leet jurisdiction in the city of Norwich during the thirteenth and fourteenth centuries: with a short notice of its later history and decline from the rolls in the possession of the corporation, ed. W. Hudson (Selden Society v, 1892)

Legendys of hooly wummen by Osbern Bokenham, ed. M. S. Serjeantson (EETS o.s ccvi, 1938, repr. 1971)

The liber celestis of St Bridget of Sweden: the Middle English version in British Library, MS Claudius Bi, together with a life of the saint from the same manuscript, ed. R. Ellis (EETS o.s. ccxci, 1987)

The life and miracles of St William of Norwich by Thomas of Monmouth, ed. A. Jessop and M. R. James, Cambridge 1896

The life of solitude by Francis Petrarch, ed. and trans. J. Zeitlin, Urbana 1924

Love, N., *Mirror of the blessed life of Jesus Christ*, ed. M. G. Sargent, Exeter 2005

Lydgate's minor poems, ed. O. Glauning (EETS e.s. lxxx, 1900)

The making of Kings Lynn: a documentary survey, ed. D. M. Owen, Oxford 1984

'Marie d'Oignies: the *Life* of Marie d'Oignies by Jaques de Vitry', ed. M. King, in Petroff, *Visionary literature*, 179–83

Medical works of the fourteenth century: together with a list of plants recorded in contemporary writings, ed. G. Henslow, London 1899

Medieval English prose for women: selections from the Katherine group and Ancrene Wisse, ed. B. Millet and J. Wogan-Browne, Oxford 1992

Medieval women's visionary literature, ed. E. Petroff, Oxford 1986

Meditationes vitae Christi of the pseudo-Bonaventure, ed. and trans. J. de Vinke, Paterson 1960

Middle English sermons, ed. W. O. Ross, Oxford 1960

The Middle English stanzaic versions of the life of St Anne, ed. R. E. Parker (EETS o.s. clxxiv, 1928, repr. 1971)

Minor poems of John Lydgate, ed. H. N. MacCracken (EETS e.s. cvii, 1962)

Mirk's festial: a collection of homilies of Johannes Mirkus (John Mirk), i, ed. T. Erbe (EETS e.s. xcvi, 1905)

The myroure of Oure Ladye: containing a devotional treatise on divine service, with a translation of the offices used by the sisters of the Brigittine monastery of Sion, at Isleworth, during the fifteenth and sixteenth centuries, ed. J. H. Blunt (EETS e.s. xix, 1873)

The New Testament 1526, translated by William Tyndale, ed. W. R. Cooper, London 2000

The N-town play: Cotton MS Vespasian D.8, ii, ed. S. Spector (EETS s.s. xi, xii, 1991)

The Old English Lives of St Margaret, ed. M. Clayton and H. Magennis, Cambridge 1994

The Paston letters and papers of the fifteenth century, ed. N. Davis, Oxford 1971–

The political songs of England, from the reign of John to that of Edward II, ed. T. Wright (Camden vi, 1839)

'Prosalegenden: die legenden des MS Douce 114', ed. C. Horstmann, *Anglia* viii (1885), 102–96

Records of the city of Norwich, ii, ed. W. Hudson and J. C. Tingey, London 1910

Records of the gild of St George in Norwich, 1389–1547: a transcript with an introduction, ed. M. Grace (NRS ix, 1937)

The register of Henry Chichele, archbishop of Canterbury, 1414–1443, iv, ed. F. F. Jacob, Oxford 1943–7

Richard Rolle: the English writings, ed. R. S. Allen, London 1989

Songs, carols, and other miscellaneous poems: from the Balliol MS 354, Richard Hill's common-place book, ed. R. Dyboski (EETS e.s. ci, 1907)

The streets and lanes of Norwich: a memoir by John Kirkpatrick, ed. W. Hudson, Norwich 1889

'Symon Wynter: the *Life* of St Jerome', ed. C. Waters, in A. C. Bartlett and T. H. Bestul (eds), *Cultures of piety: medieval English devotional literature in translation*, Ithaca 1999, 141–63

Testamenta eboracensia, or, wills registered at York: illustrative of the history, manners, language, statistics, &c. of the province of York, from the year MCCC downwards, ed. J. Raine (Surtees Society liii, 1868)

'Three Carrow account rolls', ed. L. J. Redstone, *NA: The Centenary Volume* xxix (1946), 41–88

Three chapters of letters relating to the suppression of the monasteries, ed. T. Wright (Camden o.s. xxvi, 1843)

The Trotula: a medieval compendium of women's medicine, ed. M. H. Green, Philadelphia 2001

Walter Hilton: the ladder of perfection, ed. L. Sherley-Price, repr. London 1988

'The will of Margaret Paston', ed. D. Turner, *NA* iii (1852), 152–76

Wills and inventories from the registers of the commissary of Bury St Edmunds and the archdeaconry of Sudbury, ed. S. Tymms (Camden o.s. xlix, 1850)

The writings of Margaret of Oingt, ed. R. Blumenfeld-Kosinski, Woodbridge 1997

Secondary works

Abbott, C., *Julian of Norwich: autobiography and theology*, Cambridge 1999

Aers, D., 'Altars of power: reflections on Eamon Duffy's *The stripping of the altars: traditional religion in England, 1400–1580*', *Literature and History* 3rd ser. iii (1994), 90–105

Amundsen, D. W., 'Medieval canon law on medical and surgical practice by the clergy', *Bulletin of the History of Medicine* lii (1978), 22–43

Archer, R. E., '"How ladies … who live on their manors ought to manage …": women as landholders and administrators in the late Middle Ages', in Goldberg, *Women is a worthy wight*, 149–81

—— 'Piety in question: noblewomen and religion in the late Middle Ages', in Wood, *Women and religion*, 118–40.

Armstrong, C. A. J., 'The piety of Cicely, duchess of York: a study in late medieval culture', in his *England, France and Burgundy in the fifteenth century*, London 1983, 135–56

Ashley, K. and P. Sheingorn, 'Locating St Anne in gender and cultural studies, in Ashley and Sheingorn, *Interpreting cultural symbols*, 1–68

—— and P. Sheingorn (eds), *Interpreting cultural symbols: St Anne in late medieval society*, Athens, GA 1990

Aston, M., *Lollards and reformers: images and literacy in late medieval religion*, London 1984

—— 'Segregation in church', in Sheils and Wood, *Women in the Church*, 237–94

Atherton, I. and others (eds), *Norwich cathedral: church, city and diocese, 1096–1996*, London–Rio Grande 1996

Atkin, M., A. Carter and D. H. Evans, *Excavations in Norwich, 1971–8*, pt ii, Norwich 1985

Ayers, B., *The book of Norwich*, London 1994

—— *Norwich, a fine city*, Stroud 2003

—— and others (eds), *Excavations within the north-east bailey of Norwich castle, 1979*, Norwich 1985

Baird, W., 'The Gospel according to St Luke', in C. M. Laymon (ed.), *The interpreter's one volume commentary of the Bible*, Nashville 1992, 672–706

Barron, C. M. and A. F. Sutton (eds), *Medieval London widows, 1300–1500*, London 1994

Bean, J. M.W., 'Plague, population and economic decline in England in the later Middle Ages', *Economic History Review* 2nd ser. xv (1963), 423–43

Beckwith, S., *Christ's body: identity, culture and society in late medieval writings*, London–New York 1993

Bennet, H. S., 'Notes on the original statutes of the college of St John Evangelist of Rushworth, Co. Norfolk, founded by Edmund Gonville, AD 1342', *NA* x (1888), 277–382

Bensley, W. T., 'St Leonard's priory, Norwich', *NA* xii (1895), 190–227

Biller, P., 'Childbirth in the Middle Ages', *History Today* (Aug. 1986), 41–4

Blomefield, F., *An essay towards a topographical history of the county of Norfolk*, 2nd edn, London 1805–10

Bowers, J. M., *The politics of Pearl: court poetry in the age of Richard II*, Cambridge 2001

Britnell, R., 'York under the Yorkists', in Britnell, *Daily life*, 175–94

—— (ed.), *Daily life in the late Middle Ages*, Stroud 1998

Brody, S. N., *The disease of the soul: leprosy in medieval literature*, Ithaca, NY 1974

Brown, P., *The body and society: men, women and sexual renunciation in early Christianity*, New York–Chichester 1988

Bynum, C. W., *Jesus as mother: studies in the spirituality of the high Middle Ages*, Berkeley 1982

—— *Holy feast and holy fast: the religious significance of food to medieval women*, Berkeley 1987

—— *Fragmentation and redemption: essays on gender and the human body in medieval religion*, New York 1992

Cadden, J., *Meanings of sex difference in the Middle Ages: medicine, science and culture*, Cambridge 1993

Cahill, S., *Wise women: over two thousand years of spiritual writing by women*, New York–London 1996

Carlin, M., 'Fast food and urban living standards in medieval England', in M. Carlin and J. Rosenthal (eds), *Food and eating in medieval Europe*, London 1998, 27–51

Castor, H., 'The duchy of Lancaster and the rule of East Anglia, 1399–1440', in R. E. Archer (ed.), *Crown, government and people in the fifteenth century*, Stroud 1995, 53–78

—— *Blood and roses: the Paston family in the fifteenth century*, London 2004

Cattermole, P. and S. Cotton, 'Medieval parish church building in Norfolk', *NA* xxxviii (1983), 235–79

Cautley, H. M., *Norfolk churches*, Ipswich 1949

Clayton, M., 'Aelfric and the nativity of the Blessed Virgin Mary', *Anglia* civ (1986), 286–315

Coletti, T., '*Paupertas est donum die*: hagiography, lay religion, and the economics of salvation in the Digby *Mary Magdalene*', *Speculum* lxxvi (2001), 337–78

—— *Mary Magdalene and the drama of saints: theater, gender and religion in late medieval England*, Philadelphia 2004

Coster, W., 'Purity, profanity and Puritanism: the churching of women, 1500–1700', in Sheils and Wood, *Women in the Church*, 377–87

Cotton, S., 'Medieval roodscreens in Norfolk: their construction and painting dates', *NA* xl (1989), 44–54

Cressy, D., 'Purification, thanksgiving and the churching of women in post-Reformation England', *Past & Present* cxxxxi (1993), 197–210

—— *Birth, marriage, and death: ritual, religion, and the life-cycle in Tudor and Stuart England*, Oxford 1997

Cross, F. L. (ed.), *Oxford Dictionary of the Christian Church*, 2nd rev. edn, Oxford 1983

Cullum, P., '"And hir name was charite": charitable giving by and for women in late medieval Yorkshire', in Goldberg, *Woman is a worthy wight*, 182–211

—— '"For pore people harberles": what was the function of the *maison dieu*?', in

D. J. Clayton, R. G. Davies and P. McNiven (eds), *Trade, devotion and governance: papers in late medieval history*, Stroud 1994, 36–54

Delany, S., *Impolitic bodies: poetry, saints and society in fifteenth-century England*, New York–Oxford 1998

Devlin, D., 'Feminine lay piety in the high Middle Ages: the beguines', in Nichols and Shanks, *Medieval religious women*, i. 183–96

Dodwell, B., 'William Bauchon and his connection with the cathedral priory at Norwich', *NA* xxxvi/2 (1975), 111–18

Duffy, E., 'Holy maydens, holy wyfes: the cult of women saints in fifteenth- and sixteenth-century England', in Sheils and Wood, *Women in the Church*, 175–96

—— *The stripping of the altars: traditional religion in England, c. 1400–1580*, New Haven–London 1992

—— 'The parish, piety and patronage in late medieval East Anglia: the evidence of rood screens', in K. French, G. Gibbs and B. Kumin (eds), *The parish in English life, 1400–1600*, Manchester 1997, 133–62

—— *Marking the hours: English people and their prayers, 1240–1570*, New Haven–London 2006

Dunn, P., 'Trade', in Rawcliffe and Wilson, *Medieval Norwich*, 213–34,

Dupeux, C., P. Jezler and J. Wirth (eds), *Iconoclasme: vie et mort de l'image medievale*, Berne 2001

Dyer, C., *Standards of living in the later Middle Ages: social change in England, c. 1200–1520*, Cambridge 1989

Emery, P. and E. Rutledge (eds), *Norwich Greyfriars: excavations at the former Mann Egerton site, Prince of Wales Road, Norwich, 1990–5*, Norwich 2007

Erler, M. C., 'Three fifteenth-century vowesses', in Barron and Sutton, *Medieval London widows*, 165–83

—— 'English vowed women at the end of the Middle Ages', *Medieval Studies* lvii (1995), 155–82

—— *Women, reading, and piety in late medieval England*, Cambridge 2002

Fanous, S., 'Measuring the pilgrim's progress: internal emphases in *The book of Margery Kempe*', in E. Renevy and C. Whitehead (eds), *Writing religious women: female spiritual and textual practices in late medieval England*, Cardiff 2000, 168–70

Farnhill, K., *Guilds and the parish community in late medieval East Anglia*, York 2001

Finch, J., *Church monuments in Norfolk before 1850: an archaeology of commemoration*, Oxford 2000

Frost, R., 'The urban elite', in Rawcliffe and Wilson, *Medieval Norwich*, 235–53

Gasson, B., *The Burrell collection*, Glasgow 1983

Gibson, G. M., 'Bury St Edmunds, Lydgate and the *N-town cycle*', *Speculum* lxvi (1981), 56–90

—— *The theater of devotion: East Anglian drama and society in the late Middle Ages*, Chicago–London 1989

—— 'St Anne and the religion of childbed: some East Anglian texts and talismans', in Ashley and Sheingorn, *Interpreting cultural symbols*

—— *Contemplation and action: the other monasticism*, Leicester 1995

Gijsel, J., *Die unmittelbare textüberlieferung des sogenannte Pseudo-Matthaüs*, Brussels 1981

Gilchrist, R., 'The religious houses of medieval Norfolk', in S. Margeson, B. Ayers and S. Heywood (eds), *A festival of Norfolk archaeology*, Norwich 1996, 117–36

—— and M. Oliva, *Religious women in medieval East Anglia: history and archaeology, c. 1100–1500*, Norwich 1993

Le Goff, J., *The birth of purgatory*, trans. A. Goldhammer, London 1984

Goldberg, P. J. P. (ed.), *Woman is a worthy wight: women in English society, c. 1200–1500*, Stroud 1992

—— *Women, work and life cycle in a medieval economy: women in York and Yorkshire c. 1300–1520*, Oxford 1992

Goodall, J. A. A., *God's house at Ewelme: life, devotion and architecture in a fifteenth-century almshouse*, Aldershot 2001

Hanawalt, B., 'Keepers of the lights: late medieval parish gilds', *Journal of Medieval and Renaissance Studies* xiii (1984), 21–37

—— *'Of good and ill repute': gender and social control in medieval England*, Oxford 1998

Harper-Bill, C. and C. Rawcliffe, 'The religious houses', in Rawcliffe and Wilson, *Medieval Norwich*, 73–120

Harrod, H., 'Extracts from early Norfolk wills', NA i (1847), 111–28

—— 'Early Norwich pageants', NA iii (1852), 2–18

—— 'Extracts from the assize and plea rolls of the thirteenth century about Norwich thieves, etc.', NA vii (1872), 263–88

Haskins, S., *Mary Magdalen: myth and metaphor*, London 1993

Hayum, A., *The Isenheim altarpiece: God's medicine and the painter's vision*, Princeton 1989

Heale, M. R. V., 'Veneration and renovation in a small Norfolk priory: St Leonard's, Norwich, in the later Middle Ages', *Historical Research* lxxvi (2003), 431–49

Hill, C., '"Leave my virginity alone": the cult of St Margaret of Antioch in Norwich', in C. Harper-Bill (ed.), *Medieval East Anglia*, Woodbridge 2005

—— 'Julian and her sisters: female piety in late medieval Norwich', in L. Clark (ed.), *The fifteenth century*, vi, Woodbridge 2006, 165–87

Hilles, C., 'Gender and politics in Osbern Bokenham's Legendary', in W. Scase, R. Copeland and D. Lawton (eds), *New medieval literatures*, iv, Oxford 2001, 189–212

Hogg, J., 'Adam Easton's Defensorium Santae Birgittae', in M. Glasscoe (ed.), *The medieval mystical tradition: England, Ireland and Wales*, Cambridge 1999, 213–40

Hope, W. H. St J., 'Inventories of the parish church of St Peter Mancroft, Norwich', NA xiv (1900), 153–240

Horden, P., 'Disease, dragons and saints: the management of epidemics in the Dark Ages', in T. Ranger and P. Slack (eds), *Epidemics and ideas: essays on the historical perception of pestilence*, Cambridge 1992, 45–76

—— 'A non-natural environment: medicine without doctors and the medieval European hospital', in B. S. Bowers (ed.), *The medieval hospital and medical practice*, Aldershot 2007, 133–45

Horrox, R., *The Black Death*, Manchester 1994

Hughes, J., *Pastors and visionaries: religion and secular life in late medieval Yorkshire*, Woodbridge 1988

—— *The religious life of Richard III: piety and prayer in the north of* England, Stroud 1997

—— *Arthurian myths and alchemy: the kingship of Edward IV*, Stroud 2002

Hunt, T. (ed.), *Popular medicine in thirteenth-century England: introduction and texts*, Cambridge 1990

Hutton, R., *The rise and fall of merry England: the ritual year, 1400–1700*, Oxford 1994

Jacquart, D. and C. Thomasset, *Sexuality and medicine in the Middle Ages*, trans. M. Adamson, Cambridge 1988

Jansen, K. L., *The making of the Magdalen: preaching and popular devotion in the late Middle Ages*, Princeton 2000

Jantzen, G. M., *Julian of Norwich, mystic and theologian*, London 1987

—— *Power, gender and Christian mysticism*, Cambridge 1995

Jeffrey, D. L., *The early English lyrics and Franciscan spirituality*, Lincoln, NE 1975

Keene, D., 'Issues of water in medieval London to *c.* 1300', *Urban History* xxviii (2000–1), 161–79

Keiser, G. R., 'St Jerome and the Brigettines: visions of the afterlife in fifteenth-century England', in D. Williams (ed.), *England in the fifteenth century: proceedings of the 1986 Harlaxton symposium*, Woodbridge 1987, 143–52

Kelly, S., 'The economic topography and structure of Norwich *c.* 1300', in Priestley, *Men of property*, 13–39

Kerby-Fulton, K., *Books under suspicion: censorship and tolerance of revelatory writings in late medieval England*, Notre Dame 2006

King, D. J., 'A glazier from the bishopric of Utrecht in fifteenth-century Norwich', *British Archaeological Association Conference Transactions* xviii (1996), 216–25

—— *The medieval stained glass of St Peter Mancroft, Norwich*, Oxford 2006

Kirkpatrick, J., *History of the religious orders and communities, and of the hospitals and castle of Norwich, written about the year 1725*, ed. D. Turner, Yarmouth 1845

—— *The streets and lanes of Norwich*, ed. W. Hudson, Norwich 1889

Krug, R., *Reading families: women's literate practice in late medieval England*, Ithaca, NY 2002

Lacy, K., 'Margaret Croke (d.1491)', in Barron and Sutton, *Medieval London widows*, 143–64

Lander, J. R., *The Wars of the Roses* (1965), Stroud 2000

Laqueur, T., *Making sex: body and gender from the Greeks to Freud*, Cambridge, MA 1990

Lasko, P. and N. J. Morgan (eds), *Medieval art in East Anglia, 1300–1520*, Norwich 1973

Layard, N. F., 'Notes on some English paxes', *Archaeological Journal* lx (1904), 120–30

Leach, A., 'Some English plays and players', in F. J. Furnivall (ed.), *An English miscellany presented to F. J. Furnivall on the occasion of his seventy-fifth birthday*, Oxford 1901, repr. New York 1969, 205–34

L'Estrange, J., 'Description of a chamber formerly adjoining the Jesus chapel of the cathedral', *NA* vi (1864), 177–85

—— 'The church goods of St Andrew and St Mary Coslany in the city of Norwich, Temp. Edward vi', *NA* vii (1872), 45–78

—— *The church-bells of Norfolk: where, when and by whom they were made, with the inscriptions*, Norwich 1874

Leyser, H., *Medieval women: a social history of women in England, 450–1500*, London 1995

Linnell, C. L. S., 'The commonplace book of Robert Reynes of Acle', *NA* xxxii (1961), 111–27

Lloyd, T. H., *England and the German Hanse, 1157–1611: a study of their trade and commercial diplomacy*, Cambridge 1991

Lochrie, K., *Margery Kempe and translations of the flesh*, Philadelphia 1991

MacDonald, A. O., H. N. B. Ridderbos and R. M. Schlusemann, (eds), *The broken body: passion iconography in late medieval culture*, Groningen 1998

McIntosh, M., *Controlling misbehaviour in England, 1370–1600*, Cambridge 1998

McRee, B. R., 'Religious gilds and civic order: the case of Norwich in the late Middle Ages', *Speculum* lxvii (1992), 69–97

—— 'Charity and gild solidarity in late medieval England', *Journal of British Studies* xxxii (1993), 195–225

Maddern, P., *Violence and social order: East Anglia, 1422–1442*, Oxford 1992

—— 'Order and disorder', in Rawcliffe and Wilson, *Medieval Norwich*, 189–212

Manning, C. R., 'Medieval patens in Norfolk', *NA* xii (1895), 85–99

Martin, W., 'Some fragments of sculptured stone found in a barn at East Barsham', *NA* xi (1892), 257–8

Meale, C. M., 'Reading women's culture in fifteenth-century England: the case of Alice Chaucer', in P. Britani and A. Torti (eds), *Mediaevalitas: reading the Middle Ages*, Cambridge 1996, 81–101

—— (ed.), *Women and literature in Britain, 1150–1500*, Cambridge 1996

Middleton-Stewart, J., *Inward purity and outward splendour: death and remembrance in the deanery of Dunwich, Suffolk, 1370–1547*, Woodbridge 2001

Mitchell, J., 'Painting in East Anglia around 1500: the continental connection', in Mitchell, *England and the continent*, 365–80.

—— (ed.), *England and the continent in the Middle Ages: studies in memory of Andrew Martindale: proceedings of the 1996 Harlaxton Symposium*, Stamford 2000

Moorman, C., *The Pearl-poet*, New York 1968

Morant, A. W., 'Notices of the church of St Nicholas, Great Yarmouth', *NA* vii (1872), 215–48

Muller, T., *Sculpture in the Netherlands, Germany, France, Spain, 1400–1500*, trans. E. Scott and W. R. Scott, Harmondsworth 1966

Myers, A. R., 'The jewels of Queen Margaret of Anjou', *Bulletin of John Rylands Library* xlii (1959–60), 112–20

Nichols, A. E., *The early art of Norfolk: a subject list of extant and lost art including items relevant to early drama*, Kalamazoo 2002

Nichols, J. and T. L. Shank (eds), *Medieval religious women, I: distant echoes*, Kalamazoo 1984

Oliva, M., *The convent and the community in late medieval England: female monasteries in the diocese of Norwich, 1350–1540*, Woodbridge 1998

Owst, G. R., *Preaching in medieval England: an introduction to sermon manuscripts of the period, c. 1350–1450*, New York 1965

—— *Literature and pulpit in medieval England: a neglected chapter in the history of English letters and of the English people*, 2nd edn, Oxford 1966

Page-Phillips, J., *Macklin's monumental brasses*, London 1969, 1972

Park, D. and H. Howard (eds), 'The medieval polychromy', in Atherton and others, *Norwich cathedral*, 379–409

Park, K., 'Medicine and society in medieval Europe, 500–1500', in A. Wear (ed.), *Medicine in society: historical essays*, Cambridge 1992, 59–90

Parker, K., 'Lynn and the making of a mystic', in K. Lewis and J. Arnold (eds), *A companion to the book of Margery Kempe*, Cambridge 2004, 55–73

Pelling, M., *The common lot: sickness, medical occupations and the urban poor in early modern England*, London–New York 1998

Penketh, S., 'Women and books of hours', in J. H. M. Taylor and L. Smith (eds), *Women and the book: assessing the visual evidence*, London–Toronto 1997, 266–80

Peters, C., *Patterns of piety: women, gender and religion in late medieval and Reformation England*, Cambridge 2003

Pfaff, R. W., *New liturgical feasts in later medieval England*, Oxford 1970

Platt, C., *The parish churches of medieval England*, London 1995

Pound, J., *Tudor and Stuart Norwich*, Chichester 1988

Power, E., *Medieval women*, Cambridge 1997

Priestley, U. (ed.), *Men of property: an analysis of the Norwich enrolled deeds, 1285–1311*, Norwich 1983

Puddy, E., *Litcham*, Dereham n.d.

Pugh, R. B., *Imprisonment in medieval England*, Cambridge 1968

Pullan, B., *Poverty and charity: Europe, Italy, Venice, 1400–1700*, Aldershot 1994

Rawcliffe, C., *The hospitals of medieval Norwich*, Norwich 1995

—— *Medicine and society in later medieval England*, Stroud 1995

—— 'Hospital nurses and their work', in Britnell, *Daily life*, 43–64

—— *Medicine for the soul: the life, death and resurrection of an English medieval hospital: St Giles, Norwich, c. 1249–1550*, Stroud 1999

—— 'Learning to love the leper: aspects of institutional charity in Anglo-Saxon England', in J. Gillingham (ed.), *Anglo-Norman Studies, XXIII: Proceedings of the Battle conference, 2000*, Woodbridge 2000, 231–50

—— 'Women, childbirth and religion in later medieval England', in Wood, *Women and religion*, 91–117

—— 'Sickness and health', in Rawcliffe and Wilson, *Medieval Norwich*, 301–26

—— and R. Wilson (eds), *Medieval Norwich*, London 2004

Richmond, C., 'The English gentry and religion *c.* 1500', in C. Harper-Bill (ed.), *Religious belief and ecclesiastical careers in late medieval England*, Woodbridge 1991, 121–50

Riddy, F., 'Women talking about the things of God: a late medieval culture', in Meale, *Women and literature*, 104–27

Robertson, E., 'The corporeality of female sanctity in the *Life* of St Margaret', in R. Blumenfeld-Kosinski and T. Szell (eds), *Images of sainthood in medieval Europe*, Ithaca, NY 1991, 268–87

Rosenthal, J. T., *Telling tales: sources and narration in late medieval England*, University Park 2003

Roskell, J., L. Clark and C. Rawcliffe (eds), *The House of Commons, 1386–1421*, Stroud 1992

Ross, E. M., *The grief of God: images of the suffering Jesus in late medieval England*, Oxford 1997

Rubin, M., *Charity and community in medieval Cambridge*, Cambridge 1987

—— *Corpus Christi: the eucharist in late medieval culture*, Cambridge 1991

Rutledge, E., 'Immigration and population growth in early fourteenth-century Norwich: evidence of the tithing roll', in R. Rodger (ed.), *Urban history yearbook, 1988*, Leicester 1988, 15–30

—— 'Before the Black Death', in Rawcliffe and Wilson, *Medieval Norwich*, 257–88.

Sabine, E. L., 'Latrines and cesspools of medieval London', *Speculum* ix (1934), 303–21

Sahlin, C. L., *Birgitta of Sweden and the voice of prophecy*, Woodbridge 2001

Salih, S., *Versions of virginity in late medieval England*, Cambridge 2001

Sautman, F., 'St Anne in folk tradition: late medieval France', in Ashley and Scheingorn, *Interpreting cultural symbols*, 69–94

Saxer, V., *Le Culte de Marie Madeleine en occident des origines à la fin du moyen âge*, Auxerre–Paris 1959

Schatzlein, J. and P. D. Sulmasy, 'The diagnosis of St Francis: the evidence for leprosy', *Franciscan Studies* xlvii (1987), 181–27.

Scherb, V., 'Violence and the social body in the Croxton *Play of the sacrament*', in J. Redmond (ed.), *Violence in drama*, Cambridge 1991, 69–78

Shahar, S., *Growing old in the Middle Ages:'winter clothes us in shadow and pain'*, Tel-Aviv 1995

Sheils, W. J. and D. Wood (eds), *Women in the Church* (Studies in Church History xxvii, 1990)

Sheingorn, P., 'Appropriating the holy kinship', in Ashley and Sheingorn, *Interpreting cultural symbols*, 169–98

Shinners, J. R., 'The veneration of saints at Norwich cathedral in the fourteenth century', *NA* xl (1989), 133–44

Siraisi, N. G., *Medieval and early renaissance medicine: an introduction to knowledge and practice*, Chicago 1990

Staley, L., *Margery Kempe's dissenting fictions*, Philadelphia 1994

Stilgoe, L. and D. Shreeve, *The round tower churches of Norfolk*, Norwich 2001

Stirland, A., *Criminals and paupers: the graveyard of St Margaret Fyebriggate in combusto*, Norwich 2009

Summit, J., *Lost property: the woman writer and English literary history, 1380–1589*, Chicago 2000

Swabey, F. F., *Medieval gentlewoman: life in a widow's household in the later Middle Ages*, Stroud 1999

Swanson, R. N., *Church and society in late medieval England*, Oxford 1993

—— 'Passion and practice: the social and ecclesiastical implications of passion devotion in the late Middle Ages', in McDonald, Ridderbos and Schlusemann, *Broken body*, 1–30

—— 'Will the real Margery Kempe please stand up!', in Wood, *Women and religion*, 141–55

Tanner, N. P., *The Church in late medieval Norwich, 1370–1532*, Toronto 1984

—— 'The cathedral and the city', in Atherton and others, *Norwich cathedral*, 255–80

—— 'Religious practice', in Rawcliffe and Wilson, *Medieval Norwich*, 137–55

Taylor, R. C. *Index monasticus: the abbeys and other monasteries, alien priories, colleges, collegiate churches and hospitals, with their dependencies, formerly established in the diocese of Norwich and the ancient kingdom of East Anglia, systematically arranged and briefly described, according to the respective orders and denominations in each country*, London 1821

Thomson, J. A. F., 'Piety and charity in late medieval London', *JEH* xvi (1965), 178–95

Thrupp, S. L., *The merchant class of medieval London, 1300–1500*, Chicago 1976

Tripps, J., 'Les Images et la devotion privee', in Dupeux, Jezler and Wirth, *Iconoclasme*, 38–45

Tristram, E. W., *English wall painting of the fourteenth century*, London 1955

Tudor-Craig, P., 'Painting in medieval England: the wall-to-wall message', in N. Saul (ed.), *The age of chivalry: art and society in late medieval England*, London 1995, 110–22

van Houts, E., *Memory and gender in medieval Europe, 900–1200*, London 1999

von Burg, C., 'Le Témoignage des sources: 1530 Baar', in Dupeux, Jezler and Wirth, *Iconoclasme*

Ward, J., 'Townswomen and their households', in Britnell, *Daily life*, 27–42

Warner, M., *Alone of all her sex: the myth and cult of the Virgin Mary*, New York 1976

—— *From the beast to the blonde: on fairy tales and their tellers*, London 1994

Warren, A. K., *Anchorites and their patrons in medieval England*, Berkeley 1985

Watson, N., 'The composition of Julian of Norwich's *Revelation of love*', *Speculum* cxviii (1993), 637–83

Watt, D., *Secretaries of God: women prophets in late medieval and early modern England*, Cambridge 2001

Wedgwood, J. C. and A. Holt, *History of parliament: biographies of the members of the Commons House, 1439–1509*, London 1936

Williams, J. F., 'Some Norfolk churches and their old-time benefactors', *NA* xxvii (1941), 333–44

Williamson, W. W., 'Saints on Norfolk rood-screens and pulpits', *NA* xxxi (1957), 299–346

Winston-Allen, A., *Stories of the rose: the making of the rosary in the Middle Ages*, University Park 1997

Wood, D. (ed.), *Women and religion in medieval England*, Oxford 2003

Woodforde, C., *Norwich school of glass-painting in the fifteenth* century, London 1950

Yoshikawa, N. K., *Margery Kempe's meditations: the context of medieval devotional literature, liturgy and iconography*, Cardiff 2007

Unpublished works

Adams, S. J., 'Religion, society and godly women: the nature of female piety in a late medieval urban community', PhD diss. Bristol 2001

Bown, J. and A. Stirland, 'Criminals and paupers: excavations at the site of the church and graveyard of St Margaret in Combusto', unpubl. report, Norfolk Archaeology Unit 1987

Dunn, P., 'Discord and dislocation: relations between Norwich and the crown, 1400–1450', MA diss. UEA 1999

Frost, R., 'The aldermen of Norwich, 1461–1509: the study of a civic elite', PhD diss. Cambridge 1996

Hill, C., 'Some incarnational aspects of late medieval female piety in East Anglia', MA diss. UEA 1999

—— 'Incarnational piety: women and religion in late medieval Norwich and its hinterlands', PhD diss. UEA 2004

Middleton-Stewart, J., 'Personal commemoration in late medieval Suffolk: the deanery of Dunwich, 1370–1547', PhD diss. UEA 1993

Noble, C., 'Aspects of life at Norwich cathedral priory in the late medieval period', PhD diss. UEA 2001

Phillips, E., 'Charitable institutions in Norfolk and Suffolk, c. 1350–1600', PhD diss. UEA 2002

Tanner, N. P., 'Popular religion in Norwich with special reference to the evidence of wills, 1370–1532', D.Phil diss. Oxford 1973

Index

Raynham St Mary, 155

reciprocal works, 99, 119, 120, 147, 150, 154, 160, 161

reciprocity, 116, 117, 121, 123–4, 166, 170

redemption, 71, 103, 137, 150, 151; and charity, 5, 124, 135–6, 167, 169, 170; and Christ's wounds, 5, 37, 84, 90, 162, 168; and the flesh, 32, 65, 84; and Mary Magdalen, 13, 89, 91, 98; and St Anne 18, 20, 23, 28, 35; and the Virgin Mary, 2–3

Reedes, John and Agnes, 51–2

Reformation, the, 17, 29, 58, 166. *See also* Dissolution of the Monasteries

regimen sanitatis, 133

relations between lay and religious, 15, 78, 112, 113–14, 151–2

religious articles, 19, 30, 46, 48, 116, 123, 155; commissioning of, 7

religious texts, 8–9, 27, 82, 167; commissioning of, 24, 39, 67, 99–100, 104; writing of, 67

resurrection, 95, 96, 98

Reynes, Emma, 27, 41, 42

Reynes, Robert, 27, 41, 42

Richard II, king of England, 39

Rolle, Richard, hermit, 34–5, 144

St Agatha, 94

St Agnes, 32

St Anne, 33–4, 167–8; and conception, childbirth, 12, 26; cult of, 17–18, 27, 57–8, 59, 170; and dynastic matters, 21, 24, 26, 41, 46, 54, 57, 83; family of, 18, 24, 26, 32, 57; feast of, 18, 26, 39, 43, 48; images of, 17, 18–19, 30, 32, 47–8, 54, 57, 59, 174–5, 176–7; and Joachim, her husband, 20, 21, 27, 28, 31; life of, 18, 21; *Lives* of, 12, 24, 41; and marriage, 23, 30, 46, 57, 83; and material success, 46, 57; as matriarch, 18, 41, 46, 57; as mother of Virgin, 17–18, 22; role of, 20, 28, 30, 37, 39, 41, 46; significance to mercantile community, 12, 18, 46, 57; and water, 132 n. 63

St Augustine of Hippo, 120 n. 11

St Barbara, 32, 69, 95, 141

St Bridget of Sweden, 12, 33–4, 41, 79, 168; images of, 108; life of, 107; role of, 41; her son, 109; writings of, 14, 107, 108–9, 111, 112, 119

St Catherine of Siena, 99, 105

St Dorothy, 32

St Elizabeth, 23, 32, 142, 161

St Elizabeth of Hungary, 98, 120–1, 142 n. 116; cult of, 27, 120, 123, 165, 170; images of, 8 n. 30, 76, 170; *Life* of, 100, 121, 136

St Francis of Assisi, 121, 142

St George, 12, 52, 72, 74, 75

St Giles, 45

St Gregory, 51

St Jerome, 12, 77–80, 81, 82, 83, 122; *Vita* of, 78–9

St John of Bridlington, 34–5

St John the Evangelist, 93

St Katherine, 32, 45, 71, 74 n. 70

St Margaret of Antioch: and blood, 83; and childbirth, 12, 26, 61, 64, 68, 83, 128, 168; cult of, 61, 64, 74, 75, 76, 77, 83; and the dragon, 62, 63, 71, 72, 74; feast of, 26, 48, 91; images of, 26, 45, 69–73, 75, 82, 178, 180–1; legend of, 61–3, 66, 67, 68, 72, 74, 141; *Life* of, 62, 66, 67; her martyrdom, 61, 62, 66, 84; role of, 64, 85; and St George, 66, 72, 74; her virginity, 61, 63, 66, 68, 84

St Michael, 69

St Paul, 69, 140

St Peter, 140

St Roche, 142

St Sebastian, 142

St Sitha of Lucca, 135

St Thomas Becket, 50

St Wulstan of Bawburgh, 80

saints: choice of as patrons and intercessors, 19, 30, 40, 44, 45, 52, 54, 64, 102, 105; name, 40, 44, 64, 75, 76, 91

Salmon, Cicely, 79, 80

Salmon, John, 79, 80

schools, 40, 105

Segryme, Agnes, 105, 143, 169

sexuality, 59, 61, 62–3, 65, 68, 98; denial of, 64, 65, 66, 84; and spirituality, 63, 66

sexual misconduct, 76, 96, 109, 110

social status, 35–6, 42, 169

Syon, Brigettine house, 2, 78, 111, 114, 138

teaching, *see* preaching and teaching

tears, gift of, 35, 91

Milton Keynes UK
Ingram Content Group UK Ltd.
UKHW021925101224
452268UK00002B/53

9 780861 933464